# *I Say Again*

# *Praise for* I Say Again

A reader's appropriate response to this book's title is "So grateful you did say it again, Your Honor." By using a diverse collection of personal and professional writing throughout many of his ninety-six years, Judge Ditter through prose and poetry, whether serious or humorous, gives us deep understanding of what goes into the making of an exemplary family man, friend, American citizen, and state and federal judge. Whether he is writing about his love of wife and family, judicial opinions, church sermons or beekeeping, he is always very warm-hearted, fair-minded, intelligent, and interesting.

*—Seymour I. "Spence" Toll*
*Author and retired Philadelphia lawyer*

With great sensitivity, perspective, and humor, Judge J. William Ditter, Jr. inspires us with stories about his family, his poetry, and his occasional Sunday morning sermons at the local Methodist Church, stories that capture deeply loving relationships and challenge our sometimes short-sighted values and behaviors.

In his annual Christmas letters, Judge Ditter introduces us to the hilariously memorable "Cousin Misty," who never fails to offer far-fetched insights about life, while offering poignant truisms about ways one can go on after the loss of a loved one.

*I Say Again* will make you laugh and cry—and give you renewed hope to move forward in your own life with a bit of a twinkle in your eye and a lightness in your step.

*—Nathalie A. Bartle, EdD.*
*Professor (Ret.), Drexel University School of Public Health;*
*author,* Venus in Blue Jeans: Why Mothers and Daughters Need to Talk about Sex

Family. Country. Faith. The Law. In *I Say Again*, Judge J. William Ditter, Jr., reveals his life's priorities and weaves together an eclectic, insightful, and humorous collection of his poems, letters, speeches, sermons, and judicial opinions, spanning over 70 years of original writing.

The book opens focusing on Judge Ditter's family, reflecting the impact of his devoted parents, his deep love for his wife, Verna, and the joys and challenges of raising four boys of whom Judge Ditter shows great admiration. Country and history pervade the text, whether in the form of poetry that celebrates Independence Day or the poems that mix a bit of fancy with history for the Upper Dublin Association for the Recovery of Stolen Horses, Horse Thieves and Obtaining Stolen Property.

Faith permeates the book, but is particularly marked throughout a series of the judge's sermons where he draws on such diverse lives as those of the reformed slaver John Newton; Jesus' companion Cleopas; a young Maine skier, Eric Wycoff Bennett; and President Abraham Lincoln.

Judge Ditter is a champion of the law and lawyers. You see Judge Ditter's respect for the role of lawyers, from the guidance he gives new lawyers during the admissions ceremony to his setting the record straight on Shakespeare's famous quote "let's kill all the lawyers," in which the bard expresses admiration for lawyers, not a death wish. You recognize Judge Ditter's characteristic humility in the small number federal judicial opinions he includes—each of which focuses on the limits of federal judicial power. You appreciate the humor in his response to the Judicial Ethics Committee regarding farm income at his place of residence and his report to the Eastern District Chief Judge regarding his service as General Services Administration Liaison Judge.

This book overflows with creativity and humor, including a compendium of the judge's annual Christmas letters, which read like holiday letters sent by no other. I Say Again could have been written by no other than Judge Ditter.

*—J. Gordon Cooney, Jr.*
*Global Litigation Practice Leader, Morgan, Lewis & Bockius LLP*
*Fellow, American College of Trial Lawyers*
*Law Clerk for the Honorable J. William Ditter, Jr. (1984–86)*

# I Say Again

J. William Ditter, Jr.

The Red Barn Press
*Publisher of Preferred Publications*

*To Verna*

She enriched my life and filled it with delight, admiration,
and pride in all of her many accomplishments.

P.O. Box 256
Woxall, PA 18979



ISBN 978-0-692-04619-7

The cover art features the author's portrait, which hangs in Courtroom 6A in the James A. Byrne United States Courthouse in Philadelphia. Commissioned by his former law clerks, the portrait is the work of Garth C. Herrick, a nationally regarded portrait painter, sculptor, and figurative fine artist.

Book and cover design by Rachael Hixon
The Red Barn Press logo, pen & ink, by Mickey Waring

Grateful acknowledgment to the Duke Law Center for Judicial Studies for permission to reprint from Gene E. K. Pratter, "Judge J. William Ditter, Jr., Gentleman Judge and Magnificent Man," in *The Storied Branch: Stories about Judges, by Judges*, vol. 4, November 2012.

Photo Credits:

Illustration of the Great Train Wreck of 1865 (p. 195) from *Frank Leslie's Illustrated Newspaper*, August 2, 1856.

Liberty Bell, Independence Hall, Philadelphia, Pa., ca. 1901. Photograph. Detroit Publishing Co. (p. 190) Retrieved from the Library of Congress, https://www.loc.gov/item/det1994005082/PP/. (Accessed February 04, 2018.)

London Is Still "Taking It," England London, 1940. [December] Photograph. (p. 221) Retrieved from the Library of Congress, https://www.loc.gov/item/98505741/. (Accessed February 04, 2018.)

Typeset in Jansen 11 pt.

Printed in the U.S.A.

# Table of Contents

# Preface

Why this book? Good question. It all started with my Christmas letters. I wrote them hoping to add to the joys of the season with a bit of humor—humor at my expense, the best kind.

It was easy to tuck a letter into the envelope with the card that Verna had created. After a few years, we started to get some flattering feedback, which, of course, fed the flame of creativity.

After a few more years came a question: why don't you put your Christmas letters into a book? I let that flattery jell—Good idea. Why don't you?—But I didn't. Then my colleague, the Honorable Gene E. K. Pratter, offered to help and I was off to the races.

Over the course of the years, I had written some verse—for our Fourth of July party invitations, fact and fancy for the Upper Dublin Association dinners, and for Verna. Humor, a show of patriotism, and storytelling. I think the Verna poems tell about her and about me.

Over the course of the years I've done some preaching, so I've included four sermons.

There's more, but that's the general idea.

In any event I hope you'll enjoy words from Cousin Misty, profit from my travel trials and shopping troubles, and remember to choose your words carefully in an adult community. Then, too, if you delve into the Upper Dublin Association section you will find that sometimes history is made up of fact and fable.

I am most grateful to the following, who have added their time, efforts, and thoughts to make my wanderings this completed endeavor.

I've mentioned Judge Pratter and her offer to help. And help she did, but didn't stop there. She encouraged, suggested how the various materials should be organized, continued offering advice, and introduced me to Ms. Catherine A. Kreyche, who became my editor, and what an editor she has been.

She has provided insight to the various steps we've had to take to go from manuscript to here. The size and shape of this effort. What to include and what to leave on the cutting-room floor. Out typos. Yes comma, no comma. Questioned. Encouraged. Accepted. Patient, but pushing gently. In sum, the snowballs may have been mine, but she was the one who helped stack them.

Then there are those who wrote section introductions:

The Reverend Alan Smith, my pastor for twelve years and friend for life. His Sunday messages were timely and scripturally inspired. His other skills range from those of a gifted musician to a trained mechanic, with a working knowledge of plumbing and electrical wiring. Never too busy to lend a hand, help, share, and carry. And always time for a prayer. A true man of God who never forgot He who said to him, "Follow me."

Frank Boni joined our Ambler High School class of 1939 when he married Julie, who had lost her husband a few years before. As time took its inevitable toll he became a mainstay of our alumni group and chauffeur for the few of us who remained. Frank also took the reins of the venerable Upper Dublin Association as its secretary, arranging for meeting programs and places, and finally helping guide it into its place in history after 178 years.

Patricia Furlong, Esq., has been my law clerk since I resumed judicial duties after Verna died. Her research is thorough, her writing a model of clarity, and her work habits unmatched. She is also office manager, secretary, and chef. Yes, she does it all.

My son David has provided technical support, guiding me through the mysteries of computers and their ilk. He is patient with his explanations and examples. Indeed, my guru.

Why this book? Although it's not what I initially had in mind, the book has turned out to be an incidental autobiography. Hopefully, and in the literary sense, you'll emulate Little Jack Horner and be as pleased as he was.

*J. William Ditter, Jr.*
*April 2018*

# Introduction

## The Honorable Gene E. K. Pratter

The Eastern District of Pennsylvania is a large, collegial trial court where quick humor and timely touches of humanity come second only to intelligence and integrity. Even though this court is one where the former characteristics abound, most of our currently serving judges would name J. William Ditter, Jr. as first among equals with the qualities that practitioners and the public place high on the list of exemplary judges and human beings.

Bill is not only strongly rooted in public service, but also in family, community, church, and love of country. With his beloved wife of more than sixty years, the late Verna B. Ditter, Bill parented four sons who, in turn, have provided Bill with eight grandchildren and several great-grandchildren. They could not ask for a more devoted and lively paterfamilias. His various hobbies have included photography, writing poetry, gardening, genealogy, softball, downhill skiing, and beekeeping.

Bill is a man of considerable gifts and talents, and I am happy he is now sharing them in the form of this book. Which leads me to the book's genesis. After receiving a few years' worth of Bill's Christmas letters, which he sends to colleagues, friends, and family, and finding myself absolutely captivated by these wonderful, legendary, and humorous diaries of self, family, and country life, I was prompted to almost bully him into publishing them. I was confident, and told a genuinely incredulous Bill so in no uncertain terms, that every recipient of his annual letters would treasure having them in one book.

The idea grew into thoughts of publishing a broader anthology of his writings—poems, speeches, sermons, and other contributions—that would reach a wider audience. Though I am ashamed to say how long I let the idea languish, I do confess to pride in having had some small formative role in creating this volume, which holds many remarkable, priceless gifts from Bill's pen and heart.

Bill's humor—dry, witty, and self-deprecating—is showcased here. The peerless file clerk in his memory, who pulls out a charming joke on any topic and on demand, is now opening an entire drawer to us with this book, one overflowing with love, humor, history, and humanity.

Bill's poetry reveals his gentle, playful, and passionate way of connecting to the world. Bill first leads us into the circle of the Ditters' multi-generational family through both poetry and prose, and in the chapter that follows he shares verses he wrote to his beloved wife, Verna, over the course of their marriage.

Bill Ditter is a man who quietly and effectively demonstrates every day that he understands and obeys the biblical admonition to do justice, love mercy, and walk humbly with God. Always a devout and humble participant in the work of his church, he has taught Sunday School and has been chosen often as a lay homilist for the congregation.

Bill has always taken a deep interest in preserving and passing on knowledge of history and appreciation of the paths that were trod before, be it by horse or train or human. In 1984 Judge Ditter helped incorporate the Historical Society of the United States District Court for the Eastern District of Pennsylvania. He has served on its board of directors and as the chairman of the calendar committee, where he has taken special care to call to our attention the many interesting communities in the environs of Philadelphia. His membership in the Upper Dublin Association reveals us not only his versifying talents, displayed in this volume, but also a unique view of history of the region.

Bill Ditter is also a patriot who loves his country. An entire section of this book is devoted to Independence Day, and woven throughout this volume are reminders of the sacrifices made to preserve freedom.

Bill Ditter loves the trial court—interacting with lawyers and litigants, settling cases, presiding over trials, writing opinions. Those privileged to watch Bill in action see clearly that he believes trial judges have the best job in the world. Certainly, no one does it better, and those of us who try to emulate Bill Ditter are better for it. He is revered by his law clerks for whom their service with him is a singular, prized badge of honor.

Bill is an enormously productive trial judge. While many of his cases were tremendously significant, he has reminded his colleagues that every case is significant to the parties involved. He never describes the cases on his docket so that the listener will be impressed by the judge. Yet his work has been impressive.

Early in his federal career Judge Ditter masterfully engineered the Reading Railroad bankruptcy. When sentencing a prominent politician convicted of public corruption, he minced no words: "Lying, cheating and scheming were a way of life for him.... When he was out of office he gave bribes, when he was in office he took bribes." While on the state court Judge Ditter was similarly direct in denying custody to a mother who had treated her children as inconvenient commodities. His decision in *Traeger v. Ritting* is included in this volume.

Judge Ditter has presided over hundreds of other cases, mammoth and minor, all of which have received the talents of a judge who is an exemplar of ability, probity, temperament, and honor. From Bill Ditter I have learned that a judge should work calmly, with integrity, treating every human being in the courtroom—parties, lawyers, victims, offenders—with dignity. Perhaps next to fairness, the most important thing Bill has brought to the job is the respectful and dignified treatment of each person before him.

However, Bill will point out silliness whenever it manifests itself. Among the most memorable Ditter letters are those responses to judicial bureaucratic inquiries. Reporting as the district's liaison judge to the GSA for 1977, a year in the then-still-early life of our new courthouse, Judge Ditter described it as a year of significant achievement with regard to the struggles attendant to painting the judges' elevators doors, installing an "artsy" plaza water fountain as a way of handling subterranean water that was causing building subsidence, and "balancing" the building HVAC by averaging the temperatures in unrelated parts of the courthouse. Periodically this letter is reissued on its publication anniversary. It is included here.

Another classic is Judge Ditter's priceless response to an inquiry from the chairman of the Committee on Financial Disclosure seeking further explanation of $171.50 in "farm income" reported by the judge on his annual financial report. Specifically, Judge Ditter was required to explain whether one-half hog, a few dozen eggs, and some honey were "grown, manufactured, etc." at his place of residence.

I will leave you to find out how he responded to the inquiry. I can reveal that the chairman of the committee sought no further explanation. Indeed, what better example of a judge's craft could there be?

Though he rarely speaks of them, some of his colleagues know how deeply felt and indelible certain painful personal experiences have been for Bill. In each instance he has borne, and still bears, them resolutely and without complaint. His sacrifices are not worn as badges. Rather, Bill's life as a devoted husband, father, judge, friend, and community member serves as daily encouragement to the rest of us to strive to be better as we are glad to greet each day.

I learned from the late Judge Norma Shapiro (who never got these things wrong) that at the dinner to mark his assumption to senior status Judge Ditter reported that on the day of his induction as a common pleas court judge, he and his wife Verna went to a country chapel to conclude the day with a prayer. The judge prayed that God would help make him a good judge and keep him humble. Apparently, Verna quickly assured God it was only necessary to make sure Bill was a good judge because she'd make sure he stayed humble.

I am thrilled that more people will get to know Judge Ditter through the writings in this volume and learn why I and other of his friends and colleagues have such a high regard for him. Those readers who know Bill are sure to learn more, about him and about themselves. Bill's writings have a timeless quality to them, and although the reference points may be unfamiliar to a newer readership, they are well worth learning. Bill navigates the world with humor, wisdom, and humanity. I invite you on this journey with him, enjoying the book and reading it as a process of discovery.

*Note: This introduction includes material excerpted and adapted with permission of the publisher from Gene E. K. Pratter, U.S. District Court, Eastern District of Pennsylvania: "Judge J. William Ditter, Jr., Gentleman Judge and Magnificent Man," in* The Storied Branch: Stories about Judges, by Judges, *vol. 4, November 2012, published by the Duke Law Center for Judicial Studies.*

# Family

## Introduction by J. William Ditter, Jr.

I'm not sure when it was that I first realized that not everyone had a family like mine. Or when it was that I learned that the people with whom you lived were called family.

I knew of no one else whose father was a Congressman. And then there was my sister. Some of my friends had sisters, but mine was unique—she looked out for me. The other people at my house were my mother, grandmother, and great grandfather, a Civil War veteran. My mother ran the house with my grandmother's assistance. My grandmother, "Gaga," was stone deaf—"hearing challenged." She was also wise and my special friend.

Memorable holiday gatherings at the Ditters included not just my immediate family and my grandmother, but also uncles, aunts, and cousins. We would gather on Thanksgiving and Christmas, and at other times for dinners. There was lots of laughter, singing, and playing cards, a game called Michigan.

I learned from Verna that her familial pattern was the same as mine. It was only natural that when we established a home and had children we would follow the same practice. As our family grew, our gatherings included a supportive extended family.

Verna and I married on September 2, 1944, while I was still in the Navy. By the time of my second tour of duty, at the Mechanicsburg Supply Depot, we had started our family. In 1953 we moved back to Ambler into a house that my mother gave us.

The next house was on a quiet street. It had three stories, five bedrooms, and a backyard with a big tree that soon had a clubhouse—well, platform—that Verna, ever the creator, built for the boys. A few years later, Verna found just what she'd been looking for, our third house—larger, better, roomier—where we lived for thirteen years until I acquired our present land in western Montgomery County and Verna planned the house there, the ultimate house.

On this property, in view of the house, Verna and our son George built a barn…with my help, I add with all due modesty. First, each of the bents was completed, their two vertical members joined by a crosspiece. Next, the first two were lifted upright and joined, both sides by a horizontal piece. The third was then lifted and held until it was fastened to the other two by a horizontal beam.

On a fine September day, friends and members of our extended families joined us for a barn raising, with George as the raising master. George had prepared the necessary fourteen mortise and tenon joints in advance. By late afternoon, all of the joints had been pegged, and there stood the framework of a barn. How like a family: a solid foundation on which to build and achieve. That was 44 years ago. I was proud then and am still proud of each joint and every beam.

# J. William Ditter, My Father

I was only twenty-two when he died in a plane crash, but I had already realized that my father was the finest man I knew. In the more than seventy years that have passed since that awful day, I have never had a reason to think anyone could be his equal.

My father was born in Philadelphia on September 5, 1888. Although he attended public school and had a brief stint at West Chester College, trouble with his eyes delayed further education. He then became a florist, employed by his sister, my Aunt Annie, and her husband, Uncle Ed Biester. The Biesters had a good business and my father quickly became an important part of it. He made floral pieces for funerals, decorated churches, and made wreaths and sprays for Christmas.

The time came when his eyes had improved and he announced to the family that he was going to return to school and become a lawyer. Only his brother, my Uncle Harry, himself a lawyer, gave him any support. To the rest of the family the idea of more schooling had no appeal, and my father was told, "What's the matter with the florist business? Maybe someday you could have your own shop—just like Ed and Annie. They say you have a knack for it."

Yet he went back to school and, in 1913 at the age of 25, earned a law degree at Temple University. My father left his mark wherever he went. After earning his teaching certificate in 1912, while still in law school he began teaching at Northeast High School in Philadelphia. He became a beloved and respected teacher of history and commercial subjects and coach of the baseball team. One of his players, Jimmy Dykes, went on to become Connie Mack's star third baseman during the Philadelphia Athletics' glory years in the 1930s. In 1922, while still teaching in Philadelphia, Dad began practicing law part time in Ambler. Quickly the law required more time and he left Northeast in 1926. A bare six years later, he was elected to the United States Congress, a Republican from Montgomery County, Pennsylvania.

At that time, in 1932, I was eleven years old, and even though my father spent much of his time in Washington during the week, on most Friday nights my mother, my sister, and I would meet him at the North Philadelphia train station and we would drive home together. Even after I left for college in 1939, I would come home on many weekends and spend time with him.

Saturday mornings he would go to his law office—usually to see constituents or take care of other Congressional business—and get home around one o'clock. He would then often spend a few hours in his garden. Gardening was hobby, relaxation, therapy, and the formal flower garden to the left of the house, a proof of his skill and devotion. He had planned the shrubs and trees with care, so that with each passing year the total effect became more impressive. The vegetable garden yielded abundant tomatoes for canning, limas for the freezer, and asparagus for the table.

*My father, J. William Ditter, 1939*

During the summer, Saturday afternoons were also a time he spent with my sister and me. He was never too busy for us, to concern himself with our schoolwork, our projects, and our interests—and he never passed up a chance to have a catch with me. We all enjoyed a game of badminton and when company was there, we'd try croquet. The house was ideally suited for entertaining and the guests included not only my parents' friends, but also my sister's and mine.

We ate breakfast and dinner as a family—lunch was a bit more casual. Dad always read a selection of Scripture before breakfast. Religion was an important part of his life and ours. He was active in our church, Kemble Park, at Ogontz and Grange Streets in Philadelphia. On Sunday mornings, we would pile into the car for the half-hour drive to the city. For many years he was the Sunday School superintendent. I well remember how he could get the whole Sunday School singing a favorite hymn with gusto and enthusiasm. But the growing demands on his time in Washington made him turn over the job to his good friend C. H. "Preach" Longsdorf.

After church we would often go out for dinner and then visit my father's parents, Grossie and Grosspop, at 932 Erie Avenue. He was a dutiful son and as he shared his time with my mother, sister, and me, so he kept in close touch with my grandparents and Tante Betz, his sister, and her husband, Uncle Quince Shearer. He was a devoted family man and from his example I learned the importance of the extended family, its rewards and importance in building a sense of sharing, belonging, appreciation, recognition.

Before the war, Congress was often in recess on Mondays and Dad would be at home for another day. As he rose to a more important place in Congress and the national Republican Party, and as the possibility of war became a reality, there were more meetings, more speeches, more committee hearings, more

Congressional sessions, more time in Washington, and less time at home. But still he had time with my sister and me—and we took great pride in him.

From the start when he was in Washington, he wrote a letter each night to my mother, a postcard to my sister, and a postcard to me. Not often. Not usually. Every night, and once I got to college and was away from home, he often sent a letter to me. Sometimes it was written when a committee hearing began to drag. Sometimes it was written from a plane while he was on his way to a speaking engagement. Sometimes from his hotel room. I marvel at how he did it.

My father was a Republican. He made no secret of his belief that the Republican Party—its precepts, its principles, its practices, and its potential—were vital to his nation. He was also one of the leaders who successfully opposed President Roosevelt's efforts to pack the Supreme Court. Every week he would write a column for the county newspapers, "Trend of Events," which, as the name implies, was his way of informing his constituents of developments in Washington and his views about them. While he had great respect and deference for those of the Democratic Party, his was a singleness of purpose so far as politics were concerned.

As with all else in his life, he took his Congressional duties seriously. Patriotism was not a mere word—it was the bedrock of his belief, the standard against which everything else was measured. He was proud of his country—

*The* USS J. William Ditter *(DM 31), commissioned on October 28, 1944*

proud of its heritage—proud of his opportunity to keep it great and make it greater—and aware of his duty to do so.

My father was widely credited by the Navy's highest officers for his critical role in the building of the two-ocean Navy. As the ranking minority member of the Naval Appropriations Committee he gained the vision that a one-ocean Navy could no longer protect America's interests—that a Navy that could fight in both the Atlantic and the Pacific at the same time was an immediate need—and he shepherded the bills through the committee and through Congress that made possibility into reality. Admiral R. H. Stark, the U.S. Navy's Chief of Naval Operations, credited my father with having the energy and skill to get the necessary appropriations out of committee and passed on the floor. It was the two-ocean Navy that proved critical to the Allied victory in World War II.

Demonstrating his appreciation and admiration for my father and his support for the Navy, Vice Admiral John S. McCain led the military delegation in attendance at my father's funeral in Ambler in November of 1943. The delegation included four rear admirals, marine officers, and other representatives of the Navy. There were numerous other dignitaries in attendance as well—former President Herbert Hoover; more than thirty-five members of Congress from both sides of the aisle including both senators from Pennsylvania; House chaplain James S. Montgomery; and several former members of Congress.

My mother received letters of condolence from both Republicans and Democrats, including members of the Roosevelt administration and military

*J. William Ditter Memorial Chapel, Naval Air Station, Willow Grove*

leaders. In his condolence letter to my mother, Vice Admiral McCain wrote, "I am heartbroken over the death of Mr. Ditter. He was a warm friend of mine, the best I had in Congress, so I not only have lost a friend but the Navy has lost a powerful advocate." At the time, Vice Admiral McCain led the Bureau of Aeronautics; he subsequently commanded Task Force 38, a fast carrier group that destroyed the Japanese in the Pacific.

Carl Vinson, a Democrat, recognizing my father's role in the war effort, suggested that a destroyer be named after him. The *USS J. William Ditter* (DM31) was commissioned in 1944, and the chapel at the Naval Air Station, Willow Grove, was named in his honor.

Orator and statesman. Articulate and wise. A master of debate yet gentle and kind to his adversaries. Father and God-fearing. Teacher and student. Accomplished, yet humble. He was and is my hero.

*Lovers' Spat,*
*J. William Ditter, pen and ink, 1905*

*All is Well,*
*J. William Ditter, pen and ink, 1905*

*The Old Sailor's Story,*
*J. William Ditter, pen and ink, 1905*

*Perplexed. Where am I going to sit?*
*J. William Ditter, pen and ink, 1905*

## Mabel Bearne Ditter, My Mother

*My mother, Mabel S. Bearne (Ditter), 1906*

My mother never said much about her childhood—her life seemed to have started when she met my dad.

I do know that her father died when she was only sixteen and that his death ended her hopes for college. I am not sure she finished high school, because my grandmother was suddenly faced with the task of earning a living, taking care of her parents, and raising my uncle who was thirteen. Despite that, Mother's love of learning and intellectual pursuits never stopped. She was exact in grammar, well read, knew history, learned quickly, and had a wide range of interests. She was better educated than most college graduates.

Mother's first job was wrapping packages at a department store. She retained the skill of twisting a piece of string around itself and having it cut itself by giving it a quick yank.

She saved enough money to buy a piano, take lessons, and go to secretarial school. The only other job I can remember her talking about was as secretary to John Weaver, who had been the mayor of Philadelphia.

Mother and Dad were married in 1913. She was a very pretty girl and they were a devoted couple. They enjoyed each other's company and were much in love until the day he died. There were never cross words between them—on occasion they might disagree, but there was no anger, no grudge, no apparent resentment. Both must have felt that life was too short and their relationship too important to be marred by unpleasant memories. That's the atmosphere in which I grew up.

Dad wanted to be a teacher and had enrolled at West Chester State College. He actually started there, but came home after a few weeks. In one of his letters, he complained about the roaches in his room. But the real reason was a novella, *Immensee*, by Theodor Storm, which he read in his German class. It's a romance about a boy and girl. He leaves her to go away to school, and when he returns with his degree, she had married someone else. Apparently Dad was unwilling to take a chance like that. They named the house they built on Tennis Avenue *Immensee*.

Mother was the most meticulous, best organized person I have ever known. She had a place for everything and everything was in its place. And she remembered where the place was. I never heard her say, "I had that, but I can't remember where I put it."

Mother kept a cash account, writing down her expenditures as soon as she had the time—immediately if possible. She always got new bills from the bank to use for her purchases. When she wrote down the money she put in the plate at church, I would assure her that God had seen it and she didn't have to write it down!

Mother directed the household activities. We often had a maid. Minnie Lane and later Hattie Thornton would come to help with the laundry, and John Washington worked inside and out. My maternal grandmother, GaGa, lived with us until her death in 1941, and Mother utilized her talents as seamstress, cook, baker, and child-companion. They got along fabulously. I always thought that everyone must have a live-in grandmother who made peach pies and cake.

Mother ran a clipping service for the family. She read the county newspapers regularly and clipped out any items about Dad. In addition, she saved articles that would interest us—and others of instruction or inspiration. One of her self-appointed tasks during the years Dad was in Congress was to mail out a government booklet called *Infant Care* to every woman in the county who had had a baby. Each week she would get all the county papers, go through them for articles about Dad, and then clip the birth notices. If addresses were not given for the new mothers, she would check the county telephone books and hand address each envelope. Of course, this was before the computer, printed labels, and the modern techniques of mass mailing. For her it was a labor of love, a response to a need, and a way to help Dad.

After Dad was killed, Mother went into a long period of grief. She never fully got over his death although she lived almost twenty years more. The early 1940s were sad times for Mother: she lost GaGa; her brother, my Uncle Bob; and Dad in less than two years. Mother did not put on a long face or try to make others feel sorry for her. But I knew of her periods of loneliness and sadness.

She loved *Immensee* but felt she could no longer afford the help to run the place. I could not be of much help—I was married and living in Ambler—and so she sold it and moved back to Euclid Avenue, my parents' first home. It was a tough decision, but like everything else she carried it off resolutely, without self-pity or blame.

Mother had a deep faith in God and a strict code of morality. God was a part of her everyday life, and although she may not have understood why Dad died, it never affected her faith. Most things were right or wrong—there were very few gray areas admitted to debate.

She read the *Evening Bulletin*, the *Norristown Times Herald*, and the *Ambler Gazette*. She read *Readers Digest* cover to cover. She was a member of the Book of the Month Club for as long as I can remember. Since she didn't watch TV she had time to read the books she regularly borrowed from the library.

Mother gave at church and supported a variety of charities. Her three favorites were the missionary work of Carolyn Saltenberger, the Needlework Guild, and the blind. One of her girlhood friends, whom I only remember as Aunt Pat, had been a missionary to Africa. She died as a young woman and Mother felt her loss keenly—so when Carolyn became a missionary, Mother did much to support her work, as did my sister, Mabel. Mother was a Needlework Guild director. With money she collected from friends and family she would go to a wholesale outlet and buy great quantities of garments that she proudly displayed at the guild's annual ingathering. I'm not sure how she became interested in the needs of the blind, but she responded in a way that was typical for her: she learned to write Braille and spent many hours "translating" articles from *Readers Digest* into Braille. Using a small stylus, she would punch little raised dots into special paper, one letter at a time, punching in a letter's mirror image.

When my sister Mabel and I first began to practice law together, Mabel did all the office bookkeeping. It was a burden for her and took up time that she could better use as a lawyer. Whether she was asked or volunteered, Mother began to keep the office books and did her usual thorough job. She continued with this task after Ray Jenkins and I became partners, and even after I went on the bench. She took no pay—hers was the satisfaction of helping out her Mabel and me.

## Mabel Augusta Crossley (Bearne), My Grandmother

Mabel Crossley Bearne was my grandmother. We called her GaGa and she was part of our family until her death in 1941.

*My grandmother, Mabel Augusta Crossley Bearne (GaGa)*

I was the beneficiary of her love, care, interest, knowledge, and practicality. She was stone deaf and we had to shout in her ear to make ourselves heard—nonetheless, she took a full interest in all about her, especially in my sister and me.

GaGa was widowed in 1905—my mother was then sixteen, my Uncle Bob thirteen. Her father, my great grandfather Sylvester Crossley, worked little if any—he still suffered from his Civil War experiences. I do not know if my great grandmother worked. There was no Social Security or Aid to Dependent Families. It was up to GaGa to provide for her parents and children. She became a milliner and added the accent on the final syllable of Bearne (Bearné) to give her name a French sound, French milliners being more in demand than English-speaking ones. Boyd's 1908 *Philadelphia City Directory* lists her as a milliner at 1702 N. 13th Street and her home as 2262 N. Van Pelt Street.

She liked to cook and I well remember her peach pies and cakes.

She had a great sense of humor and was fond of a joke—even the ones on her.

Only a fragment of GaGa's "will" remains, but it is illustrative:

> ... I do will and bequeath my crowned tooth in case there should be a vacancy on his partial plate. To my dearly beloved mother, Caroline Virginia Matheys Crossley, I leave my good will and fixtures, the latter consisting of my false bang and black woolen underwear.
>
> To my sister, Cora Emma Weston, I leave my aristocratic carriage. To my brother, Clifford Matheys Crossley and Adalaide Patty, his wife, I leave my humpity-dumpity nose, hoping with their artistic taste they can some time in the dim vista of the future remodel it and make it useful to them and their heirs forever.
>
> The undersigned regrets the necessity of this bequest but also leaves a sufficient supply of sympathy to go therewith...

She loved hats and was constantly making them—fixing them—and trying them on. I can remember one night—I'd gotten up to go to the bathroom around 3 a.m.—and there she was, in her nightgown, standing in front of the mirror, adjusting a hat to see if she liked the little veil.

On Saturday nights, she and Cousin Bob Major would go to the movies. They would walk the quarter mile down Tennis Avenue to Bethlehem Pike and get the bus to Ambler. In bad weather, my sister or one of my parents would take them to the bus stop—or all the way to the theater. One snowy night when my parents were away, GaGa asked Mabel to take them to the corner—and Mabel properly observed that it would be dangerous because the car might skid into the ditch. GaGa replied, with perfect logic, "If skidding's the problem, don't skid."

GaGa had gall bladder troubles and was not supposed to eat butter. One time my mother saw her doing so and reminded GaGa of the doctor's instruction. Again, with absolute conviction, GaGa said, "If God had not intended us to eat butter, he would not have invented it."

Then there was the time when I was at camp, and during a ballgame I broke my wrist sliding into base. I wrote home about it with full particulars and GaGa grieved. Her knowledge of baseball was somewhere between little and nonexistent. My mother tried to reassure her that the break was not serious and that I would recover with no residual problems. But GaGa would not be comforted—she told my mother she was not concerned about the break but by the fact that it had happened while I was trying to *steal*—third base, that is.

GaGa's unexpected death during surgery near Christmas in 1941 left a large gap in our family—one that was never filled.

### *Afternote*

Why was GaGa's middle name "Augusta"? I never was told, but here is an interesting possibility.

GaGa's father was Sylvester Crossley (1839–1928), whose mother was Malvinia Bush (1817–47). Malvinia's father was George Bush (1789–?) and his father was Valentine Bush (1745/46–1824). Valentine's father was Johan (John) Jacob Bush, GaGa's great, great, great grandfather

John Jacob Bush came to America from the Palatinate, a region west of the Rhine, formerly a state of the German Empire and administered by Bavaria. In 1736, he arrived on the ship *Princess Augusta,* which had sailed from Rotterdam. "At the Courthouse of Philadelphia, before William Allen, Mayor of Philadelphia, on September 16th 1736, he took and subscribed his oath to the government."[1]

1 Ralph Beaver Strassburger, *Pennsylvania German Pioneers,* vol. 1 (Norristown, PA: Pennsylvania German Society, 1934), pp. 163–67, quoting Minutes of the Provincial Council, printed in *Colonial Records,* vol. 4, p. 72, List 42 B.

The North Atlantic has always been treacherous for wooden sailing ships and Block Island, settled in 1661, is a perfect place from which to sight ships in trouble. The *Princess Augusta* burned and sank off of Block Island. Since then people report that they have seen apparitions of a burning ship and eerie lights originating from the waters where the ship rests.

Remember, GaGa's maiden name was Mabel Augusta Crossley.

I know of no other Augustas before or since GaGa. Did the name or some legend come down through the family from John Jacob Bush, who arrived in 1736, to GaGa's birth in 1867? If not, from where did Augusta come?

There is another possibility. Just as the ship was named for a princess—there were several princesses named Augusta in Great Britain and in states of the Holy Roman Empire—so was GaGa. Or perhaps her parents just liked the name. It means *majestic dignity*—and that was my grandmother.

## Mabel Bearne Ditter (Sellers), My Sister

Mabel was my older sister and from her earliest days she believed that one of her tasks and duties in life was to look after me—and so she did. That meant punching Dick Hoyt in the nose because he wouldn't stop teasing me—and teaching me how to play bridge by regularly (with her husband Warren) outscoring Verna and me, showing me how to paddle a canoe—to enjoy poetry—to eat an ice cream cone—and so much more, great and small.

Mabel was my senior by four years and I followed her in high school and college. *Trailed* is probably a better word, for while I did well, she excelled—B+ and A- versus A+, varsity versus All-American—no, not in sports but in academics.

From my earliest days I remember how Mabel liked to read—that meant having a book on the stair above while she used the dustpan and brush on the immediate stair. Or reading in three days a whole series of books about the Bobbsey Twins, probably eight books in all.

It was a life-long passion.

Much later her husband Warren wrote of her,

> ...she read nearly all the time and remembered it all. To her a house was a library divided into rooms. She was the only person who

could successfully ride the train to law school, study, knit, and eat an apple simultaneously!

Mabel remembered not only what she read, but also what was read to her. Dad was Sunday School superintendent and had turned to Dickens' *Christmas Carol* to start his message. He began as Dickens had, "Marley was dead." He paused, and Mabel, four or five years old and sitting down front, went on, as Dickens had, "as dead as a door nail."

So much for pausing for dramatic effect!

Mabel was a good companion.

In the summer of 1940, after my first year at college and her first year at law school, we took a two-month camping trip to the West Coast and back. We would turn off the main road, find a farmer's field well away from any dwelling, and sleep in our bedrolls under the stars.

Dad had a friend in Congress who owned a dude ranch in Wyoming. We had pleasant stop there, went to a rodeo, rode horses, and helped Wyoming celebrate its fiftieth anniversary of becoming a state. We were houseguests for several nights in Elko, Nevada, again through a friend of Dad's.

Mabel and I were together twenty-four hours a day the entire trip. We had always been close. This trip brought us even closer. We—well, really Mabel—had planned things so we visited several of the West's national parks: the Grand Canyon, Yosemite and its giant Sequoias, and Yellowstone. On the way into Yellowstone, we stopped off where the Battle of Little Big Horn had been fought, which had ended with the death of General George Armstrong Custer and his 278 men sixty-four years earlier at the hands of the Lakota under Chief Sitting Bull. It didn't seem that long ago.

Then on to San Francisco—cable cars, Chinatown, Hollywood and movie studios. With no place to camp on the West Coast we stayed in motels.

After four days, we turned east and camped through the South seeing some plantations and Civil War battle sites.

A great trip we both remembered in our later years,

After my stint in the Navy and law school, we became law partners practicing in Ambler. By then Mabel had been an assistant district attorney—the first woman assistant in Montgomery County—and knew the judges and most of the county lawyers.

She again became my teacher–companion with a generous emphasis on ethics and preparation. Mabel was also an excellent wordsmith—she could take an idea and put it completely and succinctly on paper.

*Mabel Ditter Sellers,*
*my sister and law partner*

In those days, women lawyers were few and far between. But Mabel blazed the way with a high level of persistence, advocacy, and skill.

I recall a case where she represented a roofer whose bill had not been paid. Opposing counsel contended that after the underlying problems had been fixed, the slate shingles should have been put back on the roof again rather than using new composition shingles. Mabel argued that re-using the old, by-now worn and brittle slates was impossible. She had one of them on the table in front of her and "carelessly" brushed against it sending it to the floor where it shattered into a dozen pieces.

The jury returned a verdict for Mabel's client.

Not only a courtroom advocate, Mabel also provided advice and help to clients in need. More than once it was said, "I referred my friend to Mabel because she has a Christian concern, an understanding and helpful attitude that is rare indeed."

Mabel had an abiding faith in God founded upon reading, thought, and prayer. For her it was not some theory to be toyed with on Sundays, but the foundation for living and a gift to be shared. Sharing included teaching a Sunday School class of teenage boys and keeping their interest and participation high.

Mabel was also a poet. She wrote on many subjects, but I find that those poems she wrote about Dad and the two of them after Dad was killed have a particularly poignant beauty. For I was close to both Mabel and Dad, and what these poems convey may well reflect my own sense of loss.

Mabel and Warren made their own Christmas cards: a family picture and a new sonnet by Mabel each year. Her sonnets show not only her skill with words and thought, but also a deep and profound religious feeling.

I've not commented upon the fact that Mabel was a human dynamo, but Warren did:

> "Full speed ahead" was Mabel's by-word. Not to swim, but to swim laps until exhausted. Not to lounge in front of the TV, but to work a full day and then plant a garden by the light of the moon.

And finally, again from Warren:

> "Pray without ceasing" replaced Mabel's car radio. We may never see anyone who loved the Lord more or sought to serve him more earnestly. God in return put an awesome amount of woman in a single beautiful vessel.

Her time had come—far too early. Yet even as her health began to fail, her faith never did.

## Christmas at Immensee

Christmas was a time for family and friends—and a time of preparation. Dad was home from Washington, Mabel returned from college, and my high school was in recess. Things got started in earnest a week before the big day. Boxes with ornaments came down from the attic. Doors were closed so presents could be wrapped. The silverware was polished. Mother made lists of things to do – and who was to do them. Mabel and I tested the lights, both for inside and out.

Dad did the decorating—greens were cut and placed with large pine cones and holly on the mantelpieces—living room, dining room, and my parents' room. Mother and GaGa were busy in the kitchen baking pies and cinnamon buns. Mabel and I trimmed the tree—it was a live tree and always stood in the living room. Sometimes the lights were colored, other times all blue. Another year all white. We placed tinsel carefully on the tree—one strand at a time.

The turkey arrived the day before and was prepared for the oven. Knowing what the morrow would require, we exchanged our presents on Christmas Eve. With Mother at the piano, we sang a few carols. Dad read from Luke about the magic coming.

Breakfast on Christmas morning featured scrambled eggs and cinnamon buns—plenty of both. Minnie Lane would arrive and stuff the turkey and put it in the oven. There were at least two kinds of pie, pumpkin and mincemeat. Although they had been started the day before, they still had to be baked on Christmas Day and flavored with a little "stick." (Mother did not serve alcohol or countenance its use – but a little "stick" for the pies once a year was acceptable.)

Christmas included extended family—Grossie and Grosspop, the Shearers, Tante Betz and Uncle Quince, from 932 Erie Avenue, Uncle Harry and family a few houses down from 906, and the Biesters from Trevose. Dinner on Christmas was at five or five-thirty. The guests would start arriving at four. Coats would disappear into the hall closet, Dad's decorations and the tree were noted, and everyone had some cranberry juice or cider.

We then sat down at the dining room table, which mother had set with a white tablecloth and a wide red ribbon laid from one end to the other. Wedgewood and candles too. Dad carved the turkey, and serving plates were passed to load up on sweet and mashed potatoes, peas and onions, string beans or limas, stuffing, gravy, and rolls and butter.

After dinner we went into the living room to exchange more presents. With Mother at the piano, the rest of us on kazoo and fake instruments, and with Dad and Uncle Harry leading, we sang carols, partially interrupted by dessert. Lots of laughs by people who genuinely enjoyed each other's company.

Yet preparations for this day had begun well before December. Christmas, after all, is a time of joy and celebration. It should not have to be a time of apology and forgiveness, a present given to ease a troubled conscience, a gift that costs too much to make up for a year of doing too little. In that sense, preparations never stopped.

*Immensee, my childhood home*

To Mother, Dad was her joy and companion. Her friend and inspiration. No task was too great. No need or wish too small. The house was to be immaculate because when he came home from Washington that was one way to make him welcome.

To Dad, Mother was the girl of his dreams who was here and now. He showed his devotion, love, appreciation, and consideration in all he said and did.

I never heard them exchange a cross word or raise their voices to each other.

To my sister and me, Dad was our hero. Mother, ever a source of practical wisdom and direction, was our teacher and guide.

Both of them treated us as though we were the most important things in the world.

It all came together at Christmas—a diamond set in a year of love.

I was blessed to be a part of this family.

## Verna Bock Ditter

At the time of her birth on July 21, 1922, Verna's family lived in Bryn Mawr. When she was six, she started at the Bryn Mawr Elementary School. During her early years, the family—including uncles and aunts—would go camping at Belvedere, New Jersey, or to a cottage in Wildwood, New Jersey.

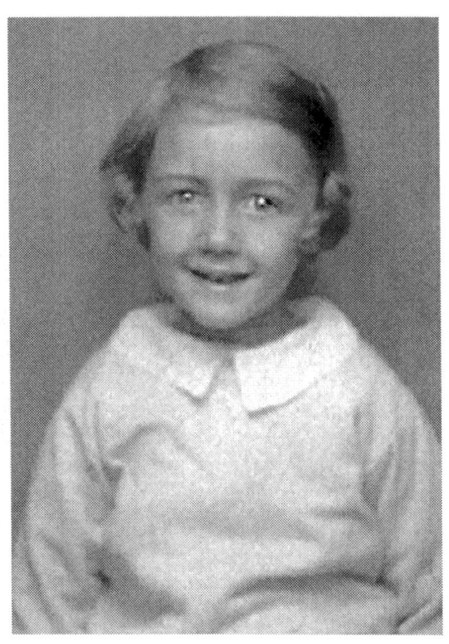

*Verna was six, 1928*

Verna was a beautiful little girl, adored by her parents, and by her extended family. There were her aunts, Mary (Mae) and Jane (Jen), neither of whom ever married. Elizabeth (Aunt Bess) and her husband, Fred White (Uncle Fred), who did not have children yet. And there

Verna and George, towards the end of barn building

were Verna's grandparents. At family gatherings, Verna was everyone's pet and little sweetheart. They played with her. Made a fuss over her. Uncle Fred would dance with her. Her grandmother would dip her finger into her wine so Verna could get a taste. They would pat her tummy after a meal and tell her what a big girl she was to have eaten so much. Yes, surrounded by love, the center of attention. And she remembered thirty, forty, fifty years later and told me. Surrounded by love, she gave in kind.

Verna attended Lower Merion Junior High School. In 1936, while she was in the ninth grade, the family moved to Collegeville and made their home at 801 Main Street, a house that was built by Robert Todd in the mid-1700s.

Verna was graduated from Collegeville–Trappe High School in 1940. After working briefly at Freed Heater in Collegeville, she worked as a secretary for an insurance broker in Norristown. She left that job for a better one at the Colonial Baking Company—and left there in 1942 to become the secretary to the president and vice-president of Ursinus College.

In 1943 she attended Mary Washington College in Fredericksburg, Virginia. Following our marriage in 1944, we lived in New Orleans for a few months, and she studied art at Sophie Newcome College, Tulane University. After the war, she worked as a secretary at American Chemical Paint Company and then at the Guidance Center at Temple University in Philadelphia.

Once our children were born, Verna devoted herself full time to them. She provided care, nurture, and love. Our children were her life and her vocation. She was their teacher, friend, guide, and companion.

Verna was always a homemaker—literally. She not only sanded and painted—but she also made the plans, bought the materials, measured, cut, and assembled shelves, bookcases, highboys, closets, and tables. She came into her own when we moved to western Montgomery County—it was a new house she had designed, where she made chair rails, ceiling trim, paneling, did the

*"Verna, did you really say that to Tip O'Neill?" at the White House with President Ronald Reagan, 1982*

mantelpiece, kitchen cabinets, china and silver closets, bookshelves, and furniture. She and son George built the barn.

Verna was a talented artist—and her watercolors and oils decorate the house. Her paintings won prizes, and she had her own art show at the Ambler Presbyterian Church in 1994. She also did ceramic work for several years, creating interesting, charming, and decorative pieces. She was an avid reader, had a wide range of interests, enjoyed conversation, and was interesting company at social gatherings, large or small.

She was radiant, beautiful, a creator of beauty, innovative, and courageous. A joy to know and be with.

God took her to be with Him on April 11, 2005.

## Our Sons

Verna and I were blessed with four sons—Bill, George, Bob, and David. The section that follows tells you a little something about each of them.

## J. William Ditter III, 1948–2013

Bill was always a straight shooter. Right from the hip. When Billy was four or five, I was on my second tour of duty in the Navy stationed at Mechanicsburg, Pennsylvania. On Saturdays I would often bring him with me while I worked at a local law library. As I researched, he did his own work, doodling and drawing pictures. One time when we were heading home in the car after one of these library sessions, hoping to start a conversation I gave him some advice, followed by a question or two, all insight and wisdom. From the backseat of the car I heard, "Daddy, I don't feel like a father-and-son chat tonight."

So much for guidance from the Voice of Experience.

Bill made friends easily and did well in Ambler's public schools.

At Wissahickon High School, an injury ended his football career and so he turned to music. He played the tuba in Wissahickon's marching band and was chosen to play in an all-district band. He is in Wissahickon High School's Hall of Fame.

After high school, he went to Gettysburg College and eventually to the Delaware Law School.

While Bill was in college, he fell in love with Deanna Hansen. They were married on June 12, 1971, and in due time had four sons, Scott, Craig, Brad, and John William Ditter IV.

Bill was always ambitious. His first job was delivering the *Evening Bulletin* (Philadelphia) from his bike. During high school and college, he had a variety of summer jobs—selling ice cream from a Good Humor truck, working as a bank teller, at a golf ball factory, as a restaurant busboy, and as a road-building inspector.

After college, Bill worked for the Montgomery County Drug and Alcohol Commission. While in law school, he was a juvenile probation officer. Following law school and his admission to the bar, he became an assistant district attorney and spent much of his legal career in that office.

With a keen eye for value, Bill acquired antiques. Even as a child, Bill collected American stamps. Photography was one of his hobbies, and he used his camera so he and Deanna could revisit the sites and sights they had seen on their vacation trips abroad. At home, he photographed many of the barns of Montgomery County, aware that these beautiful structures were rapidly disappearing owing to neglect and suburban development.

He was a volunteer tour guide and handyman at the Peter Wentz Farmstead near Lansdale. The farm, which dates back to 1744, and its stately stone German-style home, outbuildings, and programs help visitors understand Colonial life and work. It was here that George Washington and his troops rested on their way to the Battle of Germantown.

From Louis L'Amour's western novels, books about the Civil War, the Bible, and books about the Bible, Bill's reading showed a wide range of interests and understanding. He also kept up to date on current events and national politics.

Though he was quick to speak his mind and not easily dissuaded, he wore well and was a good companion, husband, father, and son. No doubt he had a father and son talk with each of his four sons. Each has gone his own way and each has found success on his chosen path.

Only sixty-four when his heart gave out on January 2, 2013, Bill's last several years were not easy ones. Myasthenia gravis caused a long hospitalization that left him weak and made swallowing and eating difficult. He required a variety of medicines, each with its own side effects. The medications lost their effectiveness, and knee replacements took their toll on his strength.

Though his body may have been weakened, Bill's faith in God and His Savior remained strong.

Losing a son leaves a void that can't be filled. But it is a blessing to know where he is.

*J. William Ditter III, 2010*

## Bill Is Six

I'd like to be a pirate bold and treasure go to seek.
Instead, I'm stuck in dumb first grade from Monday through the week.

I'll bet a figure I would cut upon a deck awash.
I'd like to hear Miss Taylor say, "It's Willie. Oh, my gosh."

I'd put my cutlass in my belt, then speaking soft and slow,
I'd say, "The tables now have turned as surely you must know."

I'd start like this, "Now learn the names of every spar and mast,
For in five minutes you'll recite. And mind, I won't be sassed."

Perhaps I'd say, "Let's all be still. We'll do a-'rith-ma-tick.
A ton of gold is what in cents? Look here, I've got a stick."

When it came to sketching maps, I'd say, "Your work's a mess.
Miss Taylor, you can try again while others have recess."

I'd like to see her draw a gun, while standing at the board,
And watch her face get hot and red while all the pirates roared.

I'd stick my pistol in my belt, then, looking in her eyes.
I'd say, "Respect must start right here. Don't call the crew, 'them guys.'"

Oh good, oh good, oh good 'twould be to send her ma a note.
"Why can't Miss Taylor ever name the front end of our boat?"

There's lots of things I could be taught, like where to dig up gold,
Instead of art, which I could take, when I have gotten old.

I have had enough of reading. Enough of Dick and Jane.
I want to go out sailoring, along the Spanish Main.

Of penmanship I've had my fill. I want to go to sea.
I've had enough of giggly girls, all twice as smart as me.

I have had enough of numbers that never add up right,
Of principals and offices, and words like, "You're a sight."

I would surely miss my mother, and chocolate cake and pies,
But livin's more than eatin', at least to little guys.

So you can take all of first grade, and staying after school,
And soap and clocks and paper, and every lunch-hall rule.

For I want to be a pirate, and feel the wind whip free.
And hear the waves a roarin', when we put out to sea.

## George B. Ditter

Verna and I worried about George. He bubbled with enthusiasm and was an interesting, delightful little boy, but he couldn't read. Try as we might—and try as the school might—Dick and Jane and their dog Spot remained a mystery to him.

Miss Mary P. Henzey ran a private school in Ambler. I had spent six years there so we turned to her to help George. Miss Henzey quickly found the problem—Dick and Jane simply bored George. She taught him to read by sharing with him a book that he found interesting, *The Swiss Family Robinson*. By the end of the summer, he was reading and to this day continues to devour vast quantities of information from the printed page. And he remembers all of it.

George is a master of history, with a good background in ancient, European, and English. But where he excels is in his knowledge of American history, from Colonial America, including its arts and crafts, to the battles of the Civil War and the naval engagements of World War II.

His formal education took him from Germantown Academy to Ursinus College and to the Villanova Law School. After law school he became a public defender for Montgomery County and then practiced law in Ambler and Lansdale.

After we acquired our present property in Lower Frederick Township and decided to build a house—well, have a house built—we also realized we would need a barn. The barn became George's project, and he built it with Verna's help. In the process, George learned carpentry, including how to use a builder's square, electric saw, drill, plumb line, and other tools. Once the barn with its accompanying forge was finished, he then acquired stone and built the dry wall in front of our house, which has served as a retaining wall along the driveway. It has both a function and beauty, and George constructed the wall just like those you see in the English countryside, with rock and no mortar.

Armed with the experience of building the barn, George built his own house, doing carpentry, painting trim, and providing other finishing touches. As he had done with the barn, George used mortise and tenon joints for the large supporting timbers for the house. On an occasion when he was having trouble with a mortise (the recess into which the tenon will fit), he said to Maryanne, "Remind me the next time I build a house not to use oak beams." Having her own trouble with the project, she replied, "The next time you decide

*George B. Ditter, 1985*

to build a house, remind me not to be your wife." (While it is true that George built the house, he did receive help from his wife, her father, and his father.)

Over the ensuing years, George acquired furniture, art, and knick-knacks large and small that make the house both beautiful and interesting. Christmas decorations include miniature villages, ponds with skaters, and toys, as well as the traditional wreaths and tree.

Outside the house George has built trellises, garden fencing, and laid down walks.

All that I have mentioned was the culmination of steady efforts over months and years.

George has also been an active participant in the work of the Goschenhoppen Historians and during its annual folk festival has donned 18th-century dress and demonstrated wood craftsmanship. One summer he added to his skills by learning to make a Windsor chair.

When his church expanded its building, George provided the legal work without charge. He has preached, taught a Sunday School class, headed the church's board of trustees, and used his mechanical skills to make minor repairs. One summer he headed a church group that went to Appalachia to renovate houses.

George is a true Renaissance man.

Last, but hardly least, George is a family man. He and Maryanne raised a daughter and a son. Biking, hiking, camping, and family games were part of their children's growing up, with George leading the way. Both of the children have left the nest to build lives of their own.

Generous with his time and assistance, he is a dutiful son and a worthy companion.

## To George—He's Four

Twinkle, twinkle, little star,
I know what you really are,
Childhood's just a game you play,
So the Lord will let you stay
Where there's laughter, lots of noise
Trucks and dogs and girls and boys.
I know you're an angel bright,
Waiting here until the night,
When you'll scamper up on high,
There to brighten up the sky.
As you do each day on earth
With your smile, your pranks, your mirth.
Sparkling, happy, charming one
You just pretend that you're my son.

*JWD, November 17, 1954*

## Birthday Advice to a Son

Now you are one and sixteen and we, your parents say,
Good health and best of wishes upon your natal day.

Three rules for life we give you, if happiness you'd earn,
The first is that there is no end of things that you must learn.

But learning's not enough, of course, the way that things are planned,
If you would be a man, my son, you must for something stand.

The final precept that we give to help you all life through,
you must something do.

Learn, stand, and do something. Take up the tasks we give,
And you'll not just the years pass by, but all through life you'll live.

## Robert V. Ditter

Robert V. Ditter, 1985

When Bobby was four or so Smokey the Bear in his familiar uniform and hat was his favorite toy and a constant companion. Bobby never lacked imagination and I'm sure there were times when he pretended the ten-inch Smokey was a real bear. In any event we learned that automobile trips, long or short, had to include Smokey. He had become one of the family.

The summer that Bobby was five we camped at Ricketts Glen, and of course Smokey joined us in the tent and at meals. The week hurried by, and time came when we had to break camp, roll up sleeping bags, take down the tent, and secure the rest of the gear. Finally, the car was packed and we headed for home. We'd gone about five miles when we realized Smokey was missing. Bobby didn't seem concerned but we were. We returned to our campsite. No Smokey. Bobby was no help, but I went down to the lake and found that Bobby had hollowed out some sand and pulled more up to make sides and a back. Smokey was sitting upright, carefully placed in this chair of sand.

The message was clear. Bobby had decided he was too old for any more pretending about Smokey, and this was Bobby's way of saying good-bye to his friend. We never heard from Smokey again.

The next year our camping trip took us to Lake Huron's Killbear Point on Georgian Bay. We pulled into a suitable campsite and began unloading the trailer that held most of our equipment. Bob's tricycle was one of the first things out and he immediately claimed it. After a few minutes we realized Bobby was gone. Hidden from our sight by the many cars of boaters, fishermen, and other campers was a pier. A quick look. No Bobby. He must have gotten lost. Could he have ridden out on the pier? Just as we were about to panic, he came around the cars at the far end of the parking lot and pedaled his way back to his relieved parents. It had taken some time but he had circled the area knowing exactly where the rest of us were.

For several years when Bob was an adult, he and I camped at French Creek. Bill, George, and David were working and Verna was content to mind the home fires. So it was just the two of us. Miniature golf in the evenings; after a breakfast of pancakes, a book or magazine; a short bike ride around the park stopping for a call home.

Then we'd have an early lunch, get our bikes, and head off into the countryside. Bobby was a steady and fast rider and usually left me behind. We agreed he was to stop at an intersection and wait for me, but he was to choose which way we were then to go. That plan worked and gave me a moment's rest before he'd be off again. So it went for an hour or so of this sort of thing and I'd be hopelessly lost, but not Bobby. He had an uncanny sense of direction and knew exactly which roads to take to get us back to camp. We never had to ask for directions. Never.

Our bike rides were not confined to camping trips. Except during rush hour, the roads around Ambler had comparatively little traffic. One of our favorite Saturday short rides was to Germantown Academy and its swings, its merry-go-round, and, in season, the blackberries in the nearby woods. Again Bob led the way.

A quarter mile from our present home is a nature trail, the old right-of-way of the North Penn Railroad. Designed for hiking, biking, and riding, it crosses the road on which we live. When we go to the left, the trail takes us to the Montgomery park. To the right, it leads to Spring Mount and the ski area. The trail is well maintained by Montgomery County and presents countless vistas. It far surpasses in beauty and safety the narrow roads that we might otherwise encounter elsewhere.

Born in 1955, Bob taught himself to read when he was just a toddler. He liked children's books and had a good supply left by his older brothers. Following a trade school education he was a graduate of Elwyn Institute.

Working for Ken Crest Services, Bob ran a sit-down lawn mower as a member of grounds maintenance crew that did yard work for homes and industrial plants. For financial reasons Ken Crest had to terminate the service. Bob now works as an assembler in an Indian Creek workshop.

Bob has always been our self-appointed flag master. Up early, after the watching the news and weather on TV he'll go out and raise the American and Pennsylvania flags. In addition, he'll take two or three smaller flags and tie them to preexisting posts to decorate space near the barn.

Bob is a keen observer and is blessed with a fine memory. We depend upon him to recall the various events of family life: The last time we camped the Thousand Islands....When we got the station wagon...

Like his older brother, Bob is a Civil War buff with a special interest in and knowledge of Gettysburg that have been helped by two-day trips he and I have taken. Little Round Top. Devil's Den. Seminary Ridge. The High Water Mark of the Confederacy. The Pennsylvania Monument, which includes the name Sylvester Crossley, my great grandfather, on one of its many plaques. Both of us learned more with each trip we took together.

One year he and I visited several of the war's other battlefields, including Antietam, Fredericksburg, Chancellorsville, and Petersburg. Finally we stopped at Appomattox Court House where General Robert E. Lee surrendered his Army of Northern Virginia to General Ulysses S. Grant. To complete our visit there, we stood where my great grandfather's regiment stood as the Confederates lay down their arms.

Bob has had to overcome his share of troubles and disappointments. He has always met life's challenges no matter how difficult or heartbreaking, from major surgery that left him dependent upon insulin four times a day to the loss of his mother, which was particularly devastating to him. He is brave, resolute, and determined.

I am justly proud of him.

## Our Bobby

He's here, there, and everywhere, he seldom stops his flight,
But he taught himself to read and gladly he'll recite.

*'Twas the Night Before Christmas* from its start to its end,
Too, the Cat that wore the hat and came the day to spend.

Elvis he will imitate, the Hound Dog's blame assign.
The Elvis hips, push and pull, with all the song combine.

Cars and trucks. He'll name the make, the year that it was made.
Learned, I guess, from ads he'd seen and by attention paid.

How will his talents serve him? What others will he gain?
What more to feel successful? What force in him will reign?

We wonder for our children, what will the years provide,
We can only trust in God and watch and pray and guide.

## David B. Ditter

*David B. Ditter, 2017*

There were five of us. We had just gotten off the chairlift and were poling along a narrow trail that led to the place where we'd start our next run. We came to a turn and, there, two people who'd gone off the trail had fallen. They seemed to be all right so we kept going. Except for fourteen-year-old David. He stopped—got them both up, brushed off, and ready to go.

Typical David.

As the youngest of four brothers, David was the one who was sometimes kidded and teased. Nothing bad or intended to hurt and not often, but David was perceptive and sensitive and may have been hurt. If so, he kept it to himself, didn't sulk, and remained pleasant.

Typical David.

Born on March 11, 1957, he was well prepared by his mother for kindergarten—numbers, the alphabet, and children's books all came easily to him. He attended Ambler's public schools until sixth grade when he transferred to Germantown Academy.

He joined a Boy Scout troop and did the necessary work to advance to the rank of Star Scout. In 1972, Hurricane Agnes devastated Pennsylvania's Wyoming Valley, flooding the cities of Scranton, Wilkes-Barre, and Kingston. David's scout troop volunteered to do relief work in Kingston. For two days David and the others helped a woman whose house had been flooded above the second floor.

After being graduated from Germantown Academy, David had two years at the Montgomery County Community College and then two years at Northland College in Wisconsin. During his college summers he was a guard at the Montgomery County Park near Green Lane. At Northland he broadened his wealth of knowledge with environmental studies.

Following his graduation in 1980, David got a job at the Tobias Knoblauch Private Bank in Reading. Five years later he went to work at Unisys Corporation, in Blue Bell, Pennsylvania, leaving in June of 2017 to pursue other interests. Over that same span of time, David became a self-trained computer expert specializing in software applications and business operations support.

David joined the Fort Washington Masonic Lodge, worked his way through the chairs, and was its Worshipful Master in 1989 and again in 1991. He continued his masonic work as a member of the Fort Washington Royal Arch Chapter, becoming its High Priest in 1993. In 2001 he transferred membership to the lodge in Boyertown and was its Worshipful Master in 2003. He currently serves as Lodge Secretary and as one of the trustees. David has been a member of the Finance Committee at his church since the early 1990s has served in multiple leadership roles.

David is also a devoted husband and father. On July 27, 1991, he and Kathleen Werner were married. They have two daughters, Rebecca, born February 22, 1998, and Anna Rose who joined them on December 23, 2000.

Like his older brothers, David has acquired the tools, knowledge, and skills in home-maintenance and minor repairs. He and Kathy are gardeners, both flower and vegetable. Family pets include cats and rabbits and more rabbits, and so one hutch became two hutches, and two hutches became three.

David has always been a hard worker, both in his home life and at work. Despite his business and home responsibilities, he makes time to be a kind, helpful, ever-pleasant, caring son.

Typical David.

### A Worthy Man

What joy was ours when he appeared,<br>
That day in early spring,<br>
For then four boys our family made.<br>
"Four Crowns," our hearts did sing.

We watched as years went tumbling by,<br>
A baby then a lad,<br>
Who helped, was kind, and strived to please,<br>
With such his portion clad.

The virtues that we saw back then,<br>
And more, define a man.<br>
Our thanks we give in him we see,<br>
So well revealed, God's plan.

## On Becoming 80: Family Birthday Celebration

*October 19, 2001*

I am very grateful to my sons for arranging tonight's festivities and getting so many of you to show up. I will not detain you for more than a reasonable time, but you should know something about the phenomena of getting old. Some of you are older and some of you are not older.

During the first twenty-five years of life, most of us are aware that while we know something, there is a lot we don't know, so that the store of knowledge is balanced by the knowledge of ignorance. There are exceptions, of course, those who not only don't know what they do know but don't know what they don't know. We call those people teenagers.

Then comes the next twenty-five years or so when there's a balance between what we know we know on the one hand and knowing that there's a lot we don't know on the other. If we are at all articulate, we are called talkative—or voluble. People who agree with us call us mature adults.

The next twenty-five years are those of assumed wisdom. It's not that we know more than we knew before but the knowledge of what we don't know has been sucked into a black hole of our own minds—so that the balance that once saved us from ourselves is gone and we are referred to as ruminative or even loquacious.

And then you get to be eighty—and suddenly you have forgotten half of what you did know, and the half you remember you get backwards and you have forgotten all about the things you didn't know. Nature rushes into the vacuum created by the forgotten and your typical octogenarian realizes with an irresistible force that he has something to say—some words of wit or wisdom to impart—some gem of philosophy, an untold tale without which the world cannot survive—and so, the talkative and voluble, the ruminative and loquacious becomes "garrulous."

I'm glad it hasn't happened to me.

I commend you on your preparation for advancing years and cite as my authority Charles Lutwidge Dodgson, who wrote under the name of Lewis Carroll.

On of his verses deals with aging—this is how he put it:

"You are old, Father William," the young man said,
"And your hair has become very white;
And yet you incessantly stand on your head—
Do you think at your age it is right?"

I interject—as George and Bill tell you—many lawyers think that many judges spend so much time getting the law upside down that they think they are standing up when they are actually standing on their heads.

The verse goes on:

"In my youth," said his father, "I took to the law,
And argued each case with my wife;
And the muscular strength, which it gave to my jaw,
Has lasted the rest of my life."

So there you have it.

The great thing about reaching eighty is having children you are proud of—friends you are fond of—and a wonderful wife. I have all three—but I must add that even though my expectations were high, Verna has brought me more joy than I dared hope for, has displayed more talent than I thought possible in one person, and has encouraged, guided, inspired, and helped me in all things. She continues to delight me, as she has for all—that is to date—20,876 days of our marriage.

I thank you for being here tonight.

*God Bless America*

# Poetry for Verna

## Introduction by J. William Ditter, Jr.

We had been married for sixty years, seven months, and nine days when her gallant heart could take her no further. There had been a long hospitalization. When the doctors said there was little more they could do for her, I brought her back home—to the place she loved, had conceived, planned, and, yes, created.

*Planned by Verna—our home since 1973*

She was its designer and decorator. She made the curtains and cabinets. Her paintings hang on the walls. Her ceramics are useful and ornamental. The paneling in the living room—those cabinets at the end of the family room with glass doors and the bookshelves. She made them. You cannot take three steps in the house without seeing something of her handiwork. Outside she had planted and pruned, raked and scraped, tilled and sowed. No one deserved more than she did to be brought home, but it was only a few days before she left me.

Verna laughed often and easily. Her smile would light the room. Joy and happiness were her constant companions and she shared them generously. She was sunshine and radiance. Hers was the glory of springtime, the warmth of summer, the beauty of fall, and the sparkle of new-fallen snow. All woman, she was even more all girl. Youthful. Fun. Vital. Beautiful. Optimistic. Appreciative.

Charming? Yes. Diaphanous and gossamer? No. Conversation was her forte. She listened intently and would answer on point. Well read, intelligent, thoughtful, experienced, and practical in art, politics, current affairs, and much more. Living with her—seeing her—sharing life with her was joy, fun, challenge, and tremendous reward. She was my teacher and advisor—my companion and friend. The time came when I tried to use verse and poetry to express my love for Verna. She seemed to appreciate my efforts and displayed them in her art room.

Here are some of those she liked best.

*Verna: She tilled, raked, and planted at our new home, 1972*

*Verna, Spring 1942*

## And Always

I love you on the first of March,
I will upon the second.
I hope that you've consider that
As on my suit you've reckoned.

I'll love you each and every day,
As long as March shall last,
And then I'll love you just as much,
When all the month has past.

*JWD*
*March 1, 1944*

## I'll Stick with Her

I think that I shall never see,
A Valentine that's like a tree.

A tree is sticks and leaves and stuff,
It's got a bark that's black and rough.

It's in the ground and filled with birds,
That never seem at loss for words.

Contrast with that my Valentine,
She warms my blood like Grecian wine.

Her skin is smooth and cuddly soft,
No birds go "Twitter" in her loft.

Each year she doesn't give a shake,
And sheds her leaves so I must rake.

She walks and talks and comes inside,
And is as pretty as a bride.

She is my one, my only love,
Sent to me by God above.

Poets who write of trees are fine,
But I will praise my Valentine.

*JWD to VBD*
*Valentine's Day, 1985*

## The Only Way

For what's not lost, I make my quest:
The way to say, "I love you" best.

Can any sweet hope to portray
The depth of love I feel today?

By flowers that too quickly fade,
Can length of love 'ere be conveyed?

A bauble? Lots are in your drawer.
Could love be shown by adding more?

I quick reject the thought of song,
Another's words would be all wrong.

My search has failed, perhaps you knew.
I must rely on "I love you."

*Love, Bill*
*Valentine's Day, 1990*

*Our wedding day, September 2, 1944*

## On the Occasion of Our Anniversary

"Grow old along with me!" the garden sundial said,
"The best is yet to be," were words we also read.
And armed with faithfulness and hope and love, we two
Walked down the path to find if it was really true.

Now, days have passed. Nay, years have come to speed away,
So with me pause, my dear, on this our special day.
Was what we saw so very long ago that time
Love's promise, or a poet's empty, idle rhyme?

Once just a catchy tune, but now a symphony.
The acorn, then the sprig, and now a mighty tree.
Better this? Yes! We found the poem's theme was so,
We've shared the hopes, the joys that young loves never know.

Love, once a tiny stream, now river deep and strong,
Made so by storms of life, by every tear and song.
Better this? Yes! Though once a groom and fairest bride,
We truly walk as one, not merely side by side.

Those blossoms that were spring's make up the autumn hue,
Flowers now, colors rich, and filled with fragrance too.
Better this? Yes! 'Tis better than our wondering start,
For hand to hand's become our joining heart to heart.

*VBD from JWD*
*September 2, 1991*

## "Today is number fifty"

Today is Number Fifty of valentines to you.
I know it should be special, imaginative and new.

Was the first a card I bought with lace and flowered rhyme?
Another's sentiments and words to mark the start of time?

How frequently has candy in heart-shaped box of red
Been the messenger I sent to say what I'd not said?

Lots of cards have been home-made with unscanned poetry,
Pictures that a child could draw (stick figures challenge me).

Of course, I've sent you flowers, their beauty less than thine.
All the love they could express was still much less than mine.

You've filled my days with gladness, your smile lights up my life.
How tell of joy's contentment, since ere you've been my wife?

Is there measure for my pride in all the things you've made?
Our house shows off your knowledge of every craft and trade.

From Christmas decorations to paintings on the wall:
Cabinets, trim, and figurines. My sweet has made them all.

If flowers, words, and candy don't tell the path we've trod,
Perhaps it's for a reason, I haven't mentioned God.

My thanks go to Him daily, He blessed my life with you.
He arranged that we would meet. He made us one from two.

Number Fifty's pride and joy and thanks to God above,
Not new or very special. It's simply all my love.

*Verna from Bill*

*February 14, 1992*

## "So scant the days"

So scant the days, so short the nights,
This month of ice and snow.
The hours of sunshine are too few
To bear what I'd bestow.

Why is this time of sentiment
The shortest of them all?
I need more days than are at hand,
Fond memories to recall.

I cannot crowd in twenty-eight
Or even twenty-nine,
The words of love I want to say
To you, my Valentine.

So lengthen February!!
To give more time to hear,
The praises of my fairest one,
My wife. My life. My dear.

But even as I say these words,
My logic's on the wane,
Adding March and then April
Would be an act most vain.

Unnumbered days, uncounted hours,
Would still leave all too few,
The length of time that I must have,
To tell how I love you.

*JWD to VBD*
*Valentine's Day 1994*

## "I sit here in silence"

Dear Verna,

I sit here in silence.
Dawn is coming. I can see the faintest light toward the east.
And I think of you.
In moments few, the sun will light the day. The way you light my life. A shining radiance. A bright fulfillment.

Now He does command the world.
Banished are the shades of night and the beauty of the morn is mine.
And I think of you.
It was you who showed me where there is beauty, the unseen wonders to which my eyes you opened.

Noon and its warmth.
The glory of the day. The clouds reflect their glowing orb with admiration, wonder, awe.
And I think of you.
To me, you are warmth and glory. You fill me with admiration, wonder, awe. You are my life just as surely as sun is life to noon.

Later, to the west.
The fiery charioteer begins his journey, I see

the lengthening shadows that so intrigue me.
And I think of you.
You, my wife, intrigue me still. As if we just
had met, but known each other since time
began. When I laugh, you laugh. When I
cry, you cry. Am I shadow or are you?

Here now, the gentle, long-awaited darkness.
The clock has chimed away the stillness and
brought the stars.
And I think of you.
The stars—a gift of God—remind me that
you are my gift from Him.
The fickle goddess, Moon, ascends. Cool.
Distant. Pale. In contrast to your warmth,
vitality, and faithfulness.
And I think of you. Again?
No, not again, but still, for you are my love,
dawn to dawn, year to year, forever.

*Love, Bill*
*July 21, 1996*

*Time off from duty at the base, Algiers, Louisiana, 1944*

*Verna with Billy and George, summer 1952*

## On the Occasion of Our Fifty-Seventh Anniversary

Heinz has fifty-seven kinds—at least, I've heard that said.
I've had fifty-seven years since first that we were wed.

Of Heinz's fifty-seven, there's sweet and sour too.
But all my fifty-seven were honeyed times with you.

Heinz's fifty-seven come from out Three Rivers' town.
God gave me fifty-seven to help my earthly crown.

Forty-four to Zero-one, with joy you've filled my days:
Your charm and grace and beauty, your effervescent ways.

I marvel at your talents, expressed in things you've done,
Artistry to carpentry—with them, I've just begun.

Barns and blooms—you mastered all—four children, zest and cheers.
Proud I've been to share with you these fifty-seven years.

Give thanks to Heinz for pickles but thanks to you for life.
Thanks for all you've been to me, my darling, precious wife.

*JWD to VBD*
*September 2, 2001*

## Madonna

When first you held our first son,
You filled my heart with awe,
The fairest of Madonnas,
Was what in you I saw.

When first you held our next son,
He shared your mirth and charms,
Your talent and your joy of life,
Were nestled in your arms.

When first you held our third son,
He looked at you and smiled,
Then shut his eyes to sleep again,
So pleased to be your child.

When first you held our fourth son,
Sure sent by God above,
I thought I heard an angel sing,
About you and your love.

And now our boys are grown men,
And each has made his way,
To you all thanks and praise are due,
For them on Mother's Day.

*JWD to VBD*
*May 11, 2003*

## Valentine's Day 2004

I stood with you and did declare,
"With this ring, I thee wed."
And how the days have tumbled by,
And how the years have sped.

Those words I said though not forgot,
Today I will renew,
Another way my love to say,
My Valentine, for you.

*JWD to VBD*
*February 14, 2004*

*Verna, summer 1942*

## "May time be always"

May time be always good to you,
May love with wondrous light shine through.

May joy its treasure houses comb,
For you the best where'er you roam.

And may you always have a song,
Each hour, each day, your whole life long.

May happiness and laughter stay,
Companions yours along the way.

And may in every moment,
Of yours the whole day through,

Assured be in the knowledge,
That God is close to you.

*September 2, 2004*

*I made this toast to Verna at the party celebrating our 60th wedding anniversary.*

*Verna camping, 1964*

## Oh, Lucky Day

And so we met, oh lucky day.
It charmed me as it came my way— Your smile.

On our first date, that eve of dance,
'Twas in your eyes with every glance. Your smile.

When down the aisle, you were in white
'Twas mine again and all was right. Your smile.

You nursed a child so newly came,
Madonna-like but still the same. Your smile.

And so it's been as years rolled past.
A thrill at start. A thrill did last. Your smile.

No gift for you could e're be bought,
To match what joy that it has wrought. Your smile.

*Happy Birthday*

*JWD to VBD*
*July 21, 2004*

## "Sixty says the calendar"

Sixty says the calendar,
but that cannot be true.
Sixty is a long, long time,
yet it's been short with you.
If you count the cards I've sent,
they'd number fifty-nine.
So mark this number sixty,
and be my valentine.

*JWD to VBD*
*February 14, 2005*

## Christmas Day Has Come

A toast I thought I'd drink to you when Christmas day'd be here,
And so I started on a quest that lasted through the year.

I took nectar from the blossoms that scatter down our lane,
With just a dash of springtime dew and drops of summer rain.

For bubbles I did listen at morn in early spring,
So I could catch the first pure note a lark was sure to sing.

For life I took some light'ning that split the summer night,
For crackle and its luminesce, its heat of golden-white.

Then I shook in distant thunder, those hints of storms long gone,
Reminders that the darkest times come just before the dawn.

For memories and for laughter there was a child's first word,
The haunting sighs of lonely doves and silence undisturbed.

No ice, but coolness that I found in swirls of morning mist,
Along a sweet, swift flowing stream where elves the flowers kissed.

I climbed upon a mountain top to find twelve flakes of snow,
As powdered sugar they now float to sweeten what's below.

An autumn's sunset's dark red sky the color did provide,
The cup I made is laced with pearls, you wore them as a bride.

And now Christ's natal day has come, to you that cup I raise,
Let joy and health and happiness bless thee throughout your days.

God sent his love on Christmas day, the one we glorify,
And only He with grace divine, could love you more than I.

*JWD to VBD*
*December 25, 2001*

## When

When I have grown so old that I cannot find the word I want, I shall remember,
Your quick wit and merry heart. Your radiance. The way you filled my life with joy.

When I have grown so old that the name of an old friend escapes me, I shall remember,
The touch of your hand. The joy of coming home to you. Just being with you.

When I have grown so old that I cannot recall an hour ago, I shall remember
The night we met. Our first dance, and how you looked as you walked down the aisle.

When I have grown so old I cannot walk and wonder what they are whispering about,
Those strangers—or are they my children?
I shall remember how we walked hand in hand across the campus,
And later down the road of life, still hand in hand.

When I have grown so old I can no longer see, I shall remember,
Your smile. Your laugh. The sparkle of your eyes.

When the shadows lengthen and darkness closes about me,
My last conscious thought will be of you
And how I was blessed,
Blessed with you, my wife,
And how I've missed you.

*J.W.D.*

*Verna B. Ditter, 1995*

# Christmas Letters

## Introduction by The Honorable Gene E. K. Pratter

Turning the calendar after Thanksgiving each year brings to mind a host of reasons to eagerly anticipate treats and delights of all varieties. Without a doubt, Bill Ditter's annual Christmas letter is among the season's sweetest, most anticipated gifts.

Little did I realize when I became a federal judge in the Eastern District of Pennsylvania that high on the list of valued perks would be a place on the list of lucky recipients of these special missives that Bill prepares and shares each year.

Bill's Christmas letters are nothing—and I mean nothing—like the annual letters we may get (or send) recounting the year's births, birthdays, trips, honors, accolades, accomplishments, acquisition, events, and such. Bill is much too modest and too clever for that kind of prescription. Indeed, his letters are far from formulaic: they are utterly unique and undoubtedly special.

In the Christmas letters the lines between the real and imaginary blur. They recount an endless series of mild misadventures marked by the foibles of human nature that we all recognize but perhaps hadn't fully understood until Bill turned his storytelling talents to the task. Bill's Christmas letter parables are told with disarming detail using fictional characters like the redoubtable Cousin Misty. Who would doubt that she just is easily could be as real as you and me? (After I read the first Christmas letter I received, I had to quietly ask a fellow judge if there *was* a Cousin Misty somewhere perched in Bill's family tree.)

Each letter is a priceless Christmas gift Bill has given us that prompts the reader to laugh out loud, dab away a tear, and acknowledge long-known but perhaps temporarily forgotten truths about common and uncommon features of the human condition.[1] Sometimes a letter's lessons stem from the ubiquitous Thanksgiving feast, or emanate from the "gender wars" or fashion fads, or from some inherently silly puzzling phrase to which but for Bill's letters we would never have given a second thought.

---

1 I think it surely must have been Bill who observed one time or another—perhaps even in one of the letters—that "some people find fault like there was a reward for it."

The Christmas letters that follow here represent the wisdom and warmth of Bill Ditter and remind us that, as to Bill's big heart, his encyclopedic mind and his keen, twinkling eye (with the apologies to Cousin Misty), "the latch string is always open."

## *So Much in One Year, and Cousin Misty Too*

The Ditters' 1998 Christmas Letter

*Box 256, Hendricks, PA 18979*

December 1998

Dear Family and Friends,

Well, another year is coming to an end and that means it's time to tell you what an exciting year it was for us, as I'm sure it was for you—or at least, some of you.

January. We went down to the firehouse at the nearby community of Zieglersville and watched the spirited debate among those who were concerned with the place's name. There are two signs that mark this little town—one *with* the "S" in the middle and one *without* an "S" in the middle. Zieglersville or Zieglerville. Well, it was plain to be seen there were several factions: those who said the correct name was without the S and that's the way it should stay; those who agreed the correct name was without the S but wanted it changed so there'd be an S; those who said the correct name had an S and that's the way they wanted it kept; those who said the correct name had an S but they wanted it changed so there'd be no S; and those who wanted the signs left alone and, as one put it, didn't give an S one way or the other. We left before raucous became violent and never did hear how things turned out.

February came and went before we were really onto it. Tempus really fugits as the fellow with the pipe at the general store says.

March came in like a Lion and went out with a Lamb. Or maybe it was the other way around.

In May, we went to an Elderhostel in Nearlythere, MN, to learn about 19th-century dynamiting, tree-felling, and road building. Fascinating!! The dynamiting course was taught by Three-Fingered Jack, a veteran with a thousand stories to tell about explosives.

Tree-felling was taught by Peg-Leg Charlie, who stressed safety when you cut down the big ones. (Verna still playfully calls, "Timber," even if I'm just cutting discount coupons from the Sunday paper.)

In June Cousin Misty and her seven kids arrived. Misty explained that her mother's second cousin, once removed, was my mother's third—it doesn't matter, so forget it. I never really understood her anyway. Well, brood might be better—ages 23 years to 7 months—all named, according to Misty for their place of conception ("never got caught by the same fellow twice in the same place," Misty explains). She and hers were not expected and there was never a dull moment in the six days before they moved on. Kitchen, 18, is trying to establish a diaper service—and used the nearby Perkiomen as a laundry until a chap from the EPA came along and made her stop. The one they call "Brew" (real name Creekbank) loves to make things. Verna says I should have figured that when her welding machine disappeared—our gas grill and all the rain gutters and down spouts were gone—that someone was up to something. Well, that low flying plane was an Alcohol, Tobacco, and Firearms agent, who saw that Brew was building a still in our woods over near the Boy Scout cabin. So that was that. His brother, Bottle (real name, Sofa; they all have nicknames), said this was the seventh time ATF had made Brew quit before he really got started. Bottle said he has no respect for the government and he'll be darned "if he'll ever pay taxes to support a rotten bunch like them."

Misty is delightful in her own way. She has a philosophy that you don't see every day and you don't hear it expressed the way she expresses it: For example, right out of the blue she'll comment, "Forgive us our debts, for they know not what they do" or "God loves a cheerful, two-fisted giver who can't count" or "The difference between an optimist and a pessimist is whether the glass is full or two-thirds empty." Well, all good things must come to an end so they left although their mail is still being forwarded here. Bills and all.

We had our usual 4th of July celebration on the 4th of July. The parade around the swimming pool was a little disappointing this year because the fellow with the tuba missed his footing (or was pushed; no one who is fair-minded is really sure) and he fell in at the deep end. That was one of those things that cuts both ways. The music sounded better without him. On the other hand, I've been spending no little time with our insurance agent. Did you know that a swimming pool should have interior lights after 8:00 p.m., DST?

Our next-door neighbor's dog had pups in August and since they thought she was a male, they were quite surprised.

We closed the swimming pool for the winter in September.

We went to the church social in October and would have won a beautiful, hand-made quilt if we hadn't forgot and left the ticket home under the sugar bowl where we keep all the things like that so we'll know where they are when we want them.

We were second in line to pay our post-office box rental in November; first, if you only count people who pay in one dollar bills.

That brings us to now, and you are up to date with us. If you're nearby, drop around to see us. As Misty says, "My latch string is always open."

Until then,

*Bill and Verna*

*The barn that Verna and George built at our new home*

## *A Reindeer's Lesson*

## The Ditters' 1999 Christmas Letter

*Box 256, Hendricks, PA 18979*

December 1999

Hello There[2]

Last Christmas was the first in which we made a serious investment in time and money to have a worthy outside lighting display. While there is an honest difference of opinion on the matter, I contend that the somewhat higher than expected costs must be balanced off against the learning experience the project brought to our household. By way of illustration—and without intending to be all-inclusive:

1. A short circuit has nothing to do with the length of a particular wire. A long circuit—strange as it may seem—is not the opposite of a short circuit. In fact, when you ask about a long circuit, all you get are smirks and smiles.

2. While words like *watts, ohms, volts, sagacity, AC, DC, installation, gauge,* and *fuse* convey little meaning to you and to me—to some people they are just as important as words like *quo warranto, habeas corpus, perpetuities,* and *nunc pro tunc* are to the rest of us. *Gauge,* for example, refers to the thickness of a wire—the bigger the number, the smaller the wire. That makes sense, doesn't it?

3. The covering on a wire is called its *installation* and its color does not necessarily show the wire's *sagacity,* i.e., its ability to carry "juice." Moreover, "only a complete idiot would think that because they are Christmas lights you should connect a green wire to a red wire."

4. Just because firemen are volunteers and have learned the way to your house does not mean that they are always cheerful—after all, during the daytime they have jobs—just like everyone else—and during the evening hours before Christmas, they have a lot to do too—just like everyone else. Volunteer firemen have heard the one about red suspenders a "thousand times" and may not want to hear it again while they're packing up their equipment.

2 Last year we said "Dear Family and Friends." We've changed that because a member of our so-called extended family said please do not rub it in ever again—and three folk whom we thought were friends said we were being presumptuous.

5. If, after a well-intentioned suggestion about business methods, you have been told to take over the checkbook, do not let your fire insurance policy lapse.

6. During the yuletide season, carpenters charge an astonishing amount for a few boards, a little paint, and a few hours' work.

7. Turning off Rudolph's flashing red nose on a lawn display of Santa, his sleigh, and eight tiny reindeer ("each foot a twinkling star that will be the talk of the neighborhood") will not keep your dog from barking all night. However, he will calm down if he is permitted to go out and wet on Rudolph, Santa, his sleigh, and eight tiny reindeer. (Actually, on Rudolph three times.)

8. Once your dog shuts up, your neighbor will not necessarily view his dog's continued barking as his exclusive problem. Never answer your phone after 2:00 A.M.

9. While the little feet on a ladder have their use, they should not be used on icy ground.

10. The longer the ladder, the more important it is to have someone hold it during icy weather.

11. The fibula is the smaller of the two principal bones in the lower leg.

12. ER stands for Emergency Room. ER personnel are unmoved by another's pain and shouting.

13. PT stands for physio-therapy.

14. An orthopedist is a doctor who is concerned with bones, muscles, joints, ligaments, and tendons. An orthodontist is concerned with teeth. An orthopedist should not be referred to as an orthodontist, whether in error or jest. No doctor should be referred to as Doc. It would be absurd to have orthopedists rename their specialty Bone-Docs to avoid confusion with those who in the future would be called Tooth-Docs.

15. As a group, orthopedists have little or no sense of humor and/or seem quite unconcerned with the confusion they and orthodontists are creating among members of the public generally.

16. Female PTs, or physiotherapists, are quite inured to the fact that they may cause pain in those who are already suffering extreme pain. They are unmoved by even sincere groans.

17. If you haven't thought of a place to store Santa, his sleigh, eight tiny reindeer (each foot a twinkling star that will be the talk of the neighborhood unless you've stepped on one of them, in which case none of them twinkle), and Rudolph, give it some thought before you plunk down enough to take us to dinner 23 times.

18. Things generally get worse before they get better.

Well, enough of learning in the abstract—Now for some of the garlands we gathered since our last report to you:

Dec '98 VBD—Most Admired Patient's Wife, Grandview Hospital.

Jan '99 VBD—Most Admired Out-Patient's Wife, Grandview Hospital.

Apr '99 VBD—Chosen to throw out first ball, grandson's pee-wee baseball league.

Aug '99 VBD—Goshenhoppen Fair Apple-Peeling Contest: Longest, Quickest Peel, 2nd place.

Dec '98 JWD—Improved Patient Attitude Award, Grandview Hospital, Honorable Mention.

Dec '98 JWD—PECO Energy Innovative Lawn Display Award, Certificate of Merit.

Feb '99 JWD—Senior Adult Center Duplicate Bridge Contest, Donkey's Tail Award.

Aug '99 JWD—Goshenhoppen Fair Whistle Whittling, Certificate of Promise.

Oct '99 JWD—Cheerful Postal Patron Award, Gift Certificate, $3.50, Yoder's Market.

Some of you have inquired about Cousin Misty: She came this year with only the new baby—the oldest two boys are in jail ("I should've kept my ear to the grindstone on them two") and her daughter got married ("And just in the nickel of time too—she never was one to let politics make a bedfellow feel strange.").

I wrote down several other Misty-observations:

"As the famous Chinese philosopher Charlie Chan, said, 'There's a certain satisfaction that comes from cursing the darkness that the lighting of a single candle can't touch.'"

"Mothers are the invention of necessity."

"We have enough youth—what we need is the Fountain of Smart."

Of her some-time husband, "Half a loafer is better than one."

"Some say Y2K—I say why not Tokay?"

We hope '99 was a good year for you and yours—and that '00 will be even more so. And as Cousin Misty says, "If there's anything better than putting off until tomorrow what you don't want to do today, tell me what it is." Oh, yes, and, "The latch string is always open."

*Bill – Verna (with reservations) – Bob*

## *Of Piccolo, Pool, and Picnic Perils*

### The Ditters' 2000 Christmas Letter

*Box 256, Hendricks, PA 18979*

December 2000

Hi,[3]

We've divided this year into significant months for our annual report to you. Our 1999 letter was "event-oriented," which apparently spoiled the whole Christmas season for several of our critics and may have even tarnished the new year for them as well.

January. We spent most of the time on two projects—first, we explained, apologized for, and provided additional information on matters we put into last year's dispatch. Second, we wanted to do our 1997 Christmas card scrapbook but decided to have some rules before cutting and pasting began, considering how things went in 1998 or 1996, matters that still cast a degree of pall over the otherwise joys of that season. We discussed at some length questions such as what to do with the picture from a card like the card we sent in 1997. Or what about the people we didn't hear from in 1998 but who sent us their 1997 card in 1999? Or

3 Again we have been corrected on our greeting. Last year's "Hello There" was said to show a lack of sensitivity by three folk who said it suggested that because "there" could be anywhere, we were intimating that those to whom we wrote lacked a place to live, i.e., were homeless. Honestly, we meant no offense even to those who use a general delivery address.

what to do when three otherwise lovely folk all sent the same card? And there was more. We ran out of January before we were close to agreement so we shelved the project hoping that time would help solve some of the difficulties that common sense, logic, experience, and a completely conciliatory attitude on the part of one person failed to resolve.

February. A very cold month[4] and, as you doubtless know, the cold will bring out the best in some, though not necessarily in all of us. Take turning off the outside spigots, for example. Reminders that start in late November are helpful but what with global warming on everyone's mind, not spurring to action, as it were. Reminders in December along with discussions about what to send Aunt Sophie Bridges, who two years ago sent the homemade calf-foot jelly but nothing last year, were simply deferred and certainly not ignored. I already told you about January.

March. It got warmer in March and we had two very nice fountains at the outside spigots although their beauty was marred by a series of somewhat pointed comments. The plumber came and had apparently studied psychology as well as piping. After he had fixed things, he offered to show me how to turn off the water. I told him I'd lived in this house for 27 years and knew very well how to do it. He then suggested that some older people like to write things down on a calendar to remind them of important tasks. I was going to show him our calendar to let him know that I already did that although there was nothing wrong with my memory, but I couldn't find it. Later it turned up in the can where we keep dry dog food. How the dog got the can open remains a mystery to me.

July. About 35 friends and family showed up to help celebrate Independence Day. We'd heard about a local musical group of high school students so we engaged them to provide some patriotic tunes. In chit chat with one of them, I learned they came from three different schools and were barely getting to know each other and the full import of that comment, even though it was delivered with a smirk, didn't occur to me until later. They arrived in semi-uniforms—blue shorts, fitted white silk-like shirts, and red neckties—and serenaded us during the dinner hour. For the evening's climax, they were to march around the pool, winding up on the near side to render a final number because most of our guests were sitting on the far side. The lesson to be learned from what occurred is that you should never let an adventurous youth who plays the slide trombone march to the rear of a well-proportioned girl who wears braces and plays the piccolo. She was at the deep end poised for what I think is called the *piccolo avocado* in the *Stars and Stripes Forever* when she gave a whoop. The piccolo, braces attached, flew into the water as did she.

4 Fortunately I'd brought in the brass monkey so he was never in danger.

The trombone player later explained that he had merely looked down to be sure of his footing and declined to give any further explanation, nor will I. She was helped from the pool by three of our octogenarian friends who almost came to blows to decide who would give her a hand at the ladder, a much-needed robe was supplied, and the piccolo, braces still attached, was retrieved. As they were saying good night, several of our male friends were kind enough to say the day's festivities had opened new vistas as to what having a glorious Fourth means.

August. You will not believe how some people are willing to compromise principle by saying "what difference does it really make?" We were having corn on the cob when I noticed that little Seth was eating his corn from the thin end to the thick end of the ear. So I told him very gently to turn the cob around and eat it correctly. When he failed to respond, I reached over and gently took the corn to turn it around for him. He let out a wail—actually a scream—and lunged at my hand and as I pulled away gently, his milk got knocked over. In trying to save the milk, my elbow hit his sister's ice tea. Why parents let children put glasses practically against each other I do not know. How the water from the flowers joined the milk and the ice tea on my son's wife's dress I did not observe, as my attention was required by my life's companion who asked what did I think I was doing. She was apparently too preoccupied by the catsup that was squirting on her new frock—the bottle had gotten under my elbow—to be aware of the events that were unfolding right beside her. I gently tried to explain that I did not want my grandson to grow up to be a clod. That seemed to upset the little tyke's mother more than the milk–ice tea–flower water on her dress because she grabbed him as though I was going to go after his corn again. Apparently that was his thought too, because he put the generously buttered corn down her dress and began to blubber. When order was finally restored, I tried in a gentle way to explain about how as the bough is bent the tree will grow and a stitch in time saves nine. Without reason the child must have thought I said a stick in time, figured that I was threatening to beat him, and tried to leave the table. I suspect it was his older sister who had tucked the tablecloth into his pants because she seemed to enjoy the resulting carnage more than anyone else.

When the dust had cleared, so to speak, somebody said I was sure getting off on the right foot with my youngest grandson so I took the opportunity to explain gently that the comment didn't make any sense because when we march we don't start with our right foot but with our left. I have always believed it is best to teach when the opportunity presents itself, but, considering the comments that followed, I am reconsidering that point of view.

Later, as I sat there watching Verna clean up the mess little Seth had caused, I told her we should not hold it against him. He's only three and children make mistakes. She stopped and looked at me—there was no word, gesture, or sign—yet I knew our minds were one. Those sacred moments in our marriage when no words are necessary almost bring tears to my eyes. Verna read this and said that when she thinks back about that moment it almost makes her cry too. Do you wonder that I feel blessed?

October. Cousin Misty and her toddler arrived in a Model T Ford! She's been offered $18,500 for it but says it holds too many memories to go for less than $23,000. They stayed five days and, as usual, I wrote down some of her observations, which I am happy to share with you:

> "When its early to bed and early to rise it makes you wish you'd married three other guys."
>
> "Mark Twain said he never met a man he didn't like. I've had the same trouble ever since I was 17—well, 14 if you count the Brewster brothers and that kid that spent the summer at the Lambert farm, which I don't."
>
> "Gun control? We ought to be like the French. The highest building in Paris is the Rifle Tower."
>
> "Alfred Einstein is a genius because he had a theory about his relatives. Me too about mine."
>
> "Clinton never tells any half-truths unless he thinks they're completely accurate."
>
> "There are three things a girl has to be careful about and both of them can be summed up in one word: men."
>
> "A word to the wise is not needed."
>
> "They let my oldest out, and I'm praying he'll pass the mustard with his parole officer."

We hope 2000 has been good and 2001 will be better for you. And we remind you, in Cousin Misty's words, "The latch string is always open."

*Bill – Verna – Bob*

*Verna Bock Ditter, watercolor*

## *Fore! And French Windows*
The Ditters' 2001 Christmas Letter

*Box 256, Hendricks, PA 18979*

December 2001

Hello, Folks,

It all began blandly enough with Verna's reminding me again that I should have an annual physical this year. A man my age can't be too careful where matters of health are concerned. It's something he does for his family as well as himself. If a person just goes ahead and does it there won't be any more little notes stuck on the refrigerator door where the ice cream is kept, not to mention the mirror where a man shaves.

Now let me tell you about doctors. I would suggest that after you have been poked, pummeled, prepped, pricked, probed, prodded, and provoked you may just want to gather up your clothes and head for the safety of a six-way intersection or your job at the dynamite factory. Even good news from a doctor can be bad news in the long run. When the doctor confides in you that you are in pretty good shape, all things considered, that's the time to leave. What comes next is advice. And it will probably be to get some exercise. For example, why don't you take up golf?

In February golf shops not only sell clubs, little numbered socks to cover your clubs, bags, shoes, socks, golf balls with your initials on them, tees, wind breakers, caps, and a really nifty little umbrella that fits right in your golf bag, they also sell instruction books. One of the better ones for beginners is *Par Is in Your Head (A Thinking Man's Approach to Golf)* by Byron Nelson, which I was lucky to get because it was the shop's last copy and it has been out of print for 17 years.

Those of you who have been to our house will remember that the French doors between the living room and the dining room are never closed. Never.

Golf shoes have little spikes which make them unsuitable for the house, but that can be overcome if you have saved a piece from a perfectly good carpet that got replaced last year by the need to match the new curtains or else people will think we don't know how exciting and vibrant a color mauve really is.

If you take that piece of carpet that you thoughtfully saved and put it on the floor, the floor will absolutely not get scratched by those little cleats. When you're learning something, it's a good idea to follow the same routine until it's a habit. Doing that from the beginning, each step of the way, according to Mr. Nelson, will take strokes off your game, and are there any of you who don't want to do that? Having read to page 14, I was ready to get started with the first thing you do, which is to call out, "Fore." That alerts other drivers that you are about to address the ball.

After eight or ten attempts I was satisfied with the resonance of my "Fore" and that it would be heard all the way down the fair lane.[5] I am not being critical, but there's simply no way to know that someone is trying to read in the living room if you have your back to the French doors. On the other hand, if a person with his back to you has a golf club in his hand, I would think that should tell you not to close the French doors. Being pleased with the ease with which I had mastered the initial phase of my first golfing effort, I carefully placed my feet just as Mr. Nelson said I should, carefully placed my hands around the club just as Mr. Nelson said I should, carefully began my back swing just as Mr. Nelson said I should, and gave another lusty, "Fore."

I was so startled by the sound of breaking glass that my feet, golf shoes, and rug went out from under me and I landed in what a moment before

5 Even for the sake of harmony, I cannot agree that I was bellowing.

had been seven panes of glass complete with those little pieces of wood that are there. *Were* there, I should say.

The face-down ride in the back of the station wagon to the hospital was not a comforting one what with my agonizing pain and a certain coolness from a driver who, while sympathetic to my plight and often fair-minded in the past about many things, seemed unwilling to accept the blame for the carnage in the living room despite readily admitting that she was the one who put the notes about a man's duty to his family on the refrigerator door where the ice cream is kept.

Once at the emergency room, I was placed face down on a litter and after an interminable wait was interviewed by the intake nurse who seemed far more concerned with my age, insurance numbers, temperature, blood pressure, blood type, pulse rate, and allergies than she was with the seat of my problem. By this time, pain was starting to erode my usual cheerful disposition, and I will admit that I shouted at her, for which I am moderately sorry—I should not have called her Nurse Wicked Witch of the West, for which I am very sorry. But it is hard to be pleasant when you are lying on your stomach with pieces of wood and glass protruding from a very sensitive part of the anatomy, and I would have apologized if she had not gone off in a huff.

The doctor was ruthlessly fast with a pair of scissors considering the fact that my golf slacks ($73.75 plus tax) had been brand new just 2 hours and 40 minutes before. While he was preparing the site, as it were, he asked me what had happened. Starting with Mr. Nelson's advice in *Par Is in Your Head (A Thinking Man's Approach to Golf)*, I recounted the events that led up to my being there in as much detail as was necessary from the golfing point of view. Just as I was warming to my task, he momentarily disappeared only to return with a tape recorder and a group of folk in hospital garb who had been lounging around the area. As I was starting my story again, I noticed several of them also had recorders. When I inquired of Dr. Quick Shears why there was such an increasing gathering, he explained that today's hospital treats the whole man and while my injuries might seem to be superficial from the medical standpoint, there was no telling which professional specialty might be called upon for consultation "down the road." *Superficial? Down the road?* But it was heartening to see that the various departments had answered his call for as I was retelling how I was injured for the third time more doctors, nurses, and orderlies had drifted in I noticed OBGYN on one, ICCU on another, and PEDIATRICS on a pleasant young lady who smiled and giggled a lot. All with recorders.

I spent the better (I am not sure *better* is the right word) part of the next day at the hospital and repeated my story, now called my past medical history or PMH, to each of several shifts, including three volunteers from the information desk and the hospital dietician—all with tape recorders.

Two final things: if you have a teenager who is wondering about a lucrative field of endeavor, you might wish to suggest floor refinishing. February is apparently their busiest month and thus the reason why they charge prices that you just would not believe. And if you know anyone who is seriously interested in taking up golf and wants some equipment, minus a No. 1 wood (apparently as I was going down, it got caught in the radiator and was then released like an arrow into the china closet) but including its little numbered cover, a really nifty[6] umbrella, and a closet full of other stuff, let me know.

Fourth of July brought our usual gathering of friends and family, including our grandson Todd, who our daughter, his mother, calls Andy, and his twin sister, Shannon, who is called Sandy. Do not ask why if you have accepted a tidy sum from your father to use family names you call your children by nicknames. Now a bit of advice. If you have a pool with a plastic liner, do not set up the quoit arena within a thousand yards of the pool if you have to go and grill hamburgers, leaving behind two inquisitive seven-year-old grandchildren, even if they have been swimming like fish since infancy. And if your favorite teenager has no bent for floor refinishing, you might steer him/her toward replacing vinyl pool liners. Also a lucrative calling.

Cousin Misty came for Thanksgiving bringing only her youngest, who starts preschool next year, and on the QT I wrote down some of Misty's more interesting comments:

> "My husband was a constitutional activist in his own way—he'd never pass up a fifth."
>
> "On her son who violated his parole: I talked to that boy until he was blue in the face, but it was just like water off a truck's back—in one eye and out the other—Finally, I quit and threw up the towel, as the old saying goes. But his girlfriend was the squaw that broke the camel's back. I tell you, she didn't have a brain on her head."
>
> "Like it says in the Bible: Rent to Caesar the things that aren't Caesar's."
>
> "That's like painting the barn after the horse has been stolen."
>
> "She said she'd leave no stove unturned."

So much for Cousin Misty, but in her words, remember, the latch string is always open.

6 I have taken a solemn vow never to use the word *nifty* again.

We take our thought for 2002 from part of an old Episcopal prayer for our country:

> *In the time of prosperity, fill our hearts with thankfulness, and*
> *in the day of trouble, suffer not our trust in thee to fail.*

Our best to you —

*Verna (with reservations)*
*Bill*

## *Christmas Ornaments, and So to Fish*

### The Ditters' 2002 Christmas Letter

*Box 256, Hendricks, PA 18979*

December 2002

Dear Family and Friends,

The time may come in your life when you begin to feel concern about the attic and how you are using the space there. I would suggest that you banish those thoughts and turn to some safer endeavor such as motorcycle racing.

The burdens of life always start so innocently.

Last December as directed, I brought down the boxes, baskets, bags, and cartons—marked and unmarked, full or half-full—wherein our Christmas bric-a-brac was stored. This was a task that was accompanied by not a little feeling of remorse that my Christmas spirit could be so easily flagged by 27 steps and roughly one ton of lading.

This and that came out of this and that and the horizontal spaces of the various rooms were filled with charming decorations of Christmas Past, Christmas Present, and Christmas Yet to Come. Even the tree was done. That left roughly one-half ton of boxed, happy memories to be carried back up the same 27 steps and returned, opened or unopened, to the attic. Here fate intervened.

My helpmate suggested that we put the containers in a spare bedroom (some of the birds have flown) and after Christmas go through things "with an eye to packing everything more efficiently."

Who could say no to such a reasonable suggestion and perhaps endanger the spirit of the rapidly approaching Noel? Scrooge, maybe. Certainly not I. Besides, remarks made in the bliss of December are oft forgot in the cold light of a new year.

But not this time.

And so it was that on an otherwise pleasant day in late January I carried roughly one-half ton of freight down 14 steps to the living room, got out three card tables, including the one with the collapsing leg, pulled out the piano bench, and opened both sets of little tray tables, so that we "could see what was what."

Out came a forgotten box of tree ornaments and, improbable as this may sound, it was decreed that we put them on the tree "to fill up those bare spots you left since we're not going to take the tree down for a few days anyway." We weren't? I hadn't realized that.

Now I have a helpful comment for you. If you are ever confronted with a situation like the one I faced, do not get out the fire extinguisher and put it by the tree. Sarcasm has its place, I dare say, but with some folk it turns a half-formed idea into tight-lipped determination.

From time to time you may have wondered why they call those things that make a Christmas tree Christmas tree "needles." I suggest if you haven't figured it out for yourself that you try to put seven balls, four crystal icicles, three glass bells, and a plastic angel on an aging pine tree that was probably cut in late August near some remote hamlet in South Dakota.

That was the first box.

Numbers two and three contained lights marked "sparks," "dog chewed on wire." "Won't work in 1981," "smells like burning rubber when lit," and similar prophesies of doom. I convinced my companion of these many years that we could do without them. Well, almost. If you know anyone who would like 223 bulbs of various hues and sizes, contact me at once and I'll even throw in the plastic bucket.

As the day progressed, but only after the card table with the bad leg collapsed spilling hundreds of priceless miscellany that came to us after Aunt Bessie Hawthorne died, my usual sunny disposition began to fray a bit around the edges. There were still three boxes to go and, although the downstairs of our cottage now resembled an illustration I once saw for Dickens' *Old Curiosity Shop* and day was dying in the west, things were still being admired and put down so that we could put like with like. But I ask you, although I kept my peace at the time, what is like a three-legged reindeer that "you won't notice the leg is missing if you put it this way on something above eye level"?

Cousin Misty says that time wounds all heels. I will attest to that. The patience I had been saving for a rainy day was soon a fond memory. More pleasurable tasks were set aside. January gave way to February and the little cry of delight that had greeted each emerging bauble became a sigh as days later each was consigned to an appropriately marked box, "Religious," "Old Santas," "New Santas," etc. No, there was none marked "Middle Aged Santas," but I don't blame you for wondering.

Finally it was finished. I sleep much, much better at night knowing that a corner of the attic that once seemed chaotic with its 17 casually marked containers now gives refuge to 9 that proclaim their contents in bold, black strokes and that only the 4 big ones say, "Miscellaneous."

I read somewhere that growing old can be slowed by a man's acquiring new interests. I have followed that advice and in so doing have remained young in mind and spirit.

One fateful day when I was keeping my regular appointment with the Geriatrician, in his waiting room I saw a copy of *Field and Stream*. It was open to a glowing account of Pennsylvania fishing.

Now up to this point in my life I had always had the attitude that anyone who matches wits with a fish pretty well deserves what he gets. But, on the other hand, I was ready for new frontiers, new challenges, new triumphs. Unfortunately my reverie in this regard was interrupted by a comely lass, approximately one-fourth my age, who, to emphasize the professional nature of our relationship, called me then and thereafter by my first name. She ushered me into the inner sanctum and there broached a number of topics that if to be discussed at all would best take place in the men's locker room at the country club. In came the doctor and like Santa Claus of the *Night Before Christmas,* he went straight to his work, the nature of which would not even be fit fodder for the aforementioned locker room. When all was finished, I gathered the shards of my dignity and once outside found the day to be one of sunshine and gentle spring breezes. With *Field and Stream* in mind, I headed for *Dan's Bait and Tackle Shop* and spent a generous amount of money in preparing myself for the so-called trout season.

Here a word of caution is in order. Never let the euphoria of sunshine and gentle spring breezes motivate you toward a new quest especially if it may culminate in altering your until-then satisfactory relationship with some other species.

I tried fishing, but with mixed results. I caught nothing but my own ear.

I do enjoy bringing gladness to the hearts of my fellow man, which apparently I did when I sloshed into the emergency room in wading boots carrying my fishing pole with its line firmly attached to my person. The waiting room was crowded. From the laughter and applause I received as I made my way to the receptionist, I feel justified in saying that I alleviated the fears and pain of a fair number of troubled souls if only for a few precious moments.

No doubt another day, another burst of sunshine and another balmy zephyr will lure me to another stream, but for this year a very painful ear and more pressing matters thankfully intervened: opening the swimming pool; closing the swimming pool; and last, but hardly least, Cousin Misty's annual pilgrimage. Misty arrived with only her seven-year-old whom she calls Toddler. She hasn't gotten around to naming him yet because she wants, so she says, to get a better line on him. She reported on the other members of her brood, favorably and unfavorably, and on life in general. As usual, I wrote down some of her more cogent comments:

"Don't burn your bridges until you see the whites of their eyes."

"He's as fat as a fiddle."

"There's more here than meets the ear."

"He kept me on threads and needles."

"Don't break all your eggs in one basket."

"He says I'm clearvoyant, you know, like I had eyes in the side of my head,"

"As it says in the Bible, love your neighbor by yourself."

"Who says you can't teach a new dog old tricks?"

So much for Cousin Misty, but in her words, "Remember, the latch string is always open."

Our best to you.

*Bill – Verna (with reservations)*

## *If You've Never Archeried, Don't!*

The Ditters' 2003 Christmas Letter

*Box 256, Hendricks, PA 18979*

December 2003

Dear Family and Friends,

When one of the birds who has left the nest, raised twins, managed a husband, and in the meantime gotten a master's degree in marine biology, decides to come back to the old homestead because Randy and Sandy are in camp and Kenny will be in 15 cities in 10 days, it should come as no surprise that during the hiatus from her family, improving her father will be high on her list. At this point I should add that Terry has spent all of her life improving herself, the last 18 improving her husband, and the last 15 improving her two children. She is our pride and joy and we admire the way her husband has accepted her finer attributes. By the way, he is the highway superintendent in Springfield, Ohio, and refers to himself as a Roads Scholar, calls our daughter, "Terror," and thinks an evening discussing asphalt is about as exciting as things can get.

At the airport carousel, Terry retrieved a longish bag that gave me an eerie feeling, but I eased it out of my mind because I wanted to enjoy her visit. Now here's a bit of advice for you: if your daughter ever shows up with a longish sort of bag—too short for skis and too long for an umbrella and it's summer time anyway—you might wish to stop at the ticket counter to see what they have in the way of a flight to Pierre, South Dakota, or maybe it's North Dakota, and let mother and child have a girl-fest while you volunteer to serve with your destination's bomb disposal squad for a few days.

The next morning as I was having my second cup of coffee and raising my blood pressure by reading the editorial page of the *Inquirer*, Terry bounded into the room with exercise in her eyes, the longish bag in her hand, and me in her sights. What I needed was activity, outdoor activity, for mind and body. Being torn away from the *Inquirer* was not all that bad, although I did rather mind leaving the coffee.

Why is it that when Terry calls me "Pops" it sounds as though she is referring to something you'd eat for breakfast?

Once outside, the bag was opened and out came a bow and a quiver of arrows. The word *quiver* is well chosen to describe what should be a man's reaction to a bow and arrows in the hands of an energetic daughter.

We hauled a couple of bales of hay out of the barn and the longish sort of bag produced a piece of target canvas, and in less than half an hour, we were ready for father-improvement. Now I will confess that at this point I was thoroughly enjoying the adventure and even permitted my mind to wander to that delicious day when I would make my weekly visit to the senior center with a feather in my little jaunty cap, my forest green tights and shirt and remind all of the denizens of Errol Flynn doing his bit in Sherwood Forrest. (*Note*: My life's companion insists that I insert her comment that I would have been more likely to remind the good folk at the center of Friar Tuck rather than of Robin Hood.)

Just as Terry had gotten things ready for firing, Verna called to say that someone from the camp was on the phone about one of the twins who might have a broken arm. Terry fairly leapt toward the house, father forgotten, and a mother's concern driving her at flank speed.

Well, there I was with a bow, some arrows, and a target. I decided to give it a try. Bows and arrows are not exactly differential calculus. Yes, I will admit that Terry called back that I should wait, but I am not a child—and certainly not like her child who apparently can't slide into second base without breaking his arm.

What you do is to put the string of the bow into a convenient little notch on the after end of the arrow, pull it back, point it at the target, and let go. I only tried three and if I do say so myself, I was very careful. On my first shot, the string on the bow knocked off my glasses and a moment later there was a sort of metallic twang. I thought it interesting that the steel arrowhead would make such a noise as it hit a canvas target, but I did not let my mind dwell on the subject unduly. I retrieved my glasses, bent them back into shape, and repeated the process. This time I could see the arrow clear the target by a good ten feet and then heard a scraping noise like the sound of piece of chalk on a blackboard. The third one? To this day, I cannot guess where it went. Not wanting to have to face my daughter three arrows short as it were, I decided to go and retrieve them, put them in the quiver, and sit there with a proper look of concern about whether there are doctors in Pike County with sufficient competence to treat my grandson.

Now here is a very useful tip for you. If you ever take up bow and arrowing and you decide to go look for an arrow or two, do not carry the bow with you. Instead, take a golf club or perhaps your dog's leash. Carrying a bow is establishing the *corpus delicti* as it were. On the other hand, if you are carrying a golf club when you stroll over to your neighbor's place and you see an arrow stuck in the door of his brand new Lincoln you can maintain an air of innocence even though he is shouting and stringing together some very demeaning comments about the marital status of many of your forebears. At this point, I may observe that our neighbor qualifies for a doctorate in leaping to conclusions about another's exercise of due care.

How I was supposed to know that his new automobile had less than 2300 miles on it is one of the points he glossed over even though his voice reached a new intensity at that time. I tried to ease his discomfort by offering to remove the offending arrow. I tried to appease him further by noting that with a little kit from Pep Boys the door could be repaired. I offered to go to Pep Boys and get the kit, even though as I pointed out to him, I hadn't planned such a trip that day. I went still further: I offered to fix the door and repaint it for him. When he showed a definite lack of appreciation for that idea, I said I'd get the kit, pay for it, and he could fix the door himself. I will admit that I should not have used a certain well-known modifier when I was referring to the door, but by then my patience was wearing a bit thin and he had begun to speculate about the damage I might have caused had either his wife, Thelma, or his dog, Rover, been outside.

Having seen Thelma bent over the petunias and having been kept awake from time to time by Rover's howling, it is difficult to abstain from putting into words what momentarily went through my mind as an unfulfilled wish for the missing third arrow. Because arrow-manufacturers put feathers on arrows, a fact of which my host seemed well aware, what I said next was not necessarily a happy choice of words even though I had chosen them carefully. I inquired if there wasn't anything I could do to soothe his feathers. It only raised his concern another peg.

Next I tried to ease the conversation away from its unilateral nature. I have found that introducing an allied subject into a unilateral conversation will often provide intellectual stimulation and the opportunity for a mutual exchange of ideas. What I did was to tell my neighbor of an interesting article I had read in *Car and Driver* about the relative strengths of the metal used on car doors and their roofs, and that because the roof metal on his Lincoln was stronger than the door, the arrow that had hit its roof only made something of a furrow. Instead of broadening the conversation, this bit of knowledge, coupled with the fact that he hadn't noticed the roof business, made the conversation even more unilateral.

At that point Terry arrived and practically ordered me to go home. I am not accustomed to taking orders from someone who, only a comparatively short time ago, I was teaching to ride a tricycle, but since I was about ready to leave anyway I did as I was told while she and my neighbor continued to chat. As it turned out, they chatted at my expense:

ultimately $1,178.56 worth to be precise. And, no, I never did go to the adult center in a little green outfit, with a jaunty feather in my little green cap. They all call me Robin Hood anyway and somehow seem to see humor in an incident where there was none.

Now Terry has gone back to higher and better things, probably improving half of Springfield, Ohio, and father has now been introduced to a new outdoor activity for mind and body. And it only cost him $1,178.56. Incidentally, why did she take down the target we had made?

In mid-August, Cousin Misty arrived with only her youngest, once called Toddler, but now named Sailor. I did not inquire why, but I believe that Misty has a touch of nostalgia about her. Her oldest boy violated his parole and is back in prison. Her comment on that was, "I'm relieved. At least he won't be getting into any mischief while he's up there." I wrote down some of her other observations.

> Of her second son, "He's like two peas in a pod."
>
> "I raised him right, but not long enough."
>
> "His girlfriend looks like she just came in out of a storm and should go back outside again."
>
> On things in general: "I like to be with people. Every crowd has a silver lining."
>
> "Life is like a merry go 'round. The music is so good, you don't mind not getting anywhere."

Our best to you and yours for the year to come, and as Misty says, "The latch string is always open." She's probably right about the merry go 'round too.

*Verna – Bill*

## *Biking and Bonding*

The Ditters' 2004 Christmas Letter

*Box 256, Hendricks, PA 18979*

December 2004

Hello There,

Please note the cheery greeting.

One pleasant day this last August I decided to take my grandson for a bicycle ride on the Nature Trail that meanders around near our cottage. He's a pleasant little fellow and I thought a bit of male bonding would be in order—and their visit would end in a few days, so then was the time to put down the paper, forget the treasured second cup of coffee, and repair to the great outdoors with "Spike."

I'll have to tell you a little about the aforementioned trail. Some years ago, a group of this area's leading citizens had the foresight to plan a railroad and the drive to bring it into reality. It permitted a brisk and mutually beneficial flow of commerce between the Perkiomen Valley and the City of Philadelphia. From Red Hill, Green Lane, and Pennsburg came cigars and chewing tobacco to ennoble the denizens of the City of Brotherly Love. In return, the citizens of William Penn's Green Towne sent to their country cousins whiskey, beer, and wine to add to the already pleasant experience of living where the pump and privy still held sway.

Progress brought the motor truck and did away with the need for the railroad, and in due time, another group of leading citizens had the foresight and drive to turn the right-of-way that wound through the trees and hillside cuts into a Nature Trail. No motor-driven vehicles allowed. Progress has brought the horse to the domain of the iron horse, the in-pain jogger to where folks would ride in comfort, the backpacker to the realm of the freight car.

Here's another thing you'll need to know. It's about bicycles. You'll want a Mountain Bike if you are moved to venture onto a Nature Trail. Mountain Bike. I have always loved mountains. There is nothing that whets the appetite more than to page through the *National Geographic* and see some fellow hiking a steep trail, or to see a spot on TV which features some chap working his way to the summit of Mount McKinley. Other than that, my relationship with mountains has pretty much been live and let live, fearing as I do, that greater contacts might cause my love for them to cloy. So I should have cringed at the words *Mountain Bike*, but in one of those rare coincidences of life, my second son, who lives nearby, happened along with his Mountain Bike just after my mate and

I had decided a little excursion with Spike would be mutually beneficial, if only I had a bike.

Now I must digress for a minute to make what might be called a public service announcement. Here it is: I am going to offer my services as a husband–counselor. You see I have been tripping along the path of matrimony for some little time now and have picked up some tips that could ease the way for my fellow journeymen. A few examples will suffice. Suppose that the Voice of Authority in your hacienda comes to you one morning just as you have settled down with your second cup of coffee and says, "Don't you think you should at least do something with your grandson? They'll only be here a few more days." [Long pause] "Well?"

At a time like that feigning deafness probably won't work, nor is it wise to say, "I shall wish them Godspeed." Do not say, "Why?" and I beg of you, do not say, "Well I'd love to but I was just about to go down to the dentist's to see if he couldn't find three or four of my teeth that need root canals." Clever as a response like that may seem at first blush, it may not be received in the pleasant, jocular way you intended.

Mountain Bikes are not like the bicycles of your youth when peddling clockwise would move you forward and pushing the opposite direction meant you would stop. A Mountain Bike has cables, little wheels to carry the cables, boasts of 10 speeds (an idle rumor, by the way), and has a *derailleur* which is French for "will make the chain come off." So there I was confronting this marvel of 21st-century technology.

For some reason there seemed to be a lot of family there to wish me well. Most of them offered suggestions on Mountain Biking much to the delight of the rest of the throng. Even my neighbor was on hand and he generously offered to get the training wheels that came with his six-year-old son's two-wheeler. I did not partake of the group levity and with fitting dignity declined to show off my abilities à la Mountain Biking.

So Spike and I set forth to the Nature Trail. No longer disconcerted by the assorted well wishers that had previously manifested their interest, I looked over the Mountain Bike and suddenly felt the same kind of challenge that must have been Sir Edmund Hillary's when he decided to conquer Mt. Everest.

As for Spike: he's a pleasant little fellow with powerful legs that enable him to proceed on a miniature Mountain Bike at roughly 70 miles per hour while his bonding companion was still in the infancy of learning how to master the handles that tugged the cables that the little wheels carried to earn the thing the title of ten-speed Mountain Bike. But in a short space of time, what with my mechanical aptitude and athletic prowess, I was able to go wobbling down the trail whistling a merry tune.

I proceeded slowly not wishing to miss any of the beauty spots and not wishing to cause the bike to overheat.

Suddenly my reverie was cut short by a wailing sound, and there off to the side of the trail was a bike that I instantly recognized as Spike's. Another word about the trail. There are places where it provides a dangerous vista of the far-below Perkiomen Creek. But the wailing came not from below but from above. I looked up. Mistake Numero Uno. There was Spike on the canyon wall. I ordered him down. As soon as he heard my voice, he cried, "Help, Bill, help." Why shouldn't he call me Bill? After all, he wasn't using the name himself and his parents encouraged an informality of address. "Mom and Dad are so positively Victorian, if you know what I mean," I was told when I made a gentle inquiry. More wailing. It quickly dawned on me that he was stuck, unable to go up and afraid to come down. From his standpoint, he was fortunate that I was there. Now here's a little advice for you. If you ever feel that necessity requires the use of a ten-speed Mountain Bike as a platform before your pride in your resourcefulness goes too far, consider other alternatives. For example, maybe the ladder truck from the local fire department might come rolling by at any moment. I had the foresight to put the kickstand down and had grasped a nearby root and was bravely hauling myself up when the bike went over, and the root came loose which in turn pulled out the rock on which Spike was standing and down we went.

Although Spike bounced up and pronounced himself ready to go, it was quickly apparent that his bonding companion was another matter. The front wheel of the Mountain Bike was bent and my left knee felt as though it was going to explode. While I was lying there considering the joys of the day, some folk came along and asked if I had fallen. Despite my agony I told them I had lost an election bet and was required to warm that spot for an hour. I told two other inquiring travelers that I was starting college late in life and that my occupying the mid-section of The Trail was part of a fraternity initiation.

After that, things are a bit hazy although I apparently swallowed my pride and used my cell phone to call home. I've been told that my usual gentle nature was scarcely recognizable for the next several days, which included a trip by ambulance to the hospital, an intake interview with a nurse who asked a great many personal questions, a conference with the surgeon and anaesthesiologist, surgery, and the joys of recovery. In any event, I have a new left knee, mostly titanium or some other exotic material.

What happened to Spike? I've never asked but when my hospital sojourn was over, he and his parents were gone. Doubtless they will return. After all, I do have another knee to give to the cause.

Yes, Cousin Misty stopped by again this year and as always gave us the latest news about her family, interspersed with commentary, some of which I wrote down. Among her more interesting observations:

> "He won't turn over a new leaf and can't find the old one."
>
> "If I was dead, I'd be turning over in my grave."
>
> "It's as American as pizza and apple pie."
>
> "I hate to say this about her but she is like Caesar's wife, not above a good approach. One time she said to her husband's best friend, 'You too, Brutus.' In those days everybody wore a nightgown that they called a token when they went to the forum to watch the Christians and the gladiators. So you don't have to be a rock scientist to figure out what they wore at home. Well, anyway, they have the Tiger River there and this happened during the Tides of March, which is why they say it comes in like a lion and goes out like a lamb. They named July and August for Caesar and his wife although nobody seems to know why."

Our best to you for the new year. And remember what Cousin Misty said last year, "Life is like a merry go 'round. The music is so good you don't mind not getting anywhere."

*Verna – Bill – Bob*

## *A Picnic That Was No Picnic*

Bill Ditter's 2006 Christmas Letter

*Box 256, Woxall, PA 18979*

December 2006

Dear Family and Friends,

There it was, in small letters on our shade, "Don't Volunteer." My roommate at Midshipmen's School, Quintin Metcalf from Paint Lick, Kentucky, tugged on my sleeve to bring to my attention this nugget of wisdom. But time marches on and I admit there have been occasions when I ignored this sage advice of sixty plus years ago.

The events of this past June have caused me to rethink volunteering and to wonder where Quintin was when I needed another tug on the sleeve.

These things always start so innocently.

At the May Administrative Council meeting, Cindy Frick announced the date for the church's Sunday School picnic. Luther Barnett observed that attendance at our last three picnics was disappointing, which led me to suggest that maybe we should advertise some organized activities for this year's outing. Somehow or other this was taken as an offer on my part to plan the entertainment and be the ringmaster as it were. And so it was that for the next four Sabbaths the congregation was bombarded with a flyer that revealed a new festivity for the oncoming Sunday School picnic: the peanut scramble, the three-legged race, the married men vs. single men softball game, the egg relay, and the baby marathon. And prizes for the victors in these contests.

As I looked at the faces, happy with anticipation, of those who were examining the church bulletin while the collection plates were being circulated I could tell we were in for a wildly wonderful, gala afternoon.

I armed myself with a police whistle, a list-laden clipboard, a red shirt that said Activities Director on it, and a matching cap. Now here's a suggestion for you: If by chance you are going to head up some venture, for example a Sunday School picnic, when the matter of garb comes up you may wish to consider a camouflage suit from the nearest Army–Navy store.

The crowd duly arrived and the kiddies responded to my invitation to gather for the peanut scramble. To those of you who may have been deprived of this formerly considered innocuous activity, it consists of the leader (here, me) throwing peanuts out and having little tots race around picking them up. I had dug into my canvas bag ready to make my initial toss when Nora Mason laid a hand on my shoulder and asked coldly, *What about the environment?* She then pointed out that if the children had peanuts they would doubtless discard the shells, which would inhibit the growth of grass, which helped consume carbon dioxide which was leading to global warming which was causing the world's ice to melt and which would cause the seas to rise. Nora cited Al Gore. She demanded that there be no scramble unless I had devised a way to police all ten acres of the park for peanut shells. Confronted by her expressed grave doubt of my concern for Planet Earth (her term) and the fact that her husband, who gave every indication of a great love for Planet Earth, was standing nearby, I called off the event. Upon hearing that news, one sweet-faced little tyke came over and kicked me in the shin. I later learned he was Nora's child.

He tried to greet me in the same way at church the following Sunday, but quick of wit, I stepped backward only to sprawl over the arm of a pew and land more or less head first, actually more—into Anita Allen's lap. If you know of a way to provide a convincing explanation for having your head in the lap of another man's wife just after the close of a church service, a man who at that moment happened on the scene, I would be happy to have you share it with me.

Back to the day in question: I then organized the three-legged race, an event where the right ankle of one participant is tied to the left ankle of his or her partner. I thought this would be a good way to get the teenagers into the spirit of things and so I invited them to choose companions, which they did with a certain alacrity that should have warned me. One young swain immediately claimed as his partner a lass who blushed a bit while they were being roped together. He announced they were going to practice, and with remarkable speed they headed over behind the pavilion where they were out of sight. By the time we had the others paired off, the first two returned, she looking a bit disheveled and he with a smirk on his face. At this juncture her mother appeared and screamed at me, "My daughter's only 13 and you let her go behind the bushes with that thug." It was news to me, of course, that her child was only 13. In my own defense she was a budding 13, and dressed to emphasize the fact, so to speak. I would have guessed her age at a mature 17. Mother freed daughter from partner, slapped his face, and she with daughter in tears, in tow, and wailing, "I'm not a child any more," headed for the family auto. I have not seen them for several Sundays and it is my understanding they may be seeking divine guidance at some other institution. Well, all this took some of the *joie de vivre* out of things, as the French would say, but we pluckily went on with the race for the remaining teenagers, most of whom seemed more interested in each other than the contest at hand.

Using my megaphone, I announced that the next event would be the married men vs. single men three-inning softball game. Now here's a contest where you'd believe only goodwill would reign, but perhaps you have never considered how much enmity you can engender with a decision as to which team could rightfully claim a chap who has played semi-pro ball and has three children without the benefit of clergy, if you know what I mean, or the problems that may arise where father and son, on opposing teams, are at odds over nonsupport payments going back several years. To sum up, the game was called midway through the bottom of the second inning. Would you not think that a 230-more-or-less pound man would know better than to try to break up a double play by barreling into a 13-year-old shortstop who wears glasses and whose protective mother was standing nearby, umbrella in hand?

Pressing on, after a hearty exchange of viewpoints, a clean abdominal shot with the umbrella, and some other little discord, I announced the next part of the program would be the baby marathon. This is where fathers put their respective children, under two, down on the grass and at the proper signal, each mother, about 15 feet away, calls for her child to crawl to her (Lap 1) and after the child has done so, father calls to his child to return to the place of original departure (Lap 2). Our church is known for its brainy children and these particular children seemed unconvinced there was any reason to leave mother and return to father, who moments ago had put them down on this prickly green stuff and shooed them away. Several fathers who had made side bets all in the spirit of friendly competition suggested that their respective wives were at fault for their respective baby's indifference to racing. A certain period of marital coolness ensued. The book from which I had gotten the baby-marathon idea said it would be a hilarious event that people would talk about for weeks to come. It wasn't and they didn't.

Are you starting to get the picture? A lesser man may have been daunted by the knowledge that he was a threat to Planet Earth, an aider and abettor to a 13-year-old's possible compromise of virtue, and responsible for a bent umbrella, but I plunged forward with the potato sack race, which is where each contestant puts his or her legs into a gunny sack and then when all is in readiness hops, bag and all, to a predetermined finish line. I was about to blow my whistle to start the festivities when Woody Stansen eased up beside me and pointed out that this was an event where people could fall, the church's insurance didn't cover such contingencies, and therefore it was his advice to cancel the impending race. I threw caution to the winds, blew my whistle, and off they went. Sure enough, Pete Grendle fell, took Preston Marfit down with him, and both wound up in the ER with twisted ankles. I count the days for the running of the statute of limitations.

The rest of the exertions followed the pattern I have described for you: the egg-on-the-spoon-in-the-mouth relay produced a broken tooth for Dutch Kellogg; the watermelon seed–spitting contest was condemned as being gross; the popcorn toss attracted no contestants; the Frisbee backhand throw failed because all the Frisbees wound up in the trees.

And the blind man's pin the tail on the donkey made Heddy Corson call out in a loud voice that this was just another example of a Republican trying to pin stuff on the Democrats. Donkey–Democrats. Get it? I didn't until I got home.

From my perspective, the only bright spot of the day, if you could call it that, came when one kind soul said to me as she left, "This was the worst, the stupidest picnic I ever attended, but you tried your best."

I had planned to ask Pastor Al about presenting certificates of award during the next week's service but gave up the idea when I learned the topic of the sermon was "Forgiveness, Here and Now."

Cousin Misty came again this summer with her eight-year-old, Sailor. She explained that she had not visited last year on purpose. Before she left, this is what she told me.

"They say, 'Time heals all wounds.'"

"Don't believe it."

"But there is a certain comfort in the wounds of grief."

"It is an assurance that those thoughts of happy days are not dreams or fancy."

"It is a reminder of love that knew no bounds."

"It brings back thoughts of little things: the quick smile, the shared secrets, the melody of a laugh, the joy of coming home, the words of parting, *Be careful. I love you.*"

"And yes, the days made sweeter by a moment of misunderstanding put aside."

"Grief brings into focus what is left, not what has gone...what you have...not what you lost."

"Time heals all wounds?"

"Don't believe it, but would you have it any other way?"

Without waiting for me to respond, she left. If she had waited, I'm not sure what I would have said.

My best to you for the coming year. And remember, as Cousin Misty once said, "The latch string is always open."

*Bill*

## *Commuter Keys*

### Bill Ditter's 2007 Christmas Letter

*Box 256, Woxall, PA 18979*

December 2007

Dear Family and Friends,

In the days of my youth, there was a radio show, *The Voice of Experience*, which featured, as I recall it, a kindly voiced man who handed out advice with casual confidence. At one time, I prepared a letter suggesting to NBC that perhaps I could do a show called *The Voice of Limited Experience*. I never mailed it, but came across it the other day, which in turn made me wonder what I could give some good advice about. With all due modesty, I decided on commuting—train commuting.

Reduced to its fundamentals, train commuting is leaving here, going there, leaving there, and coming here, some of which is by train. As we all know, however, even some of life's most basic activities can profit from guidance. To illustrate the points I wish to make, I have thought up some hypothetical situations.

**Habits Are both Good and Bad.** Suppose, hypothetically, that someone regularly catches the train at Pennbrooke, a station that is four stops beyond Ambler, because that is near where he now lives. Suppose that he had an oculist who practiced in Ambler with whom he made a late afternoon appointment and therefore drove to Ambler on a particular morning. Well, as you know appointments sometimes get canceled. A careful commuter would want to keep in mind where he (or she) had parked his car because it would not be in Pennbrooke just because that is where it usually is at the end of the otherwise non-noteworthy day. You cannot believe how long it takes for the up train to come back as the down train on a chilly night. This is a hypothetical to show how habits can produce surprising results for a commuter.

Perhaps this would be a more poignant hypothetical. Suppose a certain person regularly parks at a certain station—Pennbrooke, for example—but on rare occasions will drive all the way to the City of Brotherly Love. Very rare. On a certain day, that is what he (or she) did. It would be a mistake for this person at the close of the day's activities to blithely board the train and settle down for a few restful moments only to realize as the train pulled out of Ambler, where his (or her) son had his office, that his (or her) car was back at the courthouse. The quick thinking commuter would realize at once that here was a dilemma: get off the train, it now being 5:05 p.m., catch a ride back to Ambler (next train in 30 minutes), or ride on through to Pennbrooke and get help via the phone. Another part of this hypo is that if one has a daughter-in-law who is usually voluble and cheerful but on a particular occasion is silent and tight-lipped, there's no point in asking more than three times, "Are you sure you didn't mind missing dessert with your lady friends?" This hypothetical is intended to reinforce the point that one must not become a slave to one's habits.

Of course there are some good habits. The wise commuter will put his wallet, car keys, office keys, and change at the same place each night rather than leaving his wallet, for example, over there at the phone where he had it to get his credit card when he was ordering something for someone, the importance of which a conductor who seemed to be on a particular run for the first time in his whole life couldn't quite understand and which might entail a lengthy speech on fiscal responsibility to the amusement of a railroad car full of commuters. This is a hypothetical to show the importance of good habits.

**Cell Phones.** When cell phones were just coming out, there were those who tried to impress people by talking in a loud voice when holding a cell phone to his ear. Both annoying and impressive. Here is another hypothetical. Suppose someone had just acquired a cell phone that very day with the promise of instruction the next day, but it so happened that upon boarding the train this person, cell phone and all, sat down next to a fine looking young lady. Under these circumstances it can be understood why someone might take out his cell phone, fiddle with it for a moment or two, and then begin a conversation in a conversational tone about his forthcoming speech to the United Nations. A glance might show his seatmate was listening closely. Completely captivated. About the time this person was getting to a reorganization of the Security Council, suppose the seatmate said, "I have a cell phone just like that. Would you like me to show you how to turn it on?" Now, it would be well for me to remind you of something else: if on sudden impulse you ever decide to leave a train as quickly as you can because it is just pulling into a strange station where you have never sojourned, North Hills, might be an example, and it occurs to you it would be interesting to compare its evening accommodations with those of your usual station, SEPTA's lost and found system won't necessarily result in your getting back your brand new London Fog raincoat that you left on the rack above where you had been sitting when you decided to leave for whatever the reason. By this hypothetical I am trying to get you to understand that a commuter should be respectful of technology and make haste slowly.

Here's another pointer. Suppose someone has gone to a Phillies game and returned to his (or her) office where he divested his right-hand trousers pocket where he (or she) always has car keys of such things as the day's program and scorecard, the little Phillies waving towel, ticket stub, and pencil. Who would want those things on the train? At that point, the thoughtful commuter will remember to put his car keys back in his (or her) pocket because it can be quite disheartening after a pleasant train ride to approach the only car in the parking lot and find every pocket, pants, coat, and shirt devoid of car keys and the cell phone is in the car with which someone could call his (or her) son to come to the rescue. This is another hypothetical to demonstrate that even if you had sworn off cell phones for some reason or another but reconsidered that position, it would be well not to have the cell phone in your car on an occasion when your car keys were back at the office.

**Most Commuters Are Pleasant.** Not necessarily so for the occasional rider. Another hypothetical. Suppose an otherwise cheerful commuter is trying to get his morning siesta only to have a small, mouthy child across the aisle practice his vocabulary lessons in a loud, grating voice. Despite the interruption with the day's usual start, it might be wise not to ask Mr. Little Chatter Box if he didn't have to go to the bathroom and did he know that there was an ice cream store at the next stop. This is especially true if nearby there is a grandmotherly type, wearing steel-rimmed glasses, who up to that point had been minding her own business, but who has an umbrella with which she does not mind giving someone a not too gentle tap on the knuckles. This is a hypothetical to suggest that Shakespeare was right when he said that there may be times when it is better to suffer the slings and arrows of outrageous fortune than to do anything about it on a train.

So much for commuting.

We hadn't seen Cousin Misty or her now ten-year-old, Sailor, for two years, but late one Saturday afternoon in August she stopped by—but no Sailor. As usual, I wrote down some of her comments.

> "My daughter is doing good now. She works for a germantologist in his wading (?) room. It's what they call a level-entry proposition. She should never be short of money because skin doctors really rake it in on the coals and she was never one to let the grass grow over her feet."

> "Henry VIII had eight wives, which is how he got his name, and what he did to them is mind bundling."

> "What about Helen of Troy? Her friend Homer said she had a face that would sink a thousand ships so he wrote a story about her called *The Odds at Sea*. Not all the Greeks were famous because so many of them died young. Infant morality was widespread in those days."

Abruptly, however, she got up and said a hasty goodbye, and headed toward the door. I followed her. She turned, and wiped her eyes. She was crying.

"Sailor?" I asked. She just shook her head, and this is what she said, "Do you still talk to her? I mean, there are those who say she's just around the corner. Don't you have to ask yourself, which would be worse? To just be talking to yourself when you say things—to her I mean—the way you used to—or to have her think that you've forgotten her because she never hears about the little things—the things you talked about together in quiet times? Well?"

She did not wait for an answer, but hurried off. And I'm not sure whether she was asking me a question or herself a question.

As Misty said when first she came to see us, "Remember, the latch string is always open."

Bobby joins me in wishing the best for you in the new year—and always.

*Bill*

## *Shopping Hazards and Mysteries*

## Bill Ditter's 2010 Christmas Letter

*Box 256, Woxall, PA 18979*

December 2010

Dear Family and Friends,

When something creeps up on you, one creep at a time, it may cause you stress but you may not know where it is coming from and so you blame something else like when your seven-year-old grandson, who has been thoughtfully keeping you company for two hours while your daughter did some errands on a Saturday afternoon when you had planned to take a nap, says to his mother, "Come back after while. We've only played nine games of checkers and Grandfather ain't won yet."

You know the one about when grandchildren come to call they bring you joy twice so I won't bother to repeat it.

What I'm talking about is shopping.

Unless you're still Rip VanWinkling, you know that more and more and more stores sell more and more of more and more so that more and more you'll find less and less of what you went to the store for. It used to be that triumphant shopping was reckoned by coming home with what you went for, but now your shopping score is figured by how much of what you didn't go for you didn't come home with.

The other day I went into a grocery store to get some oatmeal. Up and down the endless aisles I strode, glancing left and right, and passing breakfast foods, cereals, and health foods.

No oatmeal. On the way out, however, I saw this particular grocery store sold toboggans. Grocery Store: Oatmeal, No. Toboggans, Yes.

In search of Smith's cough drops I visited a drug store a fortnight ago. I passed stuffed animals, china, and check cashing. Never did find cough drops, they were probably displayed with batteries, or compact disks, or perhaps garden gloves.

Parking. Now that you know some of the general problems of shopping, I will give you some advice on the specifics about this modern version of trial by combat.

Stores are found in malls, and according to *Webster* ***THE*** mall is a fashionable promenade in St. James Park, London, while ***A*** mall is a variation of the word *maul,* which means to bruise or handle roughly. None of the various malls to which I have been exposed were either shaded or fashionable so I have long since concluded that the original mall-designators were gifted alternate-meaning prognosticators.

On one of my early ventures not so very long ago I noticed there were high poles atop which were large letters, A, B, C, etc. It came to me in a flash: the "A" area was for folk with last names like Adams, Allen, or Arthur; the B area for Bakers, Browns; and so on. Spotting D close by I headed toward an empty spot, arriving only a few seconds after a grizzled little old chap in a big car was lining up to pull in. Fearing he did not know the system and not wishing him to be embarrassed by his proceeding into a spot that rightly was mine, I cut him off and called out in a challenging but friendly way, "Are you a D?" Obviously he misunderstood my thoughtfulness for he snarled back, "No, I am a life-long Republican with a black belt in karate. Now get that heap of yours out of the way before I tear your front fender off and stick it behind your left ear." Greatly admiring his politics and realizing that he was younger and bulkier than I had first thought, I backed off and drove round and round, finally settling in the "J" section (for John). I then promenaded roughly 27 unshaded city blocks to the emporium of my choice.

Later experience has taught me never race a woman for a parking place. Let the rules of chivalry apply. In the unlikely event that you happen to win, invariably they will have a husky husband along or are surprisingly expert in wielding a cane if you alight from your vehicle and may not mind taking a shot or two at your windshield if you choose to stay inside.

One of the perils of parking is that of forgetting where you began your on-foot trek. This memory betrayal is exacerbated if you happen to go to a store with several entrances, each from a different parking lot. Invariably you will head out the nearest exit, which in all probability was not your point of entrance and thus the sea of vehicles will not yield the one of your choice. I have found the best way to solve this problem is to bring a grandchild along when shopping is on the Plan of the Day. Of course, doing so has its downside that can be solved with a dollar or two.

Shopping Carts. Shopping carts should be thought of as indoor pick-up trucks. If by chance you've found some item that's on your list, you pluck it unaided from the shelf, and, with a carefree air, toss it into the trundle abaft of you. Not eggs, of course. At least not over the shoulder while eyeing a short-skirted, by nature favored, and well-turned-out young lady go by. Now promptly leaving the scene of an unfortunate incident is usually a good idea, but when it involves egg yolks splashed on the new Easter dress of a seven-year-old girl accompanied by her somewhat surly father, perhaps some sort of apologies may well be in order. No, I did not wipe egg yolk off her legs. I was about to do so when my silent guardian angel suggested it would not be a good idea. So I didn't.

Another hint: Do not race your shopping cart against that of a fellow octogenarian even only once around the perimeter aisles. What paltry sums you collect from wagers are insufficient recompense for the stated displeasure of a store manager and the stone-visaged so-called mall security woman. By the way, did you know you could be charged with disorderly conduct in a grocery store? However, not all district justices are devoid of humor or of the need for older men to engage in friendly competition, but even the costs might surprise you.

Cousin Misty dropped by on Labor Day and amidst family and friends she said of her oldest son, "He spends money like a fish out of water. He has a pen pal, in fact several of them, they all got out at the same time." She observed, "If worms could talk you can bet they wouldn't go out early, but then birds might start going out later too." "Why," she asked, "if night falls why does dawn break?"

When she got up to leave I followed her to the door. She told me that one of the kind things friends can do is to say I remember her too and write down things that may be reminders. Without another word she handed me a note and was gone. This is what she had written:

> "A tinkling piano is the next apartment, those stumbling words that told you what my heart meant, a fairground's painted swings, these foolish things remind me of you."

> "The winds of March that made my heart a dancer, a telephone that rings but whose to answer, Oh, how the ghost of you clings, these foolish things remind me of you."

And then,

> "If I had a flower for every time I think of you, I could walk in my garden forever."

Bob joins me in wishing you the best for the coming year. And remember what Cousin Misty once said, "The latchstring is always open."

*Bill*

## *Questions at 90*

### Bill Ditter's 2011 Christmas Letter

*Box 256, Woxall, PA 18979*

December 2011

Dear Family and Friends,

I achieved one of life's milestones this last year and greatly enjoyed the fuss made about it although I realized that my parents' genes more deserved the tributes than did I. But colleagues, law clerks present and past, and family were most kind and left me with a continuing warm glow of appreciation. I treasure the memories of this most recent October.

This year I'll talk about aging and some mysteries and perils we may encounter as we march, nay, perhaps drift, along life's narrow way.

After you've been around for a while you realize that wisdom comes from experience and can roughly be defined as having more answers than there are questions so long as someone else's problems are on the table.

Here are two of today's mysteries:

The so-called young at heart these days do not write letters, they communicate by E-mail. Do you realize that the *Dear* which we always have used to start our correspondence is now obsolete? I certainly don't know why but E-Mailers can't or won't say dear. They'll say, *Hi, Good Morning, Hello,* or just your name, but never dear and never capital I when they use the first person singular. There's more, much more, all in derogation of the language of Shakespeare and the King James version.

Sad but true.

Then there's dancing. Recently I attended a wedding with a post-ceremony reception complete with musicians who amplified their efforts with giant speakers producing a cacophony that shook the very walls. The grim-faced dancers each did his/her own shuffling, being careful not to touch, apparently believing to do so would foster the spread of a dangerous disease. Their expressions did not suggest enjoyment.

Is there deeper meaning here? Some almost forgotten-in-the-heart manifestation of disdain? You are you and I am me. I don't need you and don't count on me for anything.

I hope not, but I wonder.

By way of contrast, the next night I watched *The Sound of Music,* set in the Austria of the late 30's, in which there is a dance scene, the men and women have their arms around each other and move together, harmoniously, gracefully, joyously, yes, to the sound of the music.

Now for some warnings:

I advise avoiding golf. It has two faults: the better you do, the more it costs per swing, and contrary to other sports (best pitcher in the whole league, they didn't block for me, etc.), a poor performance can only be blamed on one's self. My theory is that golfers suffer from some hidden, hidden even to themselves, sense of guilt and they punish themselves by buying all sorts of equipment and then pay a large fee for the privilege of seeing how little they can do.

Bowling suffers from the same no-one-else to-blame deficiency, plus it's a hazardous activity. It starts with taking a large, heavy ball that has three holes for such fingers as one chooses to commit. Having received some basic instruction on this topic, I tried my index and my middle fingers plus my arthritic thumb, which immediately refused to come out. I could picture myself wearing a bowling ball through all time to come just as poor Marley had to bear his chains. Fortunately someone at the alley (you understand, don't you, that you pay good money to go to an alley?) had some spray of some sort and after some considerable and painful wiggling I was free. And this passes for sport and recreation.

Another warning:

BE CAREFUL ABOUT SEEKING HELP.

When you think about it, hospitals are there for two reasons: first to take care of sick people and, second, to take care of people who come to visit sick people so they will get better.

From this hypothetical you will see that some hospitals have an ignore visitors policy.

Suppose that on the way to the hospital to visit a friend who turns out to be in ICU, whatever that means, this hypothetical person realizes that the band aid on his or her middle finger has come off.

Obviously hospitals have bandages with all those people bustling about, in and out of rooms, putting on rubber gloves and moments later taking off the same gloves (is it any wonder hospital bills are so high?). All this busy, busy business and no one seemingly cares about someone's need for a band aid despite a request being made in a loud voice. When suddenly, in this hypothetical case, while the person who needs a band aid is starting to become annoyed at the lack of attention, a voice comes over the intercom, "Code Blue, Room 6018," repeated several times.

In a flash, all these busy in-and-out-of-rooms rubber gloves people grab those kimonos that they put on backwards and start putting on those white masks so you won't know who they are (anonymity seems to be a goal in some hospitals) while trailing two chaps in white coats who are all but running down the hall. For all the world it reminded you of the herd of children following the pied piper, except there were two pipers and these people were casting off their rubber gloves only to grab new ones and the same with their kimonos. You would think that of all places where non-littering would be taught it would be at a hospital but apparently not so. The person in need trailed along still hoping that this bandage-rich facility could yield one small band aid. Just inside the room where the group had gathered the person saw a nicely turned out young lady who wasn't doing anything except watching a TV screen and calling out numbers from time to time. So the one in need inched toward her and said, very politely, "Could you get me a band aid, one and a half inch, please."

She snarled, "Get out of here." Yes, snarled. Now you would think, wouldn't you, that a hospital would have some kind of program to teach common courtesy? He in need was about to remonstrate with her when there was a tap on his shoulder by a uniformed, un-gloved fellow, whose visage was not entirely pleasant and who was beckoning to come out of the room. I held up my finger and pointed to it to show this new arrival my problem. For some reason he turned unfriendly. He pointed to his nightstick and beckoned again.

What occurred over the next hour and fifty minutes is quite irrelevant to the point I have tried to illustrate: Be careful about asking for help.

Cousin Misty arrived, invited for July 4 but welcome even though it was late on July 5. Most of her conversation dealt with the saga of her oldest son, Lounge (you'll remember her children's names were chosen to commemorate the places of their beginnings as it were).

> "So far as he's concerned, I'm just throwing in the trowel."
>
> "I'll tell you, truth is stranger than friction."
>
> "You know the one about give a man a fish and he'll eat for a day, teach him to fish and all he'll do is sit in a boat and drink beer. That's Lounge."

When she was ready to leave, as she has several times in the past, she pressed a paper into my hand and said, I was listening to a song, I wrote down what I could remember, I didn't hear its name, but I sure you'll like it. This was what she had written.

> "In the mist of a memory, you wander back to me, breathing my name with a sigh,"
>
> "In the still of the night, Once again I hold you tight, Though you're gone your love lives on when moonlight beams."
>
> "And as long as my heart will beat, My love we'll always meet, Here in my deep purple dreams."

I wonder how she knew.

Bobby and I wish you the best for the coming year and remember, as Cousin Misty once said, the latchstring is always open.

Sincerely,

*Bill*

## *On Undershirts Becoming Overshirts*

Bill Ditter's 2012 Christmas Letter

*Box 256, Woxall, PA 18979*

December 2012

Dear Family and Friends,

I once read that as the island of experience grows, so grows the shoreline of uncertainty.

That's close anyway. Perhaps there should have been a warning too. Something about not giving voice to your uncertainty.

Here's a hypothetical to illustrate what I mean.

Suppose that someone has noticed that many young ladies these days, no matter how well dressed and no matter the occasion, will have the lower part of a cotton undershirt floating out at the waistline. Now suppose that an experienced person and his brother-in-law are having a sandwich in a quiet corner at a busy public house when a well-endowed young lady and a male companion stroll by and you note while she is well turned out, her cotton undershirt is on display in the manner previously noted. Suppose the imaginary person, in a very quiet voice and expressing uncertainty, makes a perfectly harmless observation to his brother-in-law about the lady's habiliment. Next, if your brother-in-law is a little hard of hearing, that is always a matter to be considered when using terms such as "tomato, hot for the picking," "cotton come on," and "eager dude" when speculating about one thing or another. Finally, on this point I can never figure out why in a crowded room two persons will think that a general comment expressing uncertainty about someone's plans for later in the evening is intended to be about them and the umbrage it may cause.

But once in a while a modicum of thought will give certainty to the uncertain.

More on undershirts.

Not shaving is the response.

Young men will let the rather common, daily ritual go for several days. No, they are not starting a beard, they just don't shave. And then they do or partially do. Why?

Because ball players don't shave and movie chaps don't shave? No, although I will admit these growth-faced young men may *think* that in not shaving they are approaching their chosen role models of the arena or silver screen. That may be their belief on the conscious level. The truth lies deeper in the psyche as I shall explain.

After World War II came hand in hand the feminist revolution and the wearing by women of men's articles of clothing or the absence thereof. Bathing suits for women—at least the trim ones—approached the beachwear of men. Then ladies bought men's shirts. Next, trousers. As decade replaced decade, liberation meant suits for women that were like men's suits. Since they couldn't do anything about it anyway, men accepted the idea that what they wore, women would wear. Both genders were equal except that women were more equal.

Women smoked cigars and began to swear like men. But there was a place where the genders had not mixed—underwear—and either consciously or unconsciously. This was an area of reassurance and comfort. Here a man's underwear was his castle so to speak. Let them smoke. Let them swear. A man could tug on his cotton undershirt and from it gain reassurance.

Well, you know what happened next—inevitably next: women started not only to wear men's cotton undershirts but to flaunt them. The displayed undershirt made them look somewhat bizarre but made an unmistakable statement—to show our liberated feminism, we are wearing men's clothes, including the unmentionables.

Men reacted—not in knowing concert, not by common consent, but individually, driven in each by the same call that the knights of old felt before a joust, the thing that makes men men: "There, try this."

Now about gifts.

Throughout the year, I receive gifts and invitations in the mail—usually both in the same envelope. The gift is mine to keep, but I am invited to send money to the donor in return. Twenty-five dollars for 12 pieces of notepaper with my name on them. Calendars and Christmas cards start in August, wrapping paper and To and From labels soon after. Discs are starting to become popular. Pens and pencils. Please send whatever you can. Next year's date book. A magnifying glass and a calculator.

Sometimes I get a double mailing and quite often a follow up and another double mailing a few weeks later. That's how the gold coins with an angel on them became mine—and they are still coming. So if you want a gold coin with an angel on it, I'm your man.

Self-sticking name labels have always been a favorite with senders and I am constantly amazed at the various permutations of my name they achieve—my middle name becomes my first name, my first initial becomes a name, my last name gains a letter or two and even becomes my first name.

This shows how senders sometimes make a mistake and so you have to be careful with things that come in the mail. Directions may be incomplete and not well thought out and therefore dangerous.

Here's a hypothetical to help you understand how something bad and painful can be caused.

Suppose one day in the mail there's a little cushion exactly four and a quarter inches by four and a quarter inches. The directions say that if you put a cup of hot tea or coffee on it, you will release the aroma of the pine glades of Maine, and the glades can be renewed if they begin to fail by striking the cushion with a hammer. And that's all they say. That's all. Well, what they should have said is that when you're going to restore the glades, do not hold the cushion with the forefinger of your left hand and do not restore the glades on a glass-topped table at all.

This is only a hypothetical.

I have made light—perhaps too lightly—of the "gifts" and "invitations" that have come this year past and before. I mean not to demean or be insensitive for, yes, I know that each carries with it an appeal for those in need—those who have so little or nothing at all. And I? I have been blessed beyond all measure with so much. Mother, Father, Sister, Wife.

Sons. Health. Steadfast friends and companions along the way, even now. An ample share of this world's goods.

At this season of the year—especially this season—should I treat these cries for help as junk mail? I cannot begin to respond positively to all of them, but does that mean I should think they are unworthy? The cold? The hungry? The sick? The abused? The forgotten? The questions answer themselves. Junk mail? No, if I cannot send money to answer a particular plea, let it at least be a reminder of the manifest blessings I know and have known.

So may it be.

We were basking in the afterglow of Thanksgiving dinner when Cousin Misty arrived. She was on the way to her daughter's—"you wouldn't recognize her, she's shook the sawdust out of her head and some brains are starting to seep in"—and could only stay for a minute, long enough or a cup of non-alcoholic eggnog.

But when we got to the door, she said "I was listening to old-time radio and I heard a song—I could only get part of it, but I thought you might be reminded of someone by it." She handed me a piece of paper and was gone. This is what she had written:

> I get along without you very well, of course I do,
> Except when soft rains fall and drip from leaves, then I recall
> The thrill of being sheltered in your arms, of course I do,
> But I get along without you very well.

I needed no reminder.

Bob and I wish you the best for the year to come and remember, as Cousin Misty once said, the latch string is always open.

*Bill*

## *Sojourning in an Adult Community*
## Bill Ditter's 2015 Christmas Letter

*Box 256, Woxall, PA 18979*

December 2015

Dear Family and Friends:

I am going to call this one that is hurrying into history as the Year of the Fall. More of that later.

Let's start with last December. Christmas dinner was here at Ridge Farm with David and his family doing the decorating and preparing the feast and all that makes up a holiday's groaning board. It was magnificent.

We then repaired to the living room to await Bill's family and the exchange of presents. Number 2 grandson thoughtfully brought along his new girl friend's new puppy, Dexter. He, grandson, not puppy, explained that Madeline was going to her aunt's for the day and if Dexter is left alone, he will howl and thus disturb Madeline's neighbors. Look at it this way, as Grandson No. 2 pointed out, what kind of an impression would you make on a young lady if you favored puppy-abandonment and neighbor-annoyance? Well, that made bringing Dexter to a present-exchange reasonable, didn't it?

Dexter goes to training school. I will rejoice for Madeline when he graduates from kindergarten.

Dexter is young and hasn't mastered, "Sit," "Hush," or "No Muddy Paws on Granddaughter's New Dress." On the other hand, he has learned the importance of letting other pooches that may later arrive know that he'd been here. The west side of the Christmas tree was utilized for his calling card as it were.

Now about candy canes on Christmas trees. Why would anyone put a cane low enough that a puppy standing on his hind legs could reach it, barely, rather than low enough that a puppy could reach it easily? Good question. Grandson Number 2 has always been quick to seek answers. For the rest of the gala, the tree teetered toward the direction from whence came the Wise Men.

February: I like to recall it as a learning-time about the pelvis rather than dwell upon why I undertook this particular line of study. Well, the pelvis is really two bones. One for the left and one for the right. The pelvis (pelvises?) is the bone to which the legs fasten with ball and socket.

But first, Ridgevale, where I pursued matters of the pelvis.

Ridgevale is a place between light and darkness for folk, a way station along life's path as it were. It is divided into three sections: apartments for the well and hearty, single rooms for those who have suffered injury, and the nursing unit. The residents refer to the three units as the Pending, Mending, and Sending.

I will admit that my sense of humor was misplaced that first night. You see, I wanted to make a good impression on the diners. And what better way than to give them a good laugh?

It started with my suit, shirt, and tie. I slicked my hair down and then, satisfied I was well turned out, I headed for the dining room, limping behind my walker. Ridgevale provides tables of four with a few of six. You can sit wherever you spot a three-or-less-some, of which I did partway. The tables I passed and approached accommodated some rather hostile-looking ladies—suspicious and dour.

Could there be a better way to win and charm them—to loosen them up as it were—than by a bit of humor? Apparently some other way—any other way. But unrealized at the time. Using my stentorian voice, probably too stentorian, I announced, "I'm Bill from the Pennsylvania Board of Parole."

Now I ask you, could anyone think of a less likely place to find folk with ties to the parole board than a senior living facility? Well that's what I thought and therefore my self-identification was so obviously false it would get a good laugh. Wrong on both counts.

No sooner had I gotten the Parole part out than a nice grandmotherly type said, "Whoops" and fainted, fell forward, and hit her soup plate at just the right angle so it bisqued a lady at the next table. The next few moments are a bit dim in memory's record but I recall nurses, aides, security lads and lassies milling around and escorting me to a nearby office for discussion. To give it to you quickly. The soup lady was indeed on parole (something about funding her desires from her employer's credit cards) but hadn't bothered to report for untold months. My less than jovial (meant to be jovial) introduction gave her a flash of slammer thoughts as she passed out.

Later that evening there was a knock on my door and the lady herself was there. I hardly knew what to expect—but she came forward, gave me a hug and big kiss. She told me she was so relieved to learn I was a phony that all was forgiven. I was all set to say I'm not a phony, I'm really a judge but I thought better of it. And the fact that I was using a walker should have tipped her off, but I thought better of that too.

*Verna Bock Ditter, watercolor*

Ridgevale's food was good and hearty. By "hearty," I mean that the portions were small and categorized. Categorized? You've seen those lists on the back of a can of beans, haven't you? So many calories and fat and carbohydrates and sodium etc. Well, Ridgevale provides you with a menu for the next day's lunch and dinner so you can pick what you want, but each choice carries with it label-like information. A truly great idea, and as others advocated, upon receiving the menu, I crossed all that information out and let my pelvi make my choices. After all, I was there to have it healed.

May was devoted to the study of the collarbone. Ridgevale again.

Cousin Misty arrived on Thanksgiving Day in time for dessert. When we had finished our coffee, and there was an appropriate pause, she made some pithy observations, which included,

> "The Greeks had a word for it but nobody knew what it was because it was always in Greek."
>
> "Of course, if they'd had automobiles in those days, you could've bought one for pennies on the dollar and that's really cheap."
>
> "After they all signed the Declaration of Independence Franklin said, 'We'll all hang out together.'"
>
> "John Brown started the Civil War by taking Harper's ferry, but he didn't mean to."
>
> "As Yogi Berry said, 'It's hard to predict the future because you don't know what's going to happen.'"

She glanced at her watch, grabbed her coat, said goodbye, and stopped at the door. She handed me a piece of paper, "I tried to get it down before I'd forget it. It's been 10 years, hasn't it?" This is what she had written:

> When I grow too old to dream, I'll have you to remember,
> And when I grow too old to dream, your love will live in my heart,
> So kiss me my sweet and though we must part,
> When I grow too old to dream that kiss will live in my heart.

Misty had it right again.

Bob and I wish you and yours the best for 2016. And remember, as Misty once said, "The latchstring is always open."

*Bill*

# The Sermons

## Introduction by The Reverend Alan Smith

I have never gone for a walk along a country road with Judge Ditter, but I've been on many an adventure with him through his stories, of both tale and truth—the lines between the two which at times are uncertain.

I was Judge Ditter's pastor for twelve years, and I have known him for seventeen. Over this time, we have spoken of deep matters of faith and life and have been struck in confusion and amazement at humanity's capacity for both cruelty and love. Throughout, Judge Ditter's love and compassion for his family and his friends, his deep and sincere faith, and his connection with community have remained certain and unaltered, despite what he has seen in his years on the bench and the challenges he has encountered on his own life's journey.

In his devotions at a board meeting, in conversations that developed while seated next to one another on metal chairs in a church fellowship hall over a dish of ice cream, or while traveling to an event that neither of us may have particularly desired to attend, our conversations have never seemed to arrive at silencing conclusions. I have also learned that the best way to receive Judge Ditter's godly wisdom and insight is as if on a shared journey. When you read these sermons, imagine yourself standing with him, staring at a tombstone, eavesdropping on two grieving friends, or sitting in a library with an unhurried theologian whose heart and mind are engaged in an honest, respectful conversation, each one's view tempered by the presence and input of the other. You may find yourself mesmerized by the beauty, innocence, and hopefulness his grandchildren engender as he opens his heart and welcomes us to see life through the window of his soul.

As you read each sermon that follows, consider what's presented to you not so much as teachings to be debated as opportunities for a conversation with a mentoring friend whom you met on a journey that is already underway. You may also sense as you are reading that you are taking part in an ongoing conversation that will continue on another day, while realizing that walking in Judge Ditter's footprints is leaving its impression upon the clay of your life.

## What's Your Claim, Rebecca?

Several weeks ago I was invited to go to my grandson's third-grade class to speak to the children about government, laws, and what judges do. We all seemed to have a good time and the children paid attention and asked interesting questions.

A few days later I got a handmade card from each of the children thanking me for being with them. Many of the cards contained drawings—of a gavel—of a person in a black robe—of a judge's bench. My favorite, of course, came from my grandson—but my next favorite came from Kyle.

This is what Kyle wrote: "Thank you, Judge Ditter, for coming to our class. I couldn't draw a picture of you, so I drawed Bugs Bunny instead."

And it was a pretty good picture too.

Trying to illustrate the unknown by illustrating the known may or may not work. It may turn out to be only funny. Trying to teach about God by talking about humans may not be funny but it may result in an analogy that is inadequate, incomplete, and perhaps blasphemous. Having said that, here goes.

The title of my sermon is "What's Your Claim, Rebecca?" and what I want to talk about is God's grace—not all about it—but [about] three aspects of it—it's freely given, it's for everyone, and it leads to salvation.

Rebecca is my granddaughter. She's four months old.... She's a lovely child—sparkling eyes—a beautiful smile. Her parents are rightly proud of her and their love for her is quite apparent. And so it should be.

But I ask you—what has she ever done for them to warrant the care and attention they lavish on her? Has she washed a dish? Swept the porch? Gone on an errand? Well, of course not—and yet they care for her, provide for her every need. What's her claim on them? In the sense that I am using the word *claim*, she has none.

And in the same sense, we have no claim on God. We have done nothing for Him—much less something that would give us some claim that might cause him to do something for us.

What God does for us is a matter of his grace.

Grace is one of those words that has many meanings. As I am using it today, it means the unmerited favor of God and the position into which it puts the believer.

1. The unmerited favor of God.

2. The position into which it puts the believer.

I come from the old school of preaching that says, *Tell them what you're going to tell them, Tell them,* and then *Tell them what you've told them.*

But I am not going to do all the preaching today—I'm going to ask you to help. I've divided this sermon into sections. After I finish each section, I'm going to ask you to sing a verse from a well-known hymn which will summarize what I've just said.

That may sound complicated, but I think it will all work out.

We are now at Roman numeral two on the outline—Slavers Too?

Do you know what a slaver was?

John Newton was a slaver—he was engaged in the slave trade. If you don't know about the way black people were brought to the United States to be sold as slaves, I may tell you more in the next minute than you might want to know.

After they were captured in Africa—almost always by rival tribes—these unfortunate people were sold to white traders and were packed on sailing ships—in the hold—chained to each other by their ankles, wrists, and necks. Often the overhead was only four-feet high so they could never stand erect. They'd be brought out for a few minutes each day—for scant food and so that those who had died—and many did—could be thrown overboard. Human cargo. Men, women, children packed together so the sweat of one—and that's not all—ran onto the back of another.

John Newton was born in 1725 and had first gone to sea in the British Navy when he was eleven years old. He found the life of a midshipman unbearable and so he deserted and became a slave trader instead.

That's what he did for four years. He bought, transported, and sold human beings under the most atrocious conditions imaginable.

He left the sea—and felt a call to study for the ministry. He came under the influence of John and Charles Wesley and George Whitfield. At age 39, John Newton became an ordained minister in the Anglican Church and became a powerful preacher.

In later years he said he had been blind—but that now he could see. What do you suppose he meant by that?

A few moments ago I read to you from the second chapter of Ephesians.

There Paul says, "It is by God's grace you have been saved... It is not a result of your efforts, but God's gift....God has made us what we are and...has created us for a life of good deeds, which he has already prepared for us to do."

No—we do not earn salvation—it is a gift—but there is a joy in doing God's work—a satisfaction that comes from helping others—a reward that awaits those who hear the words," Well done, thou good and faithful servant."

John Newton was blind to what God meant him to be and do—but through grace, he gained his sight.

When John Newton could not find a hymn that served his purposes, he would write one—often with the assistance of his close friend, the poet William Cowper.

Until the time of his death, John Newton never ceased to marvel at how God's grace had so completely transformed him. In one of his last sermons he said, "My memory is nearly gone—but I remember two things: That I am a great sinner and that Christ is a great Savior."

God's grace is for everyone—it's for a hopeless wretch like John Newton.

It's for those who have strayed. It's for the prodigal son. It's for those who yearn to serve God but don't know how. It's for everyone.

Will you please turn to your sermon outline and sing with me the first verse of a hymn by John Newton.

*Amazing grace,*

*How sweet the sound*
*That saved a wretch like me.*
*I once was lost, but now am found,*
*Was blind, but now I see.*

### *How? The Mirror*

In later years, John Newton said that the turning point in his life came with one of those vicious storms that roar out of the South Atlantic. The churning, boiling sea. The gale howling through the empty rigging. The helmsman trying to hold the bow into the wind. The pounding waves. The groaning of each piece of timber as the ship fights for its life. Was it that kind of storm that taught John Newton's heart to fear? Maybe so.

A storm at sea has certainly driven many a man to his knees—but John Newton tells us there was more to it than the fear of death.

What made him really tremble was the fear of life as he was then living it. He looked into a mirror and despaired of what he saw.

Fear means more than to be afraid of some physical event. Fear also means to experience reverence and awe in the presence of God—to realize that God sees us for what we are—to realize that God did not make us just so that we will love Him—but primarily so he could love us and we have made it impossible for him to do so. To suggest that he should love us anyway—despite our own acceptance of our faults—is to expect God to be less than God.

But through His grace we can become all that He wants us to be. It's never too late.

It's really up to us.

Will you join me in singing the second verse of John Newton's hymn.

> *'Twas grace that taught my heart to fear,*
> *And grace my fears relieved.*
> *How precious did that grace appear*
> *The hour I first believed.*

## Now and Then

We opened this service with the prayer of Girolamo Savonarola.[1] We asked not for tranquility—nor for end of tribulations—but rather for the strength and grace to overcome adversity.

At least we were realists. Most of us know from observation and experience that the way is not always easy and the burden light.

The journey through life is accompanied by danger, hardship, and temptations. All of which have their purpose in developing character and ability.

As some of you know, until a few years ago I was a beekeeper—and at one time, I had eight hives. Bees are fascinating creatures. After the queen lays an egg, the nurse bees provide pollen and honey for the larva. Then—at just the right time—the cell containing the developing bee is provided with food sealed with a wax cap.

On the twenty-first day, the pupa or fully developed bee is ready to emerge. She chews a small hole in the capping of the cell and with great labor pulls

1 *Lord, we pray not for tranquility. Nor that our tribulations may cease, We pray for thy spirit and thy love That thou grant us strength and grace to overcome adversity through Jesus Christ. Amen.*

herself up through the opening she has made. In doing so, she pulls from her wings a casing that encloses them and thus she is ready to fly.

Sometimes a weak colony is invaded by moths that eat the wax of the comb. They go from cell to cell and first eat the cappings, including those where a fully developed bee is ready to emerge. Now the task is easier: there's not just a ragged hole in the capping—the whole capping is gone. The adult bee emerges with much less effort than her sisters require. She does it more quickly. We would think that such a bee is lucky—that the wax moth has provided a service for the hive.

Such is not the case. The bees that have emerged from the cells without pulling themselves through the partially chewed hole in the cap find that their wings are still in their sheaths, sheaths that have now hardened and cannot be removed. These bees cannot fly—cannot work—and are soon put to death.

What did today's scripture say? Trouble produces endurance; endurance brings God's approval; and approval creates hope.

Let us sing together the third verse of John Newton's testimonial.

> *Through many dangers, toils and snares*
> *I have already come,*
> *'Tis grace has brought me safe thus far*
> *And grace will lead me home.*

## *I Got Nothing That I Asked For*

Come with me now, if you will, to a field in Virginia. Come back in time 135 years to those days when families were divided—when brother fought brother, Americans killed Americans. Come back with me to a Virginia field in 1863.

Here in this place God has indeed loosed the fateful lightning of his terrible swift sword. But now the battle has passed on— beyond those hills. Even the muffled roar of the cannon has ceased.

A southern burial squad makes its way across the ravaged ground and stops at the body of a lad who is as fair in death as he was in life. He was not a man, but a boy of perhaps sixteen, who here gave himself in a cause he thought was noble—but in reality was so very wrong. As is his duty, the corporal of the burial squad goes through the lad's pocket—seeking identification and anything that can be returned to the family. There are a few things—and among them a paper on which the young man had penned these words:

I asked God for strength that I might achieve,
I was made weak that I might learn humbly to obey.
I asked for health that I might do greater things.
I was given infirmity that I might do better things.
I asked for riches that I might be happy,
I was given poverty that I might be wise.
I asked for power that I might have the praise of men,
I was given weakness that I might feel the need for God.
I asked for all things that I might enjoy life,
I was given life that I might enjoy all things.
I got nothing that I asked for—but everything that I had hoped for.
Almost despite myself, my unspoken prayers are answered,
I am, among all men, most richly blessed.

God in His wisdom and grace answers our prayers. Of course, sometimes the answer is no—or perhaps not now—but of this we can be sure: God is good.

Please join me in singing the fourth verse of "Amazing Grace."

*The Lord has promised good to me*
*His word my hope secures;*
*He will my shield and portion be,*
*As long as life endures.*

## *Joy Is the Serious Business of Heaven*

I take the title to this, the last part of the sermon, from the words of C. S. Lewis: "While we may be the recipients of God's grace here on earth, His ultimate gift to us is that of Salvation."

Salvation is like nothing we can imagine.

Here on earth we crave happiness and security. We are never safe—but we often have fun—a meeting with friends, a party, jokes, laughter, love, a symphony, a stroll at sunset. You name it.

These moments are like the motels where we may stop to rest on a trip—pleasant, well apportioned—but we would not mistake them for home and the joys of this life should not be mistaken for the joys of our father's heavenly home.

Let me try again.

Our experiences here are like the pencil lines an artist would make on a sketchpad to show a beautiful landscape. His lines would quickly vanish if the real thing in all its color and dimensions were imposed on the artist's paper.

A candle flame which seemed to light the room is no longer visible when the blinds are thrown open and the blazing sun comes in.

Here on earth we pursue our jobs and worry about our responsibilities. We only have a certain time for the joys— the frivolous matters of life. But those moments of gaiety, laughter, song, games, fun—those are the matters with which heaven will be concerned.

The unborn child may be both secure and safe—but has no clue—can't possibly imagine the beauty of a sunset. We are like the unborn so far as the joys of salvation are concerned.

And now join in singing the final verse of John Newton's story.

*Yea, when this flesh and heart shall fail,*
*And mortal life shall cease*
*I shall possess within the veil,*
*A life of joy and peace.*

*Let us pray.*

*Almighty and most merciful Father*
*for Thy goodness that has created us*
*for Thy bounty that has sustained us,*
*for Thy patience that has borne with us, and*
*for Thy love that has redeemed us,*
*We give Thee praise and thanks*

*Amen.*

*J. William Ditter, Jr.*
*Tabor United Methodist Church*
*June 1998*

# The Road to Emmaus

Has it ever occurred to you how many of the New Testament stories that we know best took place on the roads of Palestine?

Any number of miracles of our Lord were performed along the way. In John we read, "As Jesus was walking along, he saw a man who had been born blind. The disciples ask if the man is blind because of his sin or that of his parents. Jesus says neither—but so that God's power might be seen at work in this man. And he heals him." (John 9:1)

Luke recounts:

> Jesus went to a town called Nain....Just as he arrived at the gate of the town, a funeral procession was coming out....The dead man was the only son of a widow. Jesus was filled with pity for her and restored the widow's son to life. (Luke 7:11)

Again Luke tells us:

> As Jesus made his way to Jerusalem...He was going into a village when he was met by ten men who were lepers. They shouted to him, and he cured them. (Luke 17:11)

It was along the highways and byways of life that Jesus taught, preached, cast out demons, healed the sick, restored sight, and even raised the dead.

Jesus sometimes chose wayside scenes for his parables. One of the best known parables is that of the Good Samaritan. The story takes place on the road between Jerusalem and Jericho.

In another of our favorite parables, a father rushes out onto the highway to meet his returning, prodigal son.

One of the most dramatic encounters of the Bible is between Saul of Tarsus and the risen Christ. It takes place on the road to Damascus. Saul, the persecutor, is struck blind. When his sight is restored, he becomes Paul, the great teacher and missionary.

But of all the New Testament stories, none to me is more filled with meaning, or more beautiful, than the story of the two followers of Jesus who left Jerusalem to take the lonely road that still crawls over the Judean hills to Emmaus. Two disheartened, beaten wayfarers wandering along a winding road in the heat of the day, recalling the stillness and the horror of the forty-eight hours just past.

They were, after all, the disciples of a dead man.

Come back with me in your mind's eye to that dusty road. Who are these travelers? Come back with me across the centuries to that Sabbath which we now commemorate as the most holy day of the Christian year. But for these two there is no joy...no song...no reassurance...no praise...no promise...no hope.

They lost. They are going home.

As we walk with these men for a little while, we learn that the name of one of them is Cleopas. The name of the other we never do learn. Now, from our reading of the New Testament, we know that Cleopas is not included in the inner circle of twelve disciples. But we also know that Luke wrote that Jesus chose seventy-two other men and sent them to teach and preach in his name. Perhaps Cleopas and his companion were among that wider circle.

In any event, they had been followers of Jesus. No doubt they had left home and hearth, friends and family, put aside their tools and their trades, and had been caught up in a cause which they recognized as greater than themselves. They had gone where Jesus directed...had done what he asked.

From them there was the gift of full commitment, all that they had...all that they were...and all that they had ever hoped to be...had been given to Him.

But let us listen to what they say:

They mention the joy of only a week ago when the Master rode triumphantly into Jerusalem to the cheers of the multitude.

They try to sort out the events that followed. The appearance of Jesus at the temple. How he taught there. Then came the arrest...a sham that barely passed as a trial... And the ghastly horror of the crucifixion... Then too, there was the rumor they had heard this very morning just as they had left Jerusalem.

The tomb was empty. Angels said Jesus had risen. Absurd.

And so here they were going home to Emmaus. Their hopes shattered... Their dreams gone... Their illusions carried away... They are stricken with grief over the pain and death of the man they loved... But yet, there is also a hint in their voices that He had somehow tricked them.

He had promised so much.

He had achieved so little.

They had enlisted in His cause. They had believed His words... They had seen His vision.

And yet, when the moment of truth came...when all the chips were down... when he was given the opportunity to overthrow the tyranny and power of Rome and at the same time establish God's kingdom on earth, He was helpless.

There was no miracle.

There was no voice from heaven. There was no sign.

Instead, there was just another Jew nailed to just another cross in the quick, efficient way the Romans had for troublemakers.

He did not even unsheathe His sword, says Cleopas.

He did not even have a sword, his companion complains.

They are bitter. They are disillusioned. They had never expected the noble crusade of which they were a part to end like this.

And so they are doing a perfectly natural, human thing: They are going back to the old life. To the old ways.

They are turning their backs on earthly kingdoms and noble causes. They are turning their backs on Jerusalem and the cross and what they had perceived to be the promises which had died there.

They have had enough. They are going home.

Not that the prospect of going home is so great... It was just that there is no other place to go.

They know what to expect in Emmaus... Emmaus is where there are friends.

Emmaus is where they are known. In the crowds of Jerusalem there was anonymity... It won't be like that in Emmaus.

There will be the old men who had seen them grow up.

There will be their earnest contemporaries. *I don't want to say I told you so, Cleopas. But I told you so.*

There will be the kids in the street.

In Emmaus they can expect averted eyes and the smirks and smiles of satisfaction that people reserve for someone who has gotten his due for daring to be daring.

The road to Emmaus is seven miles long. Cleopas and his companion were in no hurry to get there.

Dear Friend, Does any of this have a familiar ring to you? Have you ever found yourself on the Emmaus road? Was there a time when you enlisted in some cause...some new beginning...a time when you pulled yourself up from the ordinary affairs of life to join something that was noble and brave and gallant? And then came the next day with its frustrations and compromise and defeat and failure?

Was there someone you loved and trusted and with whom your whole life was entwined? And then did that person die...or worse yet, prove false?

For whatever reason, did you suddenly find yourself with your pennants and banners caught in the dust, your halyards cut?

Did you stand there with all that brave vision of a new and better world destroyed...your soul naked and neglected in an uncaring world?

Like Cleopas and his companion, did you turn your back on the whole business and call it quits? That is what it is to walk the road to Emmaus...your head down and your feet dragging in the dirt and dust of despair.

Many years ago, there was a young man who loved his father with a deep, unswerving devotion. He was not alone. Those who knew his father—and many did—warmed to him instinctively. And why not? He was a fine Christian, respected in his profession, a brilliant speaker, and prominent in the affairs of this nation. The young man was an only son. He was secure in the knowledge that the love he gave was returned, measure for measure. And more.

Late one autumn day, the young man went with his father to an airport. The older man boarded a waiting plane. The young man watched until it was out of sight. He noted the sun was setting on what had been a beautiful day. In the years to come, he would remember that sunset and its meaning.

Early the next morning as he waited for breakfast, someone thrust a newspaper his way. A headline screamed that the plane had crashed.

His father was dead.

His father was dead.

The young man arranged to go home to his family.

Much, much later that day his uncle met him at the train station, and the bitterness...the grief...the shock...the anger...the disappointment all poured out in a torrent of words and tears.

The young man said—and this was by no means the worst—"There is no God. If by chance there is a God, I want nothing to do with him. He is cruel. He is uncaring. And if there was ever a Jesus, I don't want to hear about him either."

There was more, but that was the general idea.

His uncle tried to console him, but with no success. Finally, at one point the young man said, "You don't seem to understand. I've lost my father."

And his uncle answered, "And you don't seem to understand, I've lost my brother. And your mother, her husband. And America, its servant. Do you think you are the only one who suffered loss last night?"

The young man in his hour of great need, like the men who journeyed toward Emmaus that Sabbath day so long ago, had turned his back on the cross and all its meaning...and on his savior too.

Though he knew better, he ignored the source of comfort and strength. Rather than seek help, he added to his own helplessness.

The story doesn't end there, however. More than forty-one years have passed since that gray November day. The years have brought acceptance and patience...perhaps even a degree of wisdom, although that is by no means certain. But he does know that God had forgiven his outburst. He now knows that in Jesus there is source of strength and comfort for the darkest of times. Like the men on the road to Emmaus. He had turned from the Master. He has now turned back. How? Why? There was an infinite love that would not let him go...we'll sing about it in a few minutes.

But let us return to Cleopas and the other disciple whose name we do not know. As they walk along, trying to sort out the fragments of their broken dreams, suddenly a stranger appears. They pour out to him the whole burden of their great adventure with that man from Galilee who only the day before yesterday had failed them so, dying with two common thieves.

We trusted he would redeem Israel. What fools we were. At least we weren't taken in by that wild story those crazy women told. Angels. Empty tomb. Angels indeed.

And then the stranger stops them, places his hands upon their arms, and with great patience begins to unfold the mysteries they had never before understood. Failures?... Broken hopes?... Frustrated aspirations?... Despair?

Theirs perhaps. But not God's. For God, says the stranger, intends his kingdom should be built block by heavy block, by heroic souls who will fight the good fight. Many will stumble. Many will fall. Not all will arise. But there will be few who will find the courage and the strength to get up and struggle onward to advance God's cause.

This is what the prophets have been saying.

Perhaps this man of whom you speak, this Jesus, was sent by God as an example for all mankind. Not just for here and now, but everywhere and always. Was not his sacrifice on the cross a necessary part of all this?

And then there followed that immortal scene which Rembrandt has painted... the supper at Emmaus. There the stranger takes and breaks the peasant bread and blesses it...and suddenly their unseeing eyes are opened and Cleopas and his companion knew Him.

He immediately vanished, but not the memory of Him or His presence. Cleopas and the other disciple became the apostles of a new religion, of a deathless Christ. As they take the road from Emmaus to Jerusalem to tell their friends... and later to tell countless others...what comes from their lips are among the most eloquent words ever uttered:

"Did not our hearts burn within us, while He talked with us by the way?"

The road to Emmaus became the road from Emmaus.

The road of disappointment and despair and defeat became the road back—the road of resurrection, reassurance, promise, and triumphant living.

For Cleopas and his companion, it was never the same road again. Nor will any road. Nor any will any life be the same for those who turn to the cross and the savior.

*Let us pray,*

*O, God our Father, we would find Thee in the privacy*
*of our own hearts, in the quiet of the moment.*

*We know that Thou art near us and beside us, that Thou dost love us*
*and Thou art concerned about all our affairs. Let us be truly aware of*
*the companionship of Him who will walk every road with us.*

*When we feel bereaved and forsaken, may we know the presence*
*of the comforter who will bind up our broken hearts.*

*O, God, help us to know that when we reach up to Thee, Thou art reaching down to us.*

*All this we ask in the name of Jesus, our Lord.*

*Amen.*

*J. William Ditter, Jr.*
*Laymen's Sunday*
*Old Christ Church, Philadelphia*
*April 29, 1984*

# Check It Out

I shall read to you from the eighth chapter of Romans, verse 28:

> *And we know that in all things God works for the good of those who love him, who have been called according to his purpose.*

Some few summers ago my wife and I spent a week at an Elderhostel near Bethel, Maine. As you probably know, Elderhostels are educational programs for senior citizens.[2]

Verna was taking a three-hour afternoon art class to hone her already considerable artistic skills. Since I have trouble with stick figures, I skipped the class and decided to take some pictures instead.

On the second day, I got my bike and with my camera explored the countryside. The hills were gentle and the weather warm. I had been out for about an hour when I came to a small, well-kept cemetery surrounded by a low stone wall.

For two reasons I stopped to see if there were any graves of men who had served with the 20th Maine Volunteer Infantry Regiment during the Civil War.

First of all, my great grandfather's regiment, the 118th Pennsylvania Volunteers, had fought beside those men from Maine on several occasions.

Second, the 20th Maine was the regiment of Joshua Chamberlain, Bowdoin College professor turned army colonel who had been ordered at Gettysburg to hold Little Round Top, the anchor of the Union left, "at all hazards" and who, with his 386 men, had done so. Often outnumbered two or more to one, Chamberlain and his men had beaten back attack after attack coming from three sides and finally routed the remaining rebels with a bayonet charge. I had long admired their courage and Colonel Chamberlain's leadership.

There were no men from the 20th Maine but I found four graves close together.

On one tombstone it said,

*Alexander P. Eames, 1828-1884*
*I am the resurrection and life.*

On the next stone was written:

*Huldah J. Eames, His Wife, 1827-1915*
*He giveth his beloved sleep.*

---

2 In 2010 Elderhostel was renamed Road Scholar.

Then there are two small markers. One said,

*Putnam A., only son of A.P. and H.J. Eames, age 11 months,*
*Of such is the kingdom of heaven.*

On the next stone I found these words:

*Augusta Howe, daughter of Alexander P. and Huldah J. Eames,*
*age 2 years, 7 months & 4 days*
*This lovely child so young and fair,*
*Called to an early tomb,*
*Just came to show how sweet a flower*
*In paradise would bloom.*

Not too far from where the Eames family is buried, there is another stone. On it is carved the figure of a young man who is skiing. These words are carved below:

*Jesus Loves Me*
*Eric Wycoff Bennett*
*August 12, 1971–February 13, 1990*
*"Check It Out"*
*Romans 8:28*

The "Check It Out," because it is in quotes, suggests to me that this was an expression he used. I am not sure how he died, but the February date, the ski figure, and the fact that we were near Sunday River, a ski area, suggests it was in a ski accident.

There it is. There on the tombstone of Eric Wycoff Bennett, dead at the age of 18, Romans 8:28, our text of the morning: "In all things God works for the good of those who love him." And the other words: "Jesus Loves Me." And in quotes, "Check It Out."

While I was standing at Eric's grave, a question came to me: suppose I had been the minister at their church 160 years ago—and I had gone to comfort Mr. and Mrs. Eames on the death of their daughter, that "lovely child so young and fair"—knowing as I would have known, that their only son had also died, age 11 months. Would I have talked to them about Romans 8:28?

For that matter, if I had been the father of Eric Wycoff Bennett, would I have put on his stone, "Jesus Loves Me." "Check It Out," "Romans 8:28"?

All things? In all things for good? I wondered.

In most things, sure. But in all things?

Over the next several weeks and months, from time to time, I thought back about that little cemetery and what was written on those five stones: "I am the resurrection and life," "He giveth his beloved sleep," "Of such is the kingdom of heaven," "This lovely child so young and fair," and especially, "Romans 8:28."

Again I wondered, "In all things?"

I thought of the many experiences of life. Do not our own—and those of people we know—suggest the terrible pain that surrounds us?

Listen to our own Prayer and Praise sessions.

Venture out to our cemetery and there you will find the grave of one of the young women of our church, an accomplished rider and avid competitor. During a steeplechase event, her horse tripped and fell on her and she died even as her parents watched in horror.

I wondered and decided that the suggestion of Eric Wycoff Bennett was a good one—I'd check it out. Ideas came to me. Some I kept. Some I discarded. I did some reading.

*Verna Bock Ditter, watercolor*

Let me tell you about my on-and-off thoughts of the next several months.

It was Paul of Tarsus who said, "And we know that in all things God works for the good of those who love him."

They were not the thoughts of a man who sat in his living room engaging in abstract rationalization or propounding theories from books on the shelf. The words I was pondering did not come from a man whose life had been serene and trouble free, untouched by stress and strain, filled with peace and tranquility. Quite to the contrary, Paul was a man who knew perplexity and pain first hand. He knew tragedy and turmoil, danger and deceit, suffering and humiliation. He knew the anguish of derision, sarcasm, rejection, betrayal. He knew the agony of the leather lash with its metal ends.

In Corinthians he tells how he has been "unbearably crushed" and that he "despaired of life itself." He recounts that he was "afflicted in every way." He says he was "perplexed," "persecuted," and "struck down." He experienced "beatings," "imprisonments," "hardships," and "hunger."

He had walked trackless deserts in the blazing heat and suffered through the biting cold of winter nights outdoors. He had survived storms at sea and three shipwrecks.

Paul was no armchair philosopher. When he speaks of persecution, poverty, and pain he is speaking from experience.

And what is one of the tenets of the faith that he affirms? *In all things God works for the good of those who love him.* Not some things. All things. Not in just the joyful experiences of life, but in all things. Not just on the mountaintop of triumph but in the valley of tragedy and despair. Not just when the sea is tranquil and the breeze gentle, but when the wind howls through the halyards, the ship shudders and staggers. Every door is dogged down and checked, and the bravest of the brave are filled with terror.

It is evident that when Paul says "in all things" he means in all things. Paul speaks with the voice of experience and conviction. I accept the sincerity of what he says.

But still I had questions.

One is easy to answer—Paul's words, "those who love him, who are called according to his purpose" are not words of limitation or exclusion any more than when Jesus said, "Let the little children come unto me," he meant "and keep every one else away."

When Paul says, "those who love him," he is reminding his Jewish brethren that God's good is for the gentiles as well as for them.

But what does he mean by "good"? The immediate good? Today's good? Or the long-term good?

I thought of my own hopes, disappointments, and how it turned out.

Early on in my career I sought a job for which I was well qualified and experienced. It went to another lawyer.

Later there was another opportunity. Again, another was chosen.

Then came the third, and this time the doors were opened for me. I realized that my earlier disappointments had made possible a far better good. In my life I could see the truth of Roman 8:28.

While it was impossible to ignore what Paul proclaimed and my own experience, still there were lingering doubts.

A trip to the theater gave me a new thought. I realized that we must always keep in mind that we are players on the stage for but a little while. We have scant knowledge of the other players and what is for their good. Infinity stretches before us and behind us. We have practically no understanding of the earlier parts of the drama that is unfolding even as we act out our little plans and stumble over our lines. We have only a hazy notion of what the climax of the play will be or when that will come about. Much less do we know of the author–director or His plans. So how can we know what is for our good or of any of it—much less for it all?

With that in mind I took a look at the words again: In all things, God works for the good of those who love him. At this point I realize what the words do not say.

For example, they do not say that surely goodness and mercy will follow us all the days of our lives. The psalmist may have said it, but not Paul.

They do not say that God guarantees us freedom from pain and tragedy if we are good.

They do not say that God works for the good of the Methodist Church—or for the good of America—or for what I perceive to be my benefit or what I perceive will benefit my family.

The words say none of those things—and so I am left with the realization that what God works for is quite different than any of the things that I would call good. That can mean only one thing—if it's not my call and not your call, it must be God's call. It's not the good that in my thoughts so often puzzles me, but the good that God sees with his infinite wisdom.

I turned back to chapter 8 of Romans and read what else Paul of Tarsus said. He asks the rhetorical question: is there anything that can separate us from the love of Christ: trouble? hardship? persecution? hunger? poverty? danger? death?

He answers his own question in this way. Neither death nor life; neither heavenly nor earthly powers; neither height nor depth; neither the world we know nor the world to come; no creature—nothing at all—can separate us from the love of God which is ours through Jesus Christ our Lord.

So now I found that Paul has told me what he means by "good"—nothing can separate me from God's love. I am strengthened by this reassurance.

I thought back about the men of the 20th Maine and the men of the 4th Alabama that opposed them that terrible day on Little Round Top. I asked whether I could accept the words of Julia Ward Howe that while God had "loosed the fateful lightning of His terrible, swift sword, His truth is marching on." And what was that truth, that good? In that day of agony and bloodshed, the ultimate good was that men would be free.

I was asking whether I could accept the idea that even in the awful throes of war God could be working for the good that men might be free? Was his truth really marching on? Could war and agony and sacrifice and dying men bring God's purposes closer to realization?

But then there was this.

On March 4, 1865, Abraham Lincoln stood in the East Portico of the Capitol and took the oath of office that would begin his second term as president of the United States.

The war that had ravaged his first four years in office was almost at an end. It was no longer a question of whether but only a question of when. Indeed, in about a month Lee would surrender to Grant at Appomattox and Joseph Johnston to Sherman in North Carolina.

Remember that for those four years Lincoln had borne the agony of one Union defeat after another and, more recently, the terrible casualty lists from Grant's Wilderness campaign.

But now it was all but over.

And so, we might expect that Lincoln's second inaugural address would be a song of triumph, a tribute to the armies and navies that under his command had defeated the Confederates, and a reminder that to the victor belonged the spoils.

But instead, the address was a sermon about Divine judgment. In part, this is what Abraham Lincoln said,

> Both those of the North and South read the same Bible and pray to the same God, and each invoke His aid against the other. It may seem strange that any men should dare to ask a just God's assistance in wringing their bread from the sweat of other men's faces, but let us judge not that we be not judged.

Slavery, he maintained, the immediate cause of the war, was one of those offenses which must needs come and be continued through its appointed time. Now God had willed to remove it by a terrible war, but this was no departure from the Divine attributes which believers in a living God always ascribe to. He went on, "as was said three thousand years ago, so still it must said, 'the judgments of the Lord are true and righteous altogether.'"

As was said three thousand years ago, so still it must be said, "the judgments of the Lord are true and righteous altogether."

Although I had been left with some question, some lingering doubt about the truth of Paul's words in Romans 8:28, here was the answer,

As was said three thousand years ago, so still it must be said, "the judgments of the Lord are true and righteous altogether."

So now come back with me to the little cemetery in Maine past the stones that say, "I am the resurrection and life" and "He giveth his beloved sleep." Pause with me at the grave of Putnam Eames, 11 months old, and at the grave of Augusta, that lovely child so young and fair, 2 years, 7 months and 4 days, and stop at the stone that marks where 18-year-old Eric Wycoff Bennett lies buried.

Read again with me what is written on that stone, "Romans 8:28."

Repeat with me those words: *In all things God works for the good of those who love him.* Give yourself some time to consider them, who said them, and what they mean to you.

If you have some doubts about that verse, you might take to heart the sugges-tion, the challenge, that is written on that stone—

*"Check It Out."*

*Let us pray.*

*Our Heavenly Father, who by your love has made us, and through your love has kept us, and in your love would make us perfect:*

*We humbly confess that we often doubt when we should believe, we are deaf when we should hear, we stand mute when we should speak, and we watch when we should work.*

*And then we wonder why the life triumphant seems to avoid us. Forgive what we have been; help us to amend what we are; and in Your Spirit direct what we shall be.*

*Through Jesus Christ Our Lord. Amen.*

*J. William Ditter, Jr.*
*Tabor United Methodist Church*
*2002*

## The Road to Damascus

There's a type of movie—I've seen several—they start out the same way. There's a poster—Wanted Dead or Alive. Then boots—we don't see who is wearing them—but a hand reaches up—tears up the poster and it is scattered to the wind.

Those of us who have watched our share of cowboy movies remember the bounty hunter. He rode into town—usually alone. There were questions. Sometimes he had a picture from a "wanted" poster—and a warrant. Some-times a description of a hat or horse. Sometimes only a hunch. On the trail, hot or cold.

The bounty hunter was after men with a price on their heads—fugitives from a bank or train robbery—a man who had escaped from jail. Wanted men. Desperate men who would became more desperate if they knew a bounty hunter was on their trail.

These were the days before states and extradition—before fingerprints and DNA—before a centralized FBI identification system. These were the days of shoot first and ask questions afterwards. Bring them in, dead or alive.

What drove the bounty hunter? They were a rough lot. Often ruthless. What drove them? For many it was money—the rewards were often high. For some it was the challenge and the chase. For some it was the only way of life they knew. For some, it was just another job. For some, it was a desire to help establish law and order. But while the reasons were complex and many, I never saw a movie about a bounty hunter who was motivated by religious reasons—by a desire to stamp out heresy—to keep the faith pure and unadulterated.

But before there were bounty hunters in America, there was a such a man. He hunted to keep the faith pure. He hunted to stamp out heresy. He hunted to defend the law and the temple.

We know him as the Apostle Paul.

When he was a bounty hunter, he was Saul the Rabbi.

I shall read to you from the ninth chapter of Acts, verses one and two:

> ...Saul, still breathing threats and murder against the disciples of the Lord, went to the high priest and asked him for letters to the synagogue in Damascus, so that if he found any who belonged to the Way, men or women, he might bring them bound to Jerusalem.

What sort of man was Saul whom we now call Paul?

He was born in the Greek city of Tarsus, a renowned center of education and philosophy. Paul came from a religious family. His father was a successful man, able to buy Roman citizenship for himself and his son. Paul's family lived in the two worlds of Greek and Jewish culture. Paul described himself as a "Hebrew born of Hebrews," and as a "Pharisee, a son of a Pharisee." His parents gave him the name Saul in honor of King Saul, like them of the tribe of Benjamin. He also had the Latin name, "Paulus," and was proud to be a citizen of both Greece and Rome.

Apparently while Paul was still a youth, his family moved to Jerusalem and he studied for thirteen years under Rabban Gamaliel, a member of the Sanhedrin, and an outstanding teacher and headmaster. The purpose of the school was to pass to the next generation Jewish oral traditions—so there was much memorization, including all the rules and ceremonies that governed Jewish life—the interpretations of the scriptures—and teaching methodology. Saul was an excellent student—hard working—able—dedicated. The head of his class. Later of this training he would say, "I advanced in Judaism beyond many of my own age among my people, so extremely zealous was I for the traditions of my fathers, and as to righteousness under the law, blameless."

By the time he was in his mid- to later twenties, Paul was recognized as one of the bright stars of the Jewish temple, a leader. He was marked for greatness and religion was the center of his life.

Let me remind you of the death of Stephen. Stephen was one of the leaders of the Christian church in Jerusalem. In Acts 6 it is said of him, "Stephen, full of grace and power, did great wonders and signs among the people." Any Christian who was full of grace and power—who did great wonders among the people was sure to offend the Jews. And Stephen did so one time too often. He was seized and brought before the Sanhedrin, the Jewish council that ruled both religious and civil affairs—the same council that had put Jesus on trial. Like Jesus before him, Stephen was accused of blasphemy.

Given a chance to respond, Stephen traced the history of the Jewish people, highlighting their repeated rebellions against Moses and the other prophets sent by God. He contended that God could not be confined to a single temple in Jerusalem, however ornate it might be—but that God was everywhere. Finally, he denounced his listeners for having persecuted the prophets and for murdering Jesus.

The speech turned the judicial council into an enraged mob. Stephen was taken outside of the city, thrown into a pit, and stoned to death. Those who were about to kill Stephen laid their robes at the feet of Rabbi Saul, showing that he not only approved of what they did but was also, in effect, a participant.

Stephen died with a prayer on his lips for those who had killed him.

Saul was deeply affected by the words he had heard from Stephen—more deeply affected than he could then know. His immediate reaction was to take a leading role in the persecution of the Christians. This is how it is described in Acts 8:1–3:

> That day a severe persecution began against the church in Jerusalem, and all except the apostles were scattered throughout the countryside of Judea and Samaria. Devout men buried Stephen and made loud

> lamentation over him. But Saul was ravaging the church by entering house after house. Dragging off both men and women, he committed them to prison.

A few moments ago, I read how Paul then obtained authority from the Sanhedrin to pursue the Christians, many of whom had fled to Damascus. Armed with what today we would call a general arrest warrant, Saul and his companions took off for Damascus.

All of which brings us to the question: Why did Saul, a man of God, blameless under the law, turn to persecuting Christians in Damascus? In his own mind, Saul was acting swiftly to stamp out blasphemy. There could be no reconciliation between true Judaism and the message preached by men like Stephen. Saul's mission was to destroy those would destroy the temple. Nonetheless, he was haunted by the memory of Stephen's death. A prayer for those who were killing him? What sort of nonsense was that? And yet...

Saul couldn't quite put a finger on it. So he tried to put it out of his mind. But it wouldn't go away. Saul had seen men die before. But Stephen actually prayed for those who killed him. How strange!

And Stephen's speech to the Sanhedrin. Somehow, much of what Stephen had said was true. The Jews had turned away from God—had done so more often than Saul liked to admit. And could God be confined to a single temple? Saul looked for answers in his own vast store of knowledge. And the more he searched his conscience—the more he looked for answers to Stephen's logic, the more confused he became.

So he redoubled his physical activity, seeking to blot from his mind the troubling speech from Stephen that he remembered so well. He repeated the words he had learned in rabbinical school trying to blot out those of Stephen.

We've all done that sort of thing, directing ourselves by physical activity away from things we don't want to think about. Saul threw himself into his new work: the bringing to justice those strange Jews who challenged the authority of the priests—who declared that Jesus had risen from the dead. Once a few zealots were suitably punished, Saul was sure there would be no more talk of salvation without strict adherence to the Law of Moses.

And so it was off to Damascus—to hunt down those who questioned the law and temple-authority. To imprison those who proclaimed a risen Messiah.

From Jerusalem to Damascus is about 130 miles. It's a five- or six-day walk, a little less on a horse. There's plenty of time to think when you walk for five or six days. You can be sure Paul did a lot of thinking, in spite of himself. A lot about Stephen. What kind of a man would pray for those who for those who killed him? How odd! But that's what had happened.

And, yes, it was true that time and time again the Jews had turned away from the prophets. And yes, sometimes form did seem more important than substance. No—no—no. Stephen's words were pure blasphemy. And the sooner those who thought the way Stephen thought were eliminated, the better.

Damascus was only a few miles away.

Then suddenly there was that blinding light and Saul fell to the ground. The question: "Saul, Saul, why do you persecute me?"

"Who are you, Lord?" In that response there was realization. Recognition. Acceptance.

"I am Jesus whom you are persecuting."

It was the voice of sadness. The voice of reproach. The voice of regret. "Why do you persecute me?" These were words of anguish and sorrow—of pain and of suffering. "Saul, Saul. Why do you persecute me?"

We Christians believe that someday we will see Jesus face to face. There will be that great encounter—that moment when we stand there in the presence of the one who died to take away our sins.

It may not be on the Damascus road—or any road. There may not be a flash of light, brighter than the sun. We may not be struck blind.

But for me, I'm sure it will come at the wrong time—when I least expect it—when I'm least prepared for it. Just as it happened to Paul—to Paul on his way to persecute the Christians in Damascus. For Paul it couldn't have been at a worse time.

Maybe I have nothing to worry about. If Jesus says to me, "Bill, Bill, Why do you persecute me?" I can look Him right in the eye and say, "Lord, I never have. I have never dragged a Christian from his home to be beaten. I have never turned a Christian over to the authorities to be put in prison or killed." I can say with all honesty, "Lord, I have never persecuted you."

But suppose that's not the question He asks. Suppose He says, "Bill, Bill, Why have you ignored me? Why have you been more concerned with trophies rather than truth? Why have you laid up treasures on earth and not in heaven?"

"Why have you been proud rather than humble? Why have you been arrogant rather than sincere?

"Why have you not recognized me as the man who asked for help? Why did you ignore that child in tears? Why so many times have you crossed the road and walked on the other side, averting your eyes, while I lay wounded in the ditch?

"Why have you not used the gifts I gave you?

"Why have you neglected me?"

I hope I'll have an answer.

What about you?

*J. William Ditter, Jr.*
*Tabor United Methodist Church*
*2012*

# Lawyer, the Law, and the Legal Profession

## Introduction by Patricia M. Furlong, Esquire

It is with great humility that I introduce this section of Judge Ditter's writings on the lawyers, the law, and the legal profession. Having served as his law clerk for more than ten years, I have come to realize that Judge Ditter embodies all that our citizenry should expect from those who serve in the judiciary: love of country, respect for the law and the Constitution, reverence for the institution, honesty, and compassion for those who appear before the court regardless of who they are or the nature of their cause. For Judge Ditter, the pursuit of justice is always paramount.

When you read these passages, you will understand that Judge Ditter holds his chosen profession, and those who practice it, in the highest regard. He has always enjoyed welcoming new attorneys to the bar of the District Court—the first time I heard him swear in a group of attorneys, I was moved to tears. It is not every jurist who speaks so eloquently of admission to practice before the court or explains the real meaning of Shakespeare's famous quote: "The first thing we'll do, let's kill all the lawyers!" I am witness to the fact that the newly admitted lawyers are similarly moved.

All that being said, no one could ever accuse Judge Ditter of taking himself too seriously. You can imagine that twinkle in his eye when he penned his odes to fellow members of the court. You will laugh out loud when you read his response to the Judicial Ethics Committee's inquiry into his farm income and his report to the Chief Judge as GSA liaison judge.

These few writings reveal Judge Ditter's wisdom, his generous heart, and his quick wit. I know I speak for my fellow law clerks, many of whom return to chambers each year for Judge Ditter's annual Christmas luncheon, when I say that we are all grateful to have worked with him, and to call him a mentor and a friend.

## Admission to the Bar

After spending four years in college, three more at law school, passing the bar exam, and hopefully getting a job, lawyers have to be admitted to the courts where they wish to practice, and that includes the District Court for the Eastern District of Pennsylvania. A newly minted lawyer is on the threshold of a career, a commitment, and an adventure. I believe the moment calls for ceremony beyond the oath itself, an explicit acknowledgment of the tradition and history into which they are entering, and a reminder of the importance of the law and lawyers, the values they uphold, and the need for proper comportment in carrying out their duties.

Good Afternoon, Mrs. Hahn.[1] Mr. Gallagher will you please approach the podium. Are you prepared to take the oath?

*Will you please raise your right hand and place your left on the Bible. It is open to the 6th chapter of Micah, verse 8, which says, "What does the Lord require of thee but to do justly, and to love mercy, and to walk humbly with thy God?"*

*Do you swear that you will conduct yourself as an honorable attorney of this Court, uprightly and according to the law; that you will serve this Court and your clients with integrity and diligence; that you will support and defend the Constitution and the laws of the United States against all enemies, foreign and domestic, so help you God?*

*You are hereby admitted to practice as an attorney in the United States District Court for the Eastern District of Pennsylvania.*

Will you please be seated.

It is a great pleasure for me to admit you to practice before this Court, but doubly so because you come highly recommended by Mrs. Hahn, whose judgment I have learned to trust.

Ours is a court that is steeped in tradition. It was the second district court established by the Judiciary Act of 1789 under the provisions of Article 3 of the United States Constitution—and second by only one day. The first judge of this court was Frances Hopkinson, who had served in the Continental Congress of 1776, signed the Declaration, and participated in the American Revolution. Other judges have also had distinguished careers before becoming judges on this court. There have been outstanding lawyers, teachers, law school deans, war heroes, legislators, just to name a few.

---

1 Sherry Gallagher Hahn was one of my law clerks. She was moving for the admission of her brother, Stephen P. Gallagher.

We judges hold our traditions in great respect and firmly believe that you should do the same. You'll find practicing before us will always be an interesting experience. It will be a rare day that you will find we are not prepared to hear your matter, and even rarer day when we do not expect you to provide cogent and persuasive reasons why your client should prevail.

What else do we expect of you? Promptness, civility. Remember, you can disagree with your opponent and with us without being disagreeable. Be truthful. Remember Shakespeare's words, be true to yourself, be true to us.

Remember that you are your client's advocate, not your client's partner. Think carefully about the advice you give and the services that you render. And be careful never to do for your client what you would not do for yourself.

People who say unkind things about our profession often comment that they agree with what William Shakespeare said, "Let's kill all the lawyers."

Well, that's not exactly what he said, but it is close. Shakespeare was born in 1564 and died in 1616, so we're talking about a man who lived 400 years ago. What he actually said was, "the first thing we do, let's kill all the lawyers." The line comes from *Henry VI*, a play Shakespeare wrote about the Wars of the Roses, the bloody civil war that was waged from 1455 to 1487 between two families, both claiming the right to the throne.

Just as we Americans of the year 2012 have studied and thought about our civil war, so the English of Shakespeare's time were concerned with the Houses of Lancaster and York. Englishmen had an intimate knowledge of the Wars of the Roses. They knew its battles, its generals, its intrigues, its treacheries, and the terrain where the fighting had taken place, where those who were killed were buried. And finally, they still honored the graves of those who had fought and bravely died. The terrible consequences of that civil war had not been forgotten.

Indeed, one of the reasons why Henry VIII—who was born in 1491, just one year before America was discovered and only four years after the Wars of the Roses—wanted to be divorced from Catherine of Aragon was her failure to produce for him a son. Rightly or wrongly, Henry believed that only a son who would grow up to be a strong ruler could avert resumption of civil war. And then, of course, there was Anne Boleyn, but that's a completely different story.

In Shakespeare's play *Henry VI*, part 3, act 4, scene 2, a group of tradesmen are plotting about how they will take over the government and set up a system more to their own liking. They comment that Jack

Cade the clothier means to change things, everything. It developed that Cade had been punished for stealing sheep. Cade then says there will be reformation and he will be the leader. Under his rule, things will be different. Seven half-penny loaves will only cost a penny. Three hooped pots will have ten hoops. Under Cade's rule, it will be a crime to drink a small beer. All shall eat and drink. All shall be dressed the same. All will be like brothers and worship him.

Cade and the others have captured a clerk. His crime is that he can write his own name. So they hang him with his pen-and-ink horn around his neck.

It is then that Dick the butcher suggests that the first necessary change to bring about the anarchy that Cade envisions is to kill the lawyers. That's what he says. "The first thing we'll do, let's kill all the lawyers." That's the line that people remember and quote so sanctimoniously and think they are mocking us.

But Dick the butcher's idea is hardly a condemnation of lawyers. To the contrary, Cade and the others are recognizing that their plan to make Cade ruler and do away with liberty, to set up a system where there is neither respect for person or for property, could only succeed if they first kill all the lawyers.

And so it has always been, lawyers have been the guardians of property rights, of freedom and liberty, in Shakespeare's time, and in ours.

We live in days of peril. You will help shape the future of your country. It is a solemn duty. Keep it ever in mind.

Four final things: Good luck. Enjoy the practice of the law. I hope you some money.

And, remember, God Bless America.

*In the federal courthouse in Philadelphia, there is a small, well-appointed lobby where the judges wait for the elevator that will take them to chambers. This suggestion is posted between the elevator doors and may help its reader prepare for the tasks that lie ahead. In attributing this poem to Publius, I followed the lead of the authors of the* Federalist Papers. *Publius was a Roman consul known for his patriotism.*

## Hail, Companion, and Well Met

Good Friend, Good Judge, now stop awhile in this most spacious clime,
Too soon will duty overtake and parse your thoughtful time.

Per chance a colleague will appear, philosophy to share
Of Booker or the civil rules—how charges to prepare.

Ask of the chief, if he arrives, and wisdom he'll impart,
So when in court you'll always place the horse before the cart.

Judicial privilege reigns this place: no lawyer can invade,
The time too quick will come for you to call a spade a spade.

It matters not what says the clock, proceedings won't befall,
Before you stride upon the scene. 'Till then, no bailiff's call.

'Tis truly said haste maketh waste, let not that fate be thine.
Unto yourself give moments here and better you'll opine.

Though both your lids may heavy grow, no one will think you doze,
But rather that you're deep in thought of how some case to close.

This spot of comfort's made for you where you can contemplate
The slings and arrows of the law before you elevate.

Not by chance were benches put and cushioned for your form,
So rest—enjoy—and profit from the calm before the storm.

*Publius*

*This praise and caution is posted at the door leading out from the judges' elevator lobby and is meant for those who are leaving the courthouse. Its readers are reminded that recalling their wisdom of the day will aid in the transit to come. It is attributed to Publius for the same reason as is its companion-piece, which greets those who await their elevator.*

## Hail, Companion, and Farewell

Good Friend, Good Judge, a moment's pause, this day's tasks to review,
Haste not to curtain what you've done before a venture new.

You've listened as two lawyers fought. Your gesture bid them cease,
Then patiently explained the law so they could go in peace.

Objections and exceptions both, were dealt with greatest ease,
You kept in sight the forest grand while you were citing trees.

You lectured on the common law, from vale to lofty crest,
Expounding why that east is east except when east is west.

You shared your learning practical and so left all aghast,
As you explained how they could tell a spar from mizen mast.

Of self-forged maxims you spoke well, now part of legal lore,
And why from clouds though silver lined oft' times will rain down-pour.

Here in this castle, you are lord, your gavel, scepter sure,
By West your words are heralded: Defacto and Dejure.

But once the drawbridge you have crossed, in peasant garb you'll go,
No erminned robe. No quaking clerk. No one to say, "Bon Mot."

There's many dangers, toils, and snares t'wixt here and your abode,
So gather strength from mem'ries' store before you hit the road.

*Publius*

*This is a homage to Judge Edward R. Becker, who wrote a decision in rhyme,* Mackensworth v. American Trading Transportation Co., *United States District Court for the Eastern District of Pennsylvania, 1973. 367 F. Supp. 373 (E.D. PA. 1973).*

## To Judge Becker, Re: Mackenworth (with Apologies to Joyce Kilmer)

I thought that I would never see
A case that's done in poetry.

A judge's thought so well-expressed
With metered words and lilting jest.

In verse that one could read all day,
And never stop to eat or pray.

A song that shows a craftsman's care,
The right expressed with minstrel's flair.

A rhyme on which much thought was lain,
A lyric bridge for logic's train.

If poems are used the law to teach,
You've brought new beauty to our reach.

*On special occasions, the court sits in the ceremonial courtroom. This poem is posted on the door from the robing room into the courtroom to remind each of us where to go.*

## The Ancient Order of Judges

The middle seat in the first row
Is where the CJ wants to go.
Number 23 of him's astern
This little verse all other learn:

If on the first row I alight,
I'll remember even's right
If to the second's where I trod,
I'll remember right is odd.

And so no matter where I sit,
The one I follow's opposite.
This simple rule I'll keep in mind,
My proper seat to help me find.

*This was one of many poems composed on the occasion of a judge's retirement from the bench.*

## When I Was Just a Fledgling (with Apologies to A. E. Housman)

When I was just a fledgling, I heard Judge Fullam say,
"No string cites. The Blue Book learn, You'll use it every day."

"Of errors in your grammar, Opinions should be free."
But I was just a fledgling, No use to talk to me.

Now as I've gotten older, I've learned to pay him heed.
He's my mentor and my guide, His wisdom fills each need.

Farewells have sighs a-plenty, And filled with endless rue,
John, we'll miss you at this board, Alas, alas, Adieu.

*April 14, 2011*

*Young lawyers vs. old lawyers, 2001*

## A Law Clerk Comments (with Apologies to Lewis Carroll)

You are old, Judge J. William, the law clerk said,
And your hair has become very white;
And the law you incessantly stand on its head,
Do you think at your age that is right?

In my youth, the old judge replied to his clerk,
I feared I might never be cited,
But now I find that the harder I work,
The more West-Law is delighted.

You are old, said the clerk, as I mentioned before,
And seen all your decisions reversed,
I think if you'd just let me write in your name,
By lawyers you'd seldom be cursed.

In my youth, said the judge, as he shook his gray locks,
I copied what others had written,
But now I've become most wise as a fox,
And with my own words I am smitten.

You are old, said the clerk, as I mentioned before,
And have grown most uncommonly fat,
Yet you brag that you walk from the train to this door,
Pray what is the reason for that?

In my youth, said the judge, when I studied at Penn,
I argued each case with the dean,
And the muscular strength it gave to me then,
Now makes me near fit as teen.

You are old, said the clerk, one would hardly suppose,
That your mind was as steady as ever,
Yet you balance a disk on the end of your nose,
What made you so seemingly clever?

Said the judge, We have chatted, and now I am through,
So back to your Lexis return,
I hope while I nap for a minute or two,
Some law of some kind you will learn.

## When Your Name Is Misspelled on an Affirming Opinion

Oh, fame is such a fleeting thing,
Just as a bird, it taketh wing.
A breath of air. First rays of dawn,
And in a moment all is gone.

Declares the poet, What's a name?
A rose by other'd be the same.
Or Montague? Or Capulet?
Or here's a judge, we can forget!

Though when I read it, yes, I squirmed,
For this was once I'd been affirmed,
Another's name I'd not have cursed,
When listed where I'd been reversed.

But then I realized in a beat,
Enjoy the bitter with the sweet,
Bill Shakespeare's wisdom governs here,
Just loudly this affirmance cheer.

## Officialdom in Action

Federal judges inevitably have to grapple with some requirement of the federal bureaucracy that is not intended to be humorous. But to the beholder—well, decide for yourself.

The letter from the Judicial Ethics Committee—and the response—stem from an incomplete explanation of miscellaneous income on my annual Financial Disclosure Report.

The GSA, the General Service Administration, is the "landlord" for all federal buildings. In a courthouse, the judiciary is a tenant with needs typical of every landlord–tenant relationship. Therefore the chief judge appoints one of the members of his court to be the liaison judge to the GSA. I was so honored and, as requested, provided a report.

*The James A. Byrne Federal Courthouse, Philadelphia*

Judicial Ethics Committee
Judicial Conference
of the
United States

Alfred A. Arraj
John D. Butzner, Jr.
A. Sherman Christensen
Bernard M. Decker
Edward Thaxter Gignoux
Frank M. Johnson, Jr.
William Wayne Justice
Prentice H. Marshall
John H. Pratt
Edward Allen Tamm
(Chairman)

June 29, 1981

U. S. Courthouse
Room 5128
Washington, D. C. 20001

The Honorable J. William Ditter, Jr.
United States District Judge
6614 United States Courthouse
Independence Mall West
601 Market Street
Philadelphia, Pennsylvania 19106

My dear Judge Ditter:

In accord with its current practice, a member of the Judicial Ethics Committee has reviewed the Financial Disclosure Report submitted by you and makes the following observations:

Item I - Failed to explain Farm Income, i.e., whether the items sold were grown, manufactured, etc., at his place of residence.

In replying to this letter, whether by an amended form or answering by letter, you should be certain that a copy of your response is also filed with the clerk of the court with whom you filed your original report.

Sincerely,

Edward Allen Tamm

Edward Allen Tamm
Chairman

EAT:amh

## A Matter of Ethics

July 6, 1981

The Honorable Edward A. Tamm
Judicial Ethics Committee
United States Courthouse
3rd and Constitution Avenue, N.W.
Washington, D.C. 20001

Dear Judge Tamm:

Your letter of June 29, 1981, suggests that some further explanation of my farm income of $171.50 is necessary for the discharge of your committee's duties. The items that produced this income were one-half a hog, a few dozen eggs, and some honey.

Actually, we grew both sides of the hog and sold what I believe was the starboard side— although when one tries to figure whether scrapple and sausage came from the right or the left, it may be difficult to be precise. In any event, the hog grew on the same property at which my family and I reside although not at our actual place of residence. We kept the hog in a hog pen and we occupied the house. This seemed to work out satisfactorily from the standpoint of all concerned. At least there were no complaints from the people and if the hog was unhappy, he did not let on.

Part of the farm income came from the sale of eggs. The eggs came from chickens which, although they were on our property, did not live in our place of residence. We provided a hen house for them. From what little I know of the physiology of a chicken I would believe that an egg grows. To hear the chickens discuss it, post-event, one could only conclude that each egg had been manufactured with a great deal of skill and care.

The remaining part of the farm income came from the sale of honey. Once again, the bees that produced the honey did not live in our actual place of residence. They had their own quarters which we call beehives and while one or two from time to time may have gotten into the house (a problem we did not have with either the hog or the chickens) we did not make them feel welcome and tried to make reasonable efforts to exclude them. Honey comes from nectar. I think that much of the nectar gathered by our bees was found on other persons' properties although I must admit I have made no real effort to trace it. In my judgment honey does not grow at all nor is it manufactured. Therefore, it must come under the heading "etc."

I hope this clears up any questions the committee may have about our farm income, but I will be happy to furnish further explanation if you feel it necessary for me to do so.

Yours respectfully,

*Bill*
J. William Ditter, Jr.

## GSA Liaison Judge Reporting

August 24, 1977

The Honorable Joseph S. Lord, III
Room 17614
Federal Court
Independence Mall West
Philadelphia, PA 19106

Dear Chief Judge Lord:

You have asked me to report as GSA Liaison judge.

This was a relatively new assignment for me and I confess to a slow start since it took me several months to find out what the GSA was—and how it functioned. In part this was my fault since I thought your letter of assignment was that I should be "BSA" liaison judge—and I had several meetings with the leaders of the Boy Scouts of America before I realized my mistake. By the way, they were politely puzzled about my attention and somewhat relieved when I curtly broke off negotiations as to an Explorer post for federal judges.

As to the GSA—1977 will be marked as a year of significant achievement for several reasons. First and foremost, of course, was the painting of the judges' elevator doors. In the roughly 500 days we had occupied this building the elevator doors which play such a vital part in our work had become dowdy and more than one had flecks of paint that were missing. Hence, every appropriate resource was thrown into the struggle to have them redone. Except for the one unfortunate incident when one of our colleagues was a bit slow in getting off the elevator (and was possibly standing too close to the door) and consequently got painted by an over-enthusiastic GSA worker, this project was a complete success. New rugs in the lobby and on the elevators complete this work.

A new fountain has been installed outside the courthouse. Originally it was planned as a way to get rid of the water under the building which in turn has led to settling (see below), but when passers-by complained and when the GSA found the water it sprayed out ran back in again, the fountain was declared to be a work of art and several people have commented about it.

Early in the year we were having constant complaints about the heating system. As you know, President Carter asked that we conserve energy by keeping federal thermostats at sixty-eight degrees. The ensuing battle between the red hot radiators and the air conditioning system was interesting to behold—albeit that the common cold and flu had a field day in our building. I am pleased to report, however, that there have been no—I repeat no—complaints about the heating system since early May and I feel a great deal of personal satisfactions in being able to make that report.

The air conditioning system is another matter, of course. As you know, Judge Rosen has taken that matter under his wing (or would it be under his robe?). For my part, I am happy to say that the system has now been averaged—which is not exactly the same as its being "balanced" but is close. The "averaging" method works like this: first, one must recognize that a building is a huge volume of air (width times length times height or w x l x h); second, as with any huge volume of air, it is impossible to have every cubic foot at exactly the same temperature, i.e., people breathe, open doors, move about, etc., and this constantly stirs things up; so, third, the bottom line ("bottom line" is a GSA word which I do not understand) is to have a satisfactory "mix" (another GSA word) or average temperature. Thus, if seventy-two degrees is considered the "ideal" temperature, it can be achieved by having, for example, your chambers at sixty-two and your courtroom at eighty-two in the morning. If there are complaints, the process can be reversed by mid-afternoon. I suggest no complaints, however, because I complained several days running and the GSA threatened to pump all the air out of my half of the sixth floor if I didn't stop.

The final matter is the work on the supporting columns. As you know, this building was built from the top down, in deference to the superior position of the Court of Appeals vis à vis the District Court. Building in this way has many advantages and is certainly the thing of the future. A few bugs remain to be worked out and one of them we can see in the garage and can hear as the building trembles and vibrates. Originally three columns were to be underpinned but what they found down there made it seem better to underpin a lot more. I was not consulted about this hammering and banging and probably wouldn't have learned of it if I hadn't come into work one day. Frankly, I thought I was just having a hangover—but when the same hangover went on for several weeks, I became suspicious and asked some pointed questions. That is when I discovered what was going on in the basement.

Respectfully submitted,

*Bill*

# Cases

Judges write opinions or memos to explain the reasons for decisions they make.

Federal courts are courts of limited jurisdiction, that is, they may only deal with matters assigned to them by the Constitution or by Acts of Congress. State courts, on the other hand, are courts of general jurisdiction and may hear whatever controversies are brought before them.

Jurisdiction involves not only what kind of disputes may be heard but also whether someone has been properly brought before the court. In *Massachusetts School of Law at Andover,* I dealt with this latter question. The case involved a law school's contention that the American Bar Association's standards for judging law schools were illegal and the bar association was liable to it for damages. The litigation required several procedural rulings, but finally I concluded that the bar association was not liable. My decision was affirmed by the Court of Appeals.

In *Roberts* I held that a claim for damages did not come within the provisions of a federal statute, and therefore was to be resolved by a state court, while in *Horton,* I noted that more facts were required before a decision could be reached.

Finally, *Trager v. Ritting,* a ruling that I made when I was still a state judge. It is but one example of the unlimited jurisdiction of state courts, here determining which of divorced parents should have custody of their minor children and why.

## *Massachusetts School of Law at Andover v. ABA*

MASSACHUSETTS SCHOOL OF LAW AT ANDOVER, INC.
v.
AMERICAN BAR ASSOCIATION *et al.*

846 F. Supp. 374 (1994)
United States District Court, E.D. Pennsylvania

376 MEMORANDUM AND ORDER
DITTER, District Judge.

Before me is a case involving law school accreditation and alleged violations of federal antitrust law by four organizational defendants and 22 individual defendants. Plaintiff avers in its complaint that the American Bar Association

("ABA") monopolizes the accreditation process. Defendants, plaintiff asserts, have conspired to fix the salaries of law school faculties and administrators; restrict their output; raise law school tuitions; and foreclose from legal education people in lower socio-economic classes. Twenty-one[1] of the individual defendants have filed a motion to dismiss the claims against them for lack of personal jurisdiction and improper venue. I will grant their motion.

## I. FACTS

For the purposes of the present jurisdictional motion the following allegations contained in the complaint will be accepted as true. Plaintiff, Massachusetts School of Law at Andover, Inc. ("MSL") is a non-profit corporation that operates a law school in Andover, Massachusetts. The law school opened its doors in 1988.

MSL asserts it endeavors to provide high quality, low-cost legal education to people who might otherwise be shut out of more traditional law schools. The law school prides itself on having a unique admissions procedure that encourages applicants from mid-life and from lower economic classes and on having a tuition that is currently $9,000 per year. MSL says it achieves its goals by policies and practices that it admits are in direct conflict with certain ABA accreditation criteria. MSL asserts that the ABA requires law schools to utilize the LSAT in admissions decisions, which MSL does not do. The ABA does not count adjunct faculty in computing required student-faculty ratios; MSL makes extensive use of adjunct professors, which keeps salary costs down, but does not allow MSL to reach the ABA-required ratio. The ABA criteria require a law school's library to have a certain number of hardbound volumes; MSL relies heavily on an electronic library.

MSL sought accreditation from the ABA. Such accreditation is crucial, MSL contends, because the vast majority of jurisdictions (41 states plus the District of Columbia) require that a prospective bar applicant be a graduate of an ABA-accredited law school before he or she can sit for that state's bar examination.[2] In 1993 the ABA denied MSL's application for accreditation.

MSL maintains that the ABA's accreditation criteria are anticompetitive and that the ABA has abused its monopoly power over accreditation. MSL asserts that defendants' actions have caused it to suffer competitive injury and loss of prestige. It avers that it has difficulty competing for students as a result of the ABA's denying accreditation, and it has suffered economic damage through decreased enrollments. In two counts, MSL claims that defendants have combined and conspired to organize and enforce a group boycott in restraint of trade, a violation of the Sherman Act, Section 1, and that defendants have conspired to monopolize the provision of law school training, the accreditation of law schools, and the licensing of lawyers, in violation of the Sherman Act, Section 2. 15 U.S.C. 1, 2.

A variety of motions have been filed in this case. Here I will only address the motion of 21 individual defendants to dismiss the claims against them for lack of personal jurisdiction and improper venue.[3] These defendants are, *377 or have been, members of various ABA committees and organizations that participate in the accreditation process. James White, for example, is the ABA's consultant on legal education and is the chief administrative officer of the council of the ABA section of legal education and admissions to the Bar. The council promotes the ABA's accreditation standards and determines whether individual law schools comply. Other individual defendants are or were on the council, the ABA's accreditation committee, or the site review team that visited MSL as part of its accreditation application process.

## II. PERSONAL JURISDICTION

Before this court can exercise personal jurisdiction over any of these individual defendants, there must be a constitutionally acceptable relationship between that defendant and the forum. Once a defendant challenges the exercise of personal jurisdiction, the plaintiff has the burden of proving with reasonable particularity that sufficient contacts to support jurisdiction exist between the defendant and the forum state. The plaintiff must establish a basis for either specific jurisdiction or general jurisdiction.

### *A. Personal Jurisdiction Based on Individual Defendants' Contacts With Pennsylvania*

Federal Rule of Civil Procedure 4 allows a federal district court to exercise personal jurisdiction over out-of-state defendants to the extent allowed by the law of the state where the court is located. Pennsylvania has two statutes that confer jurisdiction over persons. 42 Pa.Cons.Stat.Ann. 5301, 5322. General jurisdiction over an individual defendant is based on the individual's presence or domicile in Pennsylvania when served or on the individual's consent to jurisdiction. 42 Pa.Cons.Stat.Ann. 5301(a)(1) (Purdon 1993). Specific jurisdiction over a person is based on the cause of action arising from the person's activities and contacts in Pennsylvania. 42 Pa.Cons.Stat.Ann. 5322(a) (Purdon 1993).

Each of the individual defendants has stated in an affidavit that he or she was served outside of Pennsylvania, is not a resident[4] of Pennsylvania, and has not consented to the exercise of personal jurisdiction by courts in Pennsylvania. (Def.Mot., exh. AU). Plaintiff has not offered evidence to the contrary. Therefore, I find that there is no basis for the exercise of general personal jurisdiction over the 21 individual defendants.

Moreover, I find that plaintiff has not shown that I may exercise specific personal jurisdiction over these defendants. The exercise of personal jurisdiction over a defendant must be consistent with due process. Pennsylvania provides for jurisdiction to the fullest extent allowed by the United States Constitution and to be based on the most minimum contact with Pennsylvania allowed by the United States Constitution. 42 Pa.Cons.Stat.Ann. 5322(b). With regard to specific jurisdiction, due process is satisfied when a cause of action is related to or arises out of the defendant's purposeful contacts with the forum state so that the defendant could reasonably expect to be haled into court in that forum. See *Provident Nat'l Bank v. California Fed. Sav. and Loan,* 819 F.2d 434, 437 (citing *World-Wide Volkswagen Corp. v. Woodson,* 444 U.S. 286, 297, 100 S. Ct. 559, 567, 62 L. Ed. 2d 490 (1980)).

It is not enough to warrant the exercise of personal jurisdiction that a defendant is being sued in a forum where he or she had some contact. Rather, a court must examine the relationship among the defendant, the forum, and the litigation. *Regency Oldsmobile, Inc. v. General Motors Corp.,* 685 F. Supp. 91, 94 (D.N.J.1988). A case from the Eighth Circuit is particularly instructive. In Health Care Equalization Committee, plaintiff, a chiropractic society, alleged antitrust violations by (among other defendants) the American College of Radiology. *Health Care Equal. Comm. v. Iowa Medical Soc'y,* 851 F.2d 1020, 1022 (8th Cir.1988). Plaintiff's allegations against the ACR focused on *378 the ACR's adoption of a code of ethics that prohibited professional association with chiropractors. Id. at 1030. The district court granted the ACR's motion to dismiss for lack of personal jurisdiction. Id. at 1022. In affirming the dismissal, the Eighth Circuit examined the relationship between the ACR's contacts with the forum state and the alleged cause of action against ACR. Id. at 1030. The ACR's contacts with the forum were limited to the less than one percent of ACR members who lived there and the mailings sent to those members. Id. In holding that there were insufficient contacts with the forum to warrant jurisdiction over the ACR, the Eighth Circuit said that the plaintiff had drawn no direct connection between the ACR's adoption of its code of ethics and its limited contact with the forum. Id.

In another case, a private educational institution alleged that two professional organizations and 25 individual defendants had conspired to limit the number of practicing orthodontists in violation of the antitrust laws. *United States Dental Inst. v. American Ass'n of Orthodontists,* 396 F. Supp.565, 569 (N.D.Ill.1975). The complaint averred that the individual defendants furthered the conspiracy by adopting certain guidelines and acting to prevent the plaintiff from gaining state approval. Id. at 571. Nine of the individual defendants moved to dismiss for lack of personal jurisdiction. Id. at 569. The district court found that three of the individual defendants had been at meeting in the forum state at which the allegedly exclusionary guidelines were adopted and had been on the council that voted to approve the guidelines. Id. at 571. The court found that the plaintiffs cause of action, which arose from the exclusionary guidelines, was directly traceable to the meeting in the state at which they were adopted. Id. Therefore, the court held, the activities of the three voting defendants supported the exercise of personal jurisdiction. Id.

Here, the cause of action arises from the ABA's denial of accreditation to MSL. The ABA criteria in question were applied by an accreditation team that inspected MSL's campus and facilities in Massachusetts. The MSL faculty and students who suffer from the school's loss of prestige are in Massachusetts. The economic harms are felt by MSL in Massachusetts. The decreased enrollment is experienced in MSL's classrooms in Massachusetts.

MSL has the burden of establishing that its cause of action arose from the individual defendants' contacts with Pennsylvania. Provident Nat'l Bank, 819 F.2d at 437. MSL has not done so. It has not alleged with "reasonable particularity" the individual defendants' contacts with Pennsylvania, much less any contacts with Pennsylvania that injured MSL. Both the complaint and plaintiffs memorandum in opposition to the individual defendants' motion assert that the four organizational defendants have contacts with Pennsylvania.[5] With regard to the individual defendants, however, plaintiff does not allege with particularity any contacts they have with Pennsylvania that gave rise to MSL's claims.[6] Each individual defendant has stated in an affidavit that he or she did not take any action concerning MSL while in Pennsylvania and did not discuss MSL accreditation during any telephone conversation or correspondence with a person in Pennsylvania. (Def.Mot., exh. A-U). MSL, has not countered these affidavits with any evidence to the contrary. Instead, plaintiff merely states that the individual defendants "must have" engaged in accreditation activities in Pennsylvania, "must have" inspected law schools in Pennsylvania, and "must have" received reports written in Pennsylvania. Even if MSL were able to support its allegations of what the individual defendants "must have" done in Pennsylvania, it still cannot do what the plaintiff in *United States Dental Institute* was able to do: directly connect the *379 cause of action to the individual defendants' activities in the forum state. 396 F.Supp. at 571.

MSL has not alleged, much less established, any contacts the 21 individual defendants had with Pennsylvania. More importantly, even if MSL were able to support its supposition that the individual defendants "must have" engaged in accreditation activities in Pennsylvania regarding Pennsylvania schools, MSL has not suggested how these activities had anything to do with MSL's failure to obtain accreditation in Massachusetts. There are not a limited number of accreditations to go around, so that bestowal of accreditation on a Pennsylvania law school lowers MSL's prospect of being accredited. All this leads to my conclusion that the individual defendants do not have sufficient contacts with Pennsylvania to permit the exercise of specific personal jurisdiction over them.

***B. Personal Jurisdiction Based on Co-Conspirators' Contacts With Pennsylvania***

In addition to arguing that the individual defendants must have had sufficient contacts with Pennsylvania on other accreditation matters to warrant jurisdiction arising out of MSL's accreditation, plaintiff urges me to exercise personal jurisdiction over the 21 individual defendants based on the contacts of their alleged co-conspirators. MSL's theory of co-conspirator jurisdiction is that because the court has personal jurisdiction over four organizational defendants, and because all of the defendants are alleged to have conspired with each other, the court has personal jurisdiction over all of the defendants.[7] I conclude the co-conspirator jurisdictional theory is not applicable in this case because plaintiff has not alleged substantial acts (or any acts at all, for that matter) in Pennsylvania in furtherance of the conspiracy.

Co-conspirator jurisdiction is not a separate basis of jurisdiction apart from general or specific jurisdiction. Rather, it is based on the same contacts-with-the-forum analysis just discussed. The difference is that a court looks not only at the defendant's forum contacts, but at those of the defendant's "resident" co-conspirators. The court imputes the contacts of the "resident" co-conspirator over whom it has jurisdiction to the "foreign" co-conspirator to see if there are sufficient contacts to exercise jurisdiction over the latter. See *Ethanol Partners v. Wiener, Zuckerbrot, Weiss & Brecher*, 635 F. Supp. 15, 18 (E.D.Pa.1985); In re *Arthur Treacher's Franchisee Litig.*, 92 F.R.D. 398, 411 (E.D.Pa.1981).

The four organizational defendants in this case do not dispute that there is personal jurisdiction over them in this forum.[8] Plaintiffs alleging that the individual defendants conspired with the organizational defendants is not enough to permit an exercise of jurisdiction over the 21 individuals who contest it. Merely belonging to a civil conspiracy does not make a member subject to the jurisdiction of every other member's forum. In re *Arthur Treacher's*, 92 F.R.D. at 411. Rather, there must also be substantial acts in *380 furtherance of the conspiracy within the forum, of which the out-of-state co-conspirator was or should have been aware. Id.

MSL has not alleged in its complaint substantial acts in Pennsylvania by anyone that furthered the conspiracy and certainly nothing of which the out-of-state individual defendants would have been a part. MSL has said in its memorandum, for example, that James White communicates with all ABA-accredited law schools, including those in Pennsylvania; selects site inspection team members that visit schools in Pennsylvania; and meets with LSAC/LSAS officials. MSL has not said how these acts furthered the conspiracy that injured MSL. MSL has also stated in its memorandum (not its complaint) that phone calls, letters, reports and meetings "must have been" held in Pennsylvania. Again, plaintiff has not shown how these acts, even if proved to be more than conjecture, are substantial acts that furthered the conspiracy which injured MSL.

To be sure, MSL has alleged that the *effects* of the conspiracy were felt nationwide and therefore by law schools in Pennsylvania, but this is not the same as alleging that substantial acts to further the conspiracy took place in Pennsylvania. Therefore, I find that the individual defendants are not subject to the exercise of personal jurisdiction in Pennsylvania on the basis of co-conspirator jurisdiction.

## III. CONCLUSION

For the reasons stated above, I hold that there is no basis to support the exercise of general personal jurisdiction over 21 of the individual defendants. Similarly, I hold that those individual defendants do not have sufficient contacts with the forum either through their own acts or through co-conspirators' contacts giving rise to MSL's cause of action that would support the exercise of specific personal jurisdiction. Having decided the individual defendants' motion on the basis of personal jurisdiction, I make no decision on their venue arguments. Plaintiff's claims against the individual defendants must be dismissed for lack of personal jurisdiction. An appropriate order follows.

## NOTES

[1] The 22nd individual defendant, Carl C. Monk, has filed (with the American Association of Law Schools) a separate motion to dismiss for failure to state a claim against either Monk or AALS and for lack of personal jurisdiction and improper venue as to Monk. That motion will be addressed in another opinion.

[2] Massachusetts is not one of those states. MSL was accredited by the Massachusetts Board of Regents in 1990, and so its graduates can sit for the Massachusetts bar examination and, if successful, practice law in that jurisdiction.

[3] The 21 individual defendants who filed this motion are....

[4] For the purpose of considering general personal jurisdiction I will consider "residence" the equivalent of "domicile."

[5] For example, the ABA is a partner in ALI/ABA, a provider of continuing legal education located in Philadelphia. The Law School Admission Services, Inc. and Law School Admission Council are located in Newtown, Pennsylvania. The American Association of Law Schools has member law schools in Pennsylvania.

[6] The complaint alleges that James White "transacts business in the Eastern District of Pennsylvania" but is no more specific than that.

[7] I have serious reservations about whether the individual defendants, alleged to be on various ABA committees or carrying out the ABA's work in accrediting law schools, can conspire with the ABA. Section one of the Sherman Act applies only to concerted action, proof of which requires evidence of a relationship between at least two legally distinct persons or entities. *Oksanen v. Page Memorial Hosp.*, 945 F.2d 696, 702 (4th Cir.1991), *cert. denied,* ___ U.S. ___, 112 S. Ct.973, 117 L. Ed. 2d 137 (1992). It seems doubtful that the individual defendants are acting as distinct entities apart from the ABA during an accreditation review. See id. (medical staff indistinct from hospital during peer review process). This opinion does not address that issue; I merely note

that plaintiff's complaint, which alleged all defendants conspired with each other, may thus allege concerted activity which is legally impossible.

[8] The Clayton Act authorizes that an antitrust suit against a corporation can be brought in the judicial district where it is an inhabitant and also in any district where the corporation is found or transacts business. 15 U.S.C. 22. This provision for nationwide service of process means that a federal district court's jurisdiction is coextensive with the boundaries of the United States. *American Trade Partners v. A-1 Int'l Importing Enter., Inc.*, 755 F. Supp. 1292, 1302 (E.D.Pa. 1990). This Clayton Act provision applies only to corporate, not individual, antitrust defendants. *Delong Equip. Co. v. Washington Mills Abrasive*, 840 F.2d 843, 848 (11th Cir.1988).

## *Roberts v. Spruce Manor*

APRIL ROBERTS
v.
SPRUCE MANOR NURSING & REHABILITATION CENTER
*ET AL.*

2016 WL 693485
United States District Court, E. D. Pennsylvania

MEMORANDUM
DITTER, District Judge

This case comes before me on Defendants' motion that I reconsider my prior order that refused their motion to dismiss and Plaintiff's motion to remand. I am granting their motion and have reconsidered. The result, however, will not be what Defendants want for I will now grant Plaintiff's motion to remand.

A brief review of the facts will be helpful.

Plaintiff, April Roberts, was employed as a nurse at Spruce Manor, a skilled nursing and rehabilitation facility in Reading, Pennsylvania. As a result of an incident that occurred during the course of her employment, she was accused of improperly restraining a resident who was resisting having her blood drawn. Spruce Manor decided to terminate Plaintiff based on an investigation of this incident.

Plaintiff challenged her termination by filing a grievance with her union. During the grievance proceedings Ms. Roberts and Spruce Manor agreed to part ways and memorialized their agreement by entering into a CONFIDENTIAL SETTLEMENT AGREEMENT AND GENERAL RELEASE. In essence, this agreement provided that Ms. Roberts would be allowed to resign her employment, the company would make a small payment to her and if contacted by prospective employers, would provide Ms. Roberts with a neutral job reference that set forth only the position she held, rate of pay, and dates of employment.

In turn, Plaintiff agreed not to seek re-employment with the company and released it and the union from any claims she might have against either or both of them.

There is also a statement that the agreement contains Ms. Roberts' entire agreement and understanding with Spruce Manor and the union. It is important to note this was not a contract between a labor organization and employer but one between an individual on the one hand and a union and an employer on the other.

All parties signed the agreement in March, 2012.

In December 2013, Regal Heights Healthcare, located in Delaware, hired Ms. Roberts and as part of its hiring process asked for information about her prior employment.

Acting through one of the individual defendants and under the name, Spruce Manor Nursing & Rehab, Spruce Manor stated it was in the nursing home business, Ms. Roberts was directly involved on a daily or frequent basis providing services and/or care to clients/patients/residents/children, she had been discharged, counselled [sic], warned, reprimanded, suspended or discharged as a result of reasonably substantiated incidents involving abuse of patients/clients/residents/children, and that she would not be rehired. All this by checking off boxes on a form (called a Service Letter) provided by Regal. Despite Ms. Roberts' efforts to get Spruce Manor to send a corrected Service Letter, for all practical purposes, it did not do so and Regal discharged her.

This suit followed. It was brought in state court. The complaint noted that "Defendants were under contract not to disclose any information to a prospective employer other than giving a neutral reference." *Compl.* ¶ *79*. It then charged that Spruce Manor had defamed her by its answers to the Service Letter.[2]

Relying on Section 301 of the Labor-Management Act, 29 U.S.C. 185(a)(§ 301), Defendants removed the case to this court.

Section 301 states:

Suits for violations of contracts between an employer and a labor organization[3] representing employees in an industry affecting commerce may be brought in any District Court of the United States having jurisdiction over the parties.

---

2 Also named in the complaint are two corporations affiliated with Spruce Manor and two of its employees. Since their interests are all the same, I am including all under the Spruce Manor pennant.

3 Please note, " ...between an employer and a labor organization...," there is no reference to individual employment contracts.

I refused Plaintiff's motion to remand that followed but concluded that Ms. Roberts could pursue her defamation claim in this court as there was no mechanism for review available to a former employee. That conclusion is the basis for Defendants' motion to reconsider or certify for an appeal. They contend that § 301 provides no subject mater jurisdiction for a defamation claim and that Plaintiff's rights are governed by Spruce Manor's collective bargaining agreement with the union. I disagree. After further consideration, I conclude that this case involves enforcement of the Confidential Settlement Agreement. It does not mention the CBA and an interpretation of the CBA is not required to determine this matter.

At this, point, some law will be helpful.

Federal courts are courts of limited jurisdiction and removal is proper only if the case could have been brought in federal court. Because jurisdiction is limited, remand is favored where federal jurisdiction is not clear.

From *Lingle v. North Division of Magic Chef, Inc.*, 486 U.S. 399, 108 S. Ct. 1877 (1988):

> [I]f the resolution of a state-law claim depends upon the meaning of a collective bargaining agreement, the application of state law (which might lead to inconsistent results since there could be as many state-law principles as there are States) is pre-empted and federal labor-law principles – necessarily uniform throughout the Nation – must be employed to resolve the dispute." *Id.*, 405-406.
>
> Illinois courts have recognized the tort of retaliatory discharge ...Each of these purely factual questions pertains to the conduct of the employee and the motivation of the employer. Neither of these elements requires a court to interpret any term of a collective bargaining agreement. []Thus, the state-law remedy in this case is "independent" of the collective-bargaining agreement in the sense of "independent" that matters for § 301 preemption purposes: resolution of the state-law claim does not require construing the collective-bargaining agreement. *Id.*, 406-407.
>
> [T]he preemptive force of § 301 is so powerful as to displace entirely any state cause of action 'for violation of contracts between an employer and a labor organization. [] Conversely, ...we held that a state-law complaint brought in state court for breach of *individual* employment contracts was not 'completely pre-empted' by § 301 ...because § 301 'says nothing about the content or validity of *individual employment* contracts.' *Id.*, n. 5.
>
> In sum, we hold that an application of state law is pre-empted by § 301 of the Labor Management Relations Act of 1947 only if such application requires the interpretation of a collective-bargaining agreement.

> [T]here is nothing novel about recognizing that substantive rights in the labor relations context can exist without interpreting collective-bargaining agreements.

The Court of Appeals for the Third Circuit has weighed in with additional findings:

If a claim is brought by an individual employee against an employer, § 301 only applies if the claim also names the employee's union and alleges that it violated a duty of fair representation. *Ames v. Westinghouse Elec. Corp.*, 864 F. 2d 289, 292 (3d Cir. 1988).

The fact that a collective bargaining agreement is part of the context in which Plaintiff's claim must be addressed does not "trigger complete preemption in the absence of some substantial dispute over the collective bargaining agreement." *Kline v. Sec. Guards, Inc.*, 386 F.3d 246, 257 (3d Cir. 2004). Thus, the LMRA does not pre-empt "state rules that proscribe conduct or establish rights and obligations, independent of a labor contract, nor does the LMRA pre-empt an employee's state suit against his employer based upon an individual employment contract. *Id.* (citing *Allis-Chalmers v. Lueck*, 471 U.S. 202, 212 (1985)).

In summary, § 301 does not apply for the following reasons:

This is a state suit based upon Plaintiff's individual contract with her employer.

The LMRA says nothing about the content or validity of *individual employment* contracts.

Since the Confidential Settlement Agreement was between Plaintiff on the one hand and the employer and union on the other and not between the union and the employer, it is therefore not a collective bargaining agreement.

A state law claim is pre-empted only if its resolution requires the construing of a collective bargaining agreement. If state law provides a complete remedy for an employee, there is no pre-emption. This matter can be resolved by the application of state law, not by construing the collective bargaining agreement.

Section 301 applies to an individual's suit against an employer only if s/he has also named the union and alleged it violated its duty of fair representation. Ms. Roberts does not contend the union violated its duty of fair representation and has not sued it.[4]

Turning again to Plaintiff's complaint.

---

4 Of course in the Confidential Settlement Agreement she specifically released the union.

It is worthy of note that Plaintiff does not refer to the collective bargaining agreement between her union and Spruce Manor although her grievance procedure no doubt followed the CBA's procedures.

In 76 carefully detailed paragraphs she describes the incident at Spruce Manor, her grievance, how it was resolved, the duty imposed on Spruce Manor, her hiring by Regal Heights, and the damaging information provided by Spruce Manor.

In 15 more paragraphs she makes a claim for defamation under Pennsylvania law. While her language sets forth Spruce Manor's duty under the settlement agreement and Spruce Manor's subsequent conduct, Plaintiff does not use the words, breach of contract. Not that it matters – if there was a breach, it was of the settlement agreement and not of the collective bargaining contract between the union and the employer.

Here then we have a complaint that sets forth a state claim for defamation, a remedy with rights and obligations which the state provides.[5] There is nothing about this complaint that requires an interpretation of a collective bargaining agreement or any aspect of federal law.

I am remanding this matter to the Court of Common Pleas of Berks County. An appropriate order follows.

*My sister, Mabel, helps with robe. Swearing in ceremony, Court of Common Pleas, January 6, 1964.*

5 The merit or lack of merit of Plaintiff's claims is not for me to decide.

## *Horton v. Fedchoice*

SHEILA HORTON
ON BEHALF OF ALL OTHERS SIMILARLY SITUATED,
PLAINTIFF
v.
FEDCHOICE FEDERAL CREDIT UNION
AND DOES 1 THROUGH 10,
DEFENDANTS

2016 U.S. Dist. LEXIS 141756
United States District Court, E. D. Pennsylvania

MEMORANDUM
DITTER, District Judge

Plaintiff, Sheila Horton, has filed a class action suit challenging the fees charged for overdraft protection by a credit union, FedChoice, and unnamed individuals. Defendants allege the instant case should be stayed or dismissed because Ms. Horton and FedChoice are parties to a broad, written, enforceable arbitration agreement that governs "any dispute between" them. Because I conclude that the methods and procedures which Defendants assert give them the right to arbitration may be of questionable validity, I shall deny their motion and direct the parties to engage in discovery.

Ms. Horton opened her original checking account with the predecessor to FedChoice on February 13, 1986. On September 21, 2015, Ms. Horton may have signed up for an online service which permitted FedChoice members to make electronic transfers between their FedChoice accounts and accounts in other financial institutions. In order to avail herself of this service, Defendants contend that she was required to accept an online "Service Agreement" which contains a mandatory arbitration clause. Defendants assert that Ms. Horton agreed to the terms of the Service Agreement. Ms. Horton contends she did not and that even if she did agree, it was limited to disputes about inter-bank transfers of funds.

Defendants have attached the Declaration of Phyllis Mauck, a FedChoice employee, who described the process of registering for the online electronic transfer service. Ms. Mauck stated that the Service Agreement was provided to Ms. Horton online. Immediately following the Service Agreement was the statement, "I acknowledge that I have the disclosure (sic) and agree to all terms and conditions." Still online, there is a provision, "I accept." Unless a member had accepted the "disclosure," i.e., the Service Agreement, he or she could not use FedChoice's inter-bank service. As proof that she had accepted the Service Agreement, Ms. Mauck states Ms. Horton later used that service. Defendants have also attached a copy of the "Service Agreement" as it appeared in a pop-up window and as it would have been seen by anyone considering the service. The twelve page Service Agreement contains the arbitration clause on page ten.

Without question, the Service Agreement is a contract of adhesion. FedChoice has set the terms and conditions. Ms. Horton could either accept those terms or be denied FedChoice's inter-bank transfer service. She had no bargaining power. The contract was all or nothing.

While contracts of adhesion may be enforced, they invite an inquiry into whether they are procedurally and substantively unconscionable. Here the invitation to examine both is loud and clear: twelve pages of legalese presented online with the arbitration clause buried on page 10, and arbitration procedures that might be found to require too much with too little chance for success.

I conclude that the validity of the Service Agreement is a disputed issue. It follows that the parties are entitled to discovery on the question of arbitrability. *Guidotti v. Legal Helpers Debt Resolution, LLC,* 716 F.3d 764 (3d Cir. 2013).

An appropriate order follows.

## *Traeger v. Ritting*

Comm. ex rel. Traeger
v.
Ritting

37 Pa. D. & C.2d 515 (1965)
Aff'd per curiam on the opinion of Judge Ditter, Pa. Super. Ct. (1965)
In the Court of Common Pleas of Montgomery County Pennsylvania

Ditter, J.

The mother of five minor children brought this habeas corpus action against her former husband. After hearing, we granted visitation privileges but refused to award permanent custody to her. She has appealed our ruling to the Superior Court.

Petitioner, Mary E. Traeger, and her former husband, Richard J. Ritting, are the parents of two sons, Richard and David, aged 18 and 15, and three daughters, Susan, Deborah, and Dawn, aged 13, almost 12, and 7, respectively.

In January 1964, after approximately 20 years of marriage, petitioner, who is an attractive woman of 37, left her husband, children and the home in which the parties resided, obtained an uncontested divorce in October 1964, and remarried in December 1964. Shortly after the divorce action was instituted, she signed a settlement agreement with her then-husband, under the terms of which she conveyed to him all of her rights in their jointly owned real and personal property and agreed that he should retain custody of the children. There were only two things which she kept: her Cadillac automobile, on which there was an encumbrance of $3,000, and her personal clothing.

Sound, well-known principles must guide our determination of the issues in this case:

1. "It is basic and fundamental that the paramount consideration is the welfare of the children and that all other considerations, including the rights of parents, are subordinate to the children's physical, intellectual, moral, spiritual and emotional well-being": *Commonwealth ex rel. McNamee v. Jackson*, 183 Pa. Superior Ct. 522, 525 (1957).

2. It is the policy of the law to keep children of a family together: Commonwealth ex rel. *Doberstein v. Doberstein*, 201 Pa. Superior Ct. 102, 106 (1963). They should only be separated for good reason: *Commonwealth ex rel. Martino v. Blough*, 201 Pa. Superior Ct. 346, 351 (1963).

3. In awarding custody, consideration should be given to the preferences of the children: Commonwealth ex rel. Doberstein v. Doberstein, supra, 106. As a child grows older, greater weight will be given to his preference: *Commonwealth ex rel. Bender v. Bender*, 197 Pa. Superior Ct. 397, 401 (1962).

4. Courts are not bound by agreements between parents as to custody since these must yield to the best interests of the children. However, such an agreement may be considered in determining a question of fitness: *Commonwealth ex rel. Bordlemay v. Bordlemay*, 31 Pa. D. & C.2d 46, 51 (1963), affirmed per curiam, 201 Pa. Superior Ct. 435 (1963).

Throughout her marriage, petitioner worked as a waitress, averaging approximately $100 a week in salary and tips. Since she left home for her job at 4:30 in the afternoon and did not return until from 2 until 4 a.m., a maid was hired to look after the children. It was during this employment that petitioner met her present husband, Carl Traeger.

Mr. Traeger, age 42, is an executive in a company with offices in Philadelphia. When asked the range of his income, he modestly admitted that it was "Twenty-five plus," meaning more than $25,000. After he and petitioner were married, they took up residence at the Presidential Apartments, City Avenue and Monument Road, Philadelphia. He and Mrs. Traeger have a summer place at the shore and will buy a new house in Cherry Hill, N. J., sometime in the fall. Mr. Traeger explained that they had talked to the builder and the only question was "... what size home we are going to take, whether we are going to take a smaller home or a larger home, and we're in a position to take either one."

Once divorced and the father of a married daughter, Mr. Traeger stated he would be "happy" to have his wife's children come to live in his home. Although he had never met or talked with the four older children, he has had contact with Dawn, who is seven. He stated that he felt he would be in a position to "handle" the children and would "make every effort" to love them.

Richard J. Ritting, petitioner's first husband, has not remarried. He is 40 years of age and is a self-employed asphalt stripper, apparently not a particularly glamorous occupation. His work requires that he leave the house at approximately 6 a.m. and permits him to return from 4:30 to 6 p.m. His hours are somewhat shorter in the winter, enabling him to get the children off for school before he leaves, and he is frequently home before they arrive in the afternoon. Although his precise income was not stated, it would appear from the description of his home, the hours he is required to work and the lack of servants in the house that his financial stature does not measure up to that of petitioner's new husband.

Mr. Ritting and the children reside in a four-bedroom house in Ardsley, where they had all lived with petitioner before the separation. It has a kitchen, dining room, large basement and a recreation room. He has a bedroom, the two boys have a bedroom and the three girls share a large bedroom. Mrs. Traeger agreed that it was adequate for their needs. She also made no contention that her former husband physically abused the children or failed to furnish them with adequate food, sufficient clothing and physical necessities. However, she felt that she could make better provision for their comfort, grooming and appearance. She explained that before the breakup of the family and while she was working as a waitress, her maid took care of the housework and the girls did not have to do very much of it. Since the separation, the girls help with the cooking, cleaning, washing and ironing. If the children were with her, since she no longer works, she could "stay at home and be a good mother to the children and raise them like they should be raised."

She added that the children were fond of each other, very affectionate, normal and well-behaved, and that it would hurt them to be separated. She also testified that when she left in January 1964, the children were terribly upset, had cried, and did not want her to go.

Through the cooperation and help of friends and relatives, the children are well taken care of, both winter and summer. The younger ones have constant adult supervision, and all have adjusted well to the changes that were brought about by their mother's leaving them and their father. They share household chores, are doing satisfactorily in school, attend church and are active in its affairs, are happy and are well-behaved.

Following the testimony that was heard in open court and in the presence of their parents' respective attorneys and the court reporter, the five children were interviewed separately in chambers. All of them indicated they wanted to stay together, they wanted to live with their father and they were not particularly interested in their mother. Richard, who is 18, does not know his mother's new husband and does not want to know him, and Dawn, who is seven, says he is nice, but she likes her daddy better.

Mrs. Traeger stated that when she and the children lived together, they had loved her; there was a nice relationship; they had been a normal family group. However, since the separation, the children were embittered against her by their father. The children, however, indicated that their father had done nothing to turn them against petitioner.

If these children do not have the love for their mother which she feels they should have, she is to blame. When they lived together, she did not share holidays and vacations with them as their father did. She was rarely at home, was out at night and did not get home until late. Their father, on the other hand, was their constant companion. Where he went, they went.

Secondly, the children resent the fact that their mother left them. Jody Marion, a close friend of Mrs. Traeger's in former days, is called Aunt Jo by the children. She is Susan's godmother and close to both the boys and the girls. She testified about the break-up of the family: "... the children came out to my house. Mr. Ritting had brought them there. I know it was hard for him, but he brought them there. All the children said to me, Aunt Jo, all we want is our mother back.' They put their arms around me and begged me to go get their mother. I had promised them I would do everything I could to get their mother back to them. The next day I called where she worked and I left the message. She did not answer my phone.... Richard was 16 at that time, and he told me that he had gotten down on his knees and begged his mother to stay, and Susie did too."

Richard stated that he had no affection for his mother "...because she just went up and left us...we had affections for our mother all the way up to divorce time. We begged her to come back." Richard recounted how his father "... made a fool of himself, I think, sometimes, getting on his knees and crying to her to come on back. And this was in the street, he did that in the street." Debbie, who is not quite 12, said that she did not want to see her mother because she ran out on us "....she won't come back to us. We asked her and we begged her and she wouldn't come back."

We agree with what President Judge G. Thomas Gates, of Lebanon County, recently said:

"Children are a trust with a prior claim on parents, even before the claims of their own personal liberty. The husband or wife who puts personal happiness before the need of his family for stability is denying the true claims of his or her responsibilities and the just balance of the purposes for which marriage and the home were created. There is no God-given 'right to happiness' which can override the profound claims of children to a stable and independent home": *Commonwealth ex rel. Bordlemay v. Bordlemay*, 31 Pa. D. & C.2d 46, 49 (1963). See also *Commonwealth ex rel. Schmidt v. Schmidt*, 8 Bucks 180, 181 (1958).

For reasons not stated but which clearly appear, petitioner took her Cadillac and her clothes, left her children and has made a new life for herself. She has made her adjustment, and now, like a puppeteer returning to the stage, she wants us to place in her hands the threads that direct the lives of her children. During her absence, however, the children have also made adjustments.

These children are perceptive. They know their mother can do much for them; neatly groom their hair and iron their dresses, give them vacations at the shore, free them from housework, give them a new home in Cherry Hill, and provide them with the niceties that "twenty-five plus" will buy. Apparently, the only thing their father can offer is himself, his interest, his devotion, his companionship and his sense of spiritual values.

These are practical times. The advantages of cash, clothes and Cadillacs are so evident, the freedom from household drudgery so attractive, and the appeal of pretty baubles so enticing that the desire of these youngsters to stay with their father is a little perplexing. If, however, these unrealistic, foolish, shortsighted, wonderful children have made the wrong choice, someone else will have to instruct them upon the error of their ways.

## Upon the Retirement of My Secretary

J. William Ditter, Jr.
PO Box 256
Woxall, PA 18979

February 26, 1998

Dear Ruth,

Being the family spokesman is never easy—particularly if the family is like mine.

Were my father writing this note, he would stress your patriotism, your unfailing, unflagging love of country, your dedication, and the quality of your public service. He would comment how, rain or shine, snow or ice, you were always on the job. He would remember that clocks could be set by your daily arrival. If he was asked to put it all into a single word, I think he would say you were honorable.

Were my mother writing this note, she would stress your qualities as a wife and mother, the care and devotion with which you raised your child, the way your home is decorated and is always neat and orderly. She would recall that yours was a home where unexpected guests instinctively felt expected and welcome. She would want people to know that you were proud of your family. If she were asked to put it all into a single word, I think she would choose homemaker.

Were Mabel writing this note, it wouldn't be a note—it would be poetry with a religious overtone—quite possibly a sonnet that would make Shakespeare envious. She would stress your friendship, your helpfulness, your being her cheerful comrade in those early days. She would be reminded of the harmonious relationship you had and that you were ever a steadying influence. She would want people to know how important you were in getting her career started. If she was asked to put it all into a single word, I think she would choose loyalty.

Were Verna writing this note, she would comment with wonder about how you juggled your home and work responsibilities, excelling at each. She would relate how she shares with you a love for those special pets, cats. She would speak as one of the guild with admiration for your secretarial skills and how you have honed them to perfection. If she was asked to put it all into a single word, I think she would say proficient.

That leaves me. And though I would hesitate to suggest that the evaluations by father, mother, sister, and wife had left anything out, with trepidation I will add that you have gotten me the places where I should have gone, you have made it possible for me to do the things I should have done, and you have kept me from saying things that were better left unsaid. When seas were rough, you were calm. When days were cloudy, you were buoyant. You typed and retyped without complaint, carbons and all. You corrected without comment. Perfection was your norm and your ability to pull a case name out of the air and find a file has never ceased to amaze me. If I was asked to put it all into a single word, I couldn't do it.

For all of which—and for so much more—I thank you.

Sincerely,

J. William Ditter, Jr.

*Note: Ruth Clarke had worked for my father, my sister, and then me. She knew all my family.*

## Memorial Tribute to Raymond Jenkins

In the Court of Common Pleas of Montgomery County, Pennsylvania
March 9, 1998

You have seen the advertisements: A United States Marine standing straight and tall in his dress uniform. And the words—the Marines still need a few good men. That's the way it was in 1942. The Marines needed some good men and when Ray Jenkins graduated from college in 1942, he became a Marine.

The Marine Corps motto is *semper fidelis*—Marines consider it a code of conduct—it signifies a Marine's duty to himself, to the Marine Corps, and to his country. It means "always faithful." The Marines have shortened the Latin to *semper fi*—but whether it's Latin, long or short, or English, it means the same thing.

Let me tell you about Saipan.

Saipan is one of the chain of islands known as the Marianas. They are about two-thirds of the way between Hawaii and the Philippines and roughly 1400 miles south of the home islands of Japan. At the start of World War II they were under Japanese control. Saipan was the most important Japanese naval and air base in the western Pacific. On June 15, 1944, the 2nd and 4th Marine Divisions invaded Saipan—and in 24 days, the island was in American hands, but at a heavy cost. Captain Ray Jenkins was one of more than 13,000 Marines who were wounded there. He was an artillery observer. It was his job to get as close to the Jap positions as possible and direct artillery fire on them. He won a bronze star for his bravery.

When a man became a Marine in 1942, he knew he might end up dying for his country. Twenty-three hundred of them did on Saipan alone. *Semper fi*.

Ray Jenkins survived to live for his country. And he did it as you would expect of an ex-Marine: *Semper fi*.

Raymond Jenkins was born in Philadelphia, the son of a lawyer. He attended Germantown High School where he was an outstanding member of its football, basketball, and baseball teams. He attended Cornell University on a football scholarship, playing baseball as well, and being elected as president of Cornell's student council. He was an end on Cornell's football team and played in the North–South All Star game in 1941. An injury to his arm cut short his career as a left-handed pitcher, although he did have a tryout with the Detroit Tigers.

Following his discharge as a major from the Marine Corps, he attended the University of Pennsylvania Law School. We met there and were friends until his death in September of last year. In 1960, I persuaded him to leave Philadelphia and transfer his practice to Ambler. He was a great partner—a delight to know—a fine lawyer—popular—trusted and admired by his clients and members of the bar. People instinctively recognized him for what he was. Capable. Honest. Direct. What you saw was what you got. How did the Marines put it? *Semper fi.*

Ray was a lawyer from a lawyer's family. After I left Ambler, Ray's younger brother, Frank, joined him there, while his older brother, Harry, remained in Philadelphia with their father, Harry L. Jenkins, Sr. I am proud that I had a chance to practice with Ray—and proud that my son did too.

Ray was a man of many interests. First there was his family. He and Millicent—Dinty to everyone—were married for 55 years. Their younger daughter, Christine Smith, was always their pride and joy—but I am not sure that either Ray or Dinty ever completely got over the death of their older daughter, Ann, and her son in an automobile accident 30 years ago.

Upper Dublin Township benefited from his wisdom and service. He was one of its commissioners for 18 years, the president of its board, and its solicitor after that. Early on he recognized the importance of the township's maintaining some breathing room and led its acquisition of land to be kept as open space. In 1994, he received Upper Dublin's Outstanding Citizen award. Ray was also the solicitor for Upper Moreland Township.

For 40 years, Ray was counsel for the American Baptist Association and many of its allied organizations, missions, and ministries: The Baptist Children's Services, the American Baptist Foreign Missions Society, Elm Terrace Gardens, and the Education Ministries for American Baptist Churches, U.S.A.

And then there was golf. He was a member of Manufacturers' Golf & Country Club in Oreland and was its president from 1979 to 1982. Golf became what basketball, football, and baseball had been. He played with skill, determination, finesse—and a low handicap.

Ray's battle with cancer began 20 years ago. There was surgery. Chemotherapy. Radiation. Pain. Hospitalizations. Time and time again, he fought back and returned to the office. And to the golf course.

Golf was perhaps as much therapy as any that ever came from his doctors. He just kept playing—with a different kind of handicap. First he had to walk with a cane—then two canes—and still he played. With one cane and a club he would make his way to the ball—drop the cane—and hit a drive that would carry 150 yards.

Ray leaves behind a wife, brother, sister, daughter, four grandchildren, and two great grandchildren.

And so much more—a legacy of service, honor, integrity, courage. He lived for his country. *Semper fi.*

## Speech to the Montgomery Bar Association Dinner, May 2015

Mr. President, Honored Judges, and my fellow members of the Montgomery Bar Association.

My Father, who was a great orator and much in demand nationwide as a public speaker, once said there are three things a man cannot do: He cannot climb a fence that leans toward him, he cannot kiss a girl who leans away from him, and he cannot gracefully thank and acknowledge words of praise said in public.

He was right, of course. So rather than to try I will reminisce a bit and then ask of you that which you may already do.

Shortly after I became a common pleas judge, I was invited back to the Ambler Rotary Club to speak at the 50th anniversary of its founding.

Lou Stefan was the master of ceremonies. Lou and I had always been friendly rivals in Ambler and good social friends.

I started off by saying that I'm often asked about the difference between being a judge and a lawyer. I said, "I use the same books, I write as I did before, read briefs as I did before, but there is one difference—all the lawyers now laugh at my jokes."

After I finished the rest of my talk, it was Lou's turn and he said, "The lawyers not only laugh at Judge Ditter's jokes—they laugh at every thing he says."

Shortly before the Puritans were to disembark from the ship *Arbella* that had brought them to the new world in 1630, John Winthrop told them their new community would be a "city set on a hill" and that the eyes of all people would be upon them and that they dared not deal falsely with God in the work they had undertaken.

Three hundred thirty-one years later, President-Elect John F. Kennedy referred to Winthrop's sermon to his Puritan followers and said that Winthrop's challenge had been realized; that America was indeed a city set on a hill; the eyes of the world were upon us; and that we as a nation dared not falter in our responsibilities.

In his farewell to the nation in 1989, President Ronald Reagan said of America:

> I've spoken of the shining city all my political life, but I don't know if I ever quite communicated what I saw when I said it. But in my mind it was a tall proud city built on rocks stronger than oceans, wind-swept, God-blessed, and teeming with people of all kinds living in harmony and peace...if there had to be city walls, the walls had doors and the doors were open to anyone with the will and heart to get here. That's how I saw America and see it still.

And that brings me to you.

You have been most kind and generous to me tonight and I am grateful beyond all measure.

But there is more. It is my hope that despite her many faults and shortcomings, you share with me the belief that America is indeed a city set upon a hill. That John Winthrop's prediction has come true, that President Kennedy was correct when he said the eyes of the world are upon us and we dare not falter in our responsibilities, and that you share President's Reagan's vision of America.

Many years ago Mr. Justice Brewer observed that the mystic force that has bound our nation together and made possible its success and glories is the Law and those who have ministered at its shrine and kept alive its sacred fires.

Bear that in mind—the mystic force that has made possible our nation's success and glories is its lawyers. And that imposes a duty upon you and me and all of us whose forebearers have bound our nation together and made possible its success and glories.

And so what I am asking of you is this: When you have finished speaking to the Rotary Club, the Kiwanis, or some other civic group, and after you have told them about the Rule in Shelly's Case or the mysteries of the Rule Against Perpetuities you will pause so they will know you have finished with the law.

Then end your talk by reminding your listeners of the goodness and greatness of America—tell them the part lawyers have played and continue to play in making our nation a city set upon a hill.

It's a worthy closing and one that you should be proud to make.

Thank you—and God Bless America.

# Upper Dublin Association

## Introduction by Frank Boni

In the early 19th century, horse thievery was a boon for thieves and a bust for Atlantic seaboard farmers, who depended on horses for their livelihood. With an absence of police and sheriff protection and insurance not available, farmers rose up and formed self-help societies, a combined police force and insurance company.

In 1828, one of those societies was formed and named the Upper Dublin Association of Montgomery County for the Recovery of Stolen Horses, Detention of Horse Thieves and Obtaining Other Stolen Property. Owing to its somewhat unwieldy name, the association became better known as the Upper Dublin Association (UDA).

Founded by twenty-eight men and one woman, the members elected officers, paid dues to cover theft, and formed posses for the pursuit and capture of thieves. They advertised their presence and purpose widely in inns and taverns. Such was the UDA's notoriety that thievery declined, and the association gradually transitioned to a social organization. It continued to assemble annually lest the need arose to return to its early purpose and action. For at least 75 years, no such need had arisen, however fellowship and frivolity continued uninterrupted.

At these gatherings the members of the UDA continued the tradition of meeting each year in a regional inn or tavern, more recently at Williamson's, the William Penn Inn, and the Spring House Tavern. The annual meeting included a social hour, recitation of the pledge of allegiance, an invocation, supper, when possible a speaker related to horses (in 2016 we hosted a horse trainer), and a business meeting. As horses had become scarcer since the association's 19th-century founding, the president opened the meeting asking whether anyone has *seen* a horse during the previous year.

The Ditter family—its patriarch J. William Ditter, Jr., and his sons William, George, and David—go back to prominent members of the association. Together or singly they have been active for more than 40 years. George became president in 2013.

Bill Ditter held a special place in the program of the UDA's gatherings, both faithfully and fancifully capturing and conveying the association's history. Ten or so years ago he succeeded J. Wilson Jones as poet laureate of the association. Each year attendees at the annual meeting were graced with Bill's reading of a new poetic effort chronicling the UDA's legend and lore. What follows is a selection of his contributions.

*Note: The UDA has had an ongoing relationship with the Fort Washington Historical Society, which stores its records and history. I expect that all of Bill Ditter's contributions to the UDA will find a home there.*

# TAKE NOTICE!

TO: All horse-thieves, rustlers, highwaymen, cutpurses, vagabonds, yeggmen, footpads, reivers, larceners, filchers, chicken-thieves, moss-troopers, rapparees or others of the light-fingered gentry, BEWARE!

The owner of these Premises, to wit:

*J. William Ditter, Jr.*

is a member in good standing in and this Property is under the protection of the

UPPER DUBLIN ASSOCIATION
OF MONTGOMERY COUNTY
FOR THE RECOVERY OF STOLEN HORSES, DETECTION OF HORSE THIEVES AND OBTAINING OTHER STOLEN PROPERTY

(Organized February 14, 1828)

The members of which Association are prepared at a minute's notice to raise the hue and cry, take horse and apprehend and bring to justice all malefactors.*

N.B. Cash rewards paid to any informer, tipster or telltale whose information leads to the recovery of any stolen horse or other property and to the arrest and conviction of the thief.

BY ORDER OF THE ASSOCIATION

*Past performance is no guarantee of future results and your results may vary. Any implied or express offer of vigilante action void where prohibited by law.

# A Christmas Fable

*In the spirit of the late J. Wilson Jones and written for the 176th meeting of The Upper Dublin Association of Montgomery County for the Recovery of Stolen Horses, Detection of Horse Thieves and Obtaining Other Stolen Property*

'Twas the night of the banquet and at William-son's,
The members were checking their saddles and guns.

For a rumor was spreading around the whole inn,
That a horse had been stolen at nearby Dub-lin.

Not the Lower, but Upper, *that* Dublin, of course,
Not some weary old dobbin, but Bill Paxson's best horse.

Having fed it and stabled 'neath lock and 'neath key,
Said Bill, "How she might have been stolen mystifies me."

For the byways they scattered, each man said he'd search,
All the taprooms and taverns, the ladies, each church.

Through the Gwynedds and Whitpain, through Ambler they went,
'Till the waning of night-time in searching they spent.

But though hoof prints and horse shoes were found here and there,
They were too large or too small, said Bill of his mare.

With the coming of daylight came thoughts of a clue,
To the barn they all hurried, their plans to review.

On the frame of the barn door a note had been tacked,
It gave Bill the answer which 'till then he had lacked.

"I was mapping my route 'twixt tots naughty and neat,
When my reindeer named Dasher hurt both his front feet.

"I was caught with a sleigh full of maps. What a mess!
So I borrowed your filly, the one you call Bess,

"I'll return her some evening, as soon as a flight,
That I make with my Dasher shows he is all right."

Then Bill stopped his note-reading, and after a pause,
Said, "I guess as you've figured, its signed 'Santa Claus.'"

And so all of the members repaired to their beds,
While visions of Santa danced 'round in their heads.

Bill the barn door left open as night followed day,
In the hopes that dear Santa would bring Bess his way.

Then one eve he sat watching the barnyard below,
In the tranquil of moonlight and undisturbed snow.

When with nary a warning flakes swirled in the air,
And from out them stepped Santa installing Bill's mare.

Quick the barn door was fastened, the padlock shut tight,
Santa waved with his left hand and rose from the white.

But Bill heard Santa call as he passed out of view,
"What you do for me Christmas will come back to you."

When Bill rushed to the barnyard, his courser to greet,
The first thing he noticed were wings on her feet.

Bess then spoke to her owner, her voice low and coarse,
(The kind of a voice you'd expect from a horse.)

"It is good to be back home, back here in my stall,
It's tomorrow for talking and I'll tell you all.

"But for now I'm so sleepy, it's rest that I seek,
I've been flying for Santa each day for a week.

"So good night, dearest William, you're looking tired too,
My adventures will please you. My story's all true."

From the wall came a blanket and Bill hit the hay,
But he spent the night tossing while waiting the day,

With the coming of sunlight, the horse gave a shake,
It took only an instant and Bill was awake.

With a hearty, "Good morning," he rushed to her side,
"I am ready to hear it. My eyes open wide."

To her owner Bess listened, then words tried to say,
But she only could utter, a low, whistling neigh.

She looked down at her front feet, with pain on her face.
Bill examined all four legs, of wings, not a trace.

For the whole day Bess tried, but no words could she speak,
And Bill realized her magic was just for a week.

The week spent with Santa, until Dasher could walk,
A week for horse-flying, and a week for horse-talk.

So now it was over, with Bess back in the barn,
But a moral for all is attached to this yarn.

The Noel of Bill's lifetime, his best one, indeed.
Was he touched by the magic, all thanks to his steed?

Is there really a Santa? The answer from Bess,
"If love's given to children, the answer is yes.

"There's magic in Christmas, help their dreams to come true—
And the magic of Christmas will rub off on you."

*December 3, 2003*

# It's a Merry Christmas, Because

*In the spirit of the late J. Wilson Jones and written for the 177th anniversary meeting of The Upper Dublin Association of Montgomery County for the Recovery of Stolen Horses, Detection of Horse Thieves and Obtaining Other Stolen Property*

December first. We meet tonight to tell who stole each steed.
The way recovery came about, and crime we helped impede.

And, of course, we'll celebrate this happy time of year.
We're gathered all at Williamson's. We'll have a glass of cheer.

Tonight each worry I'll forget, the thoughts of money spent,
The list of presents still unbought, the cards that must be sent.

So hearty greetings, everyone, you make my spirits soar.
All cares and woes I pushed aside when I came in the door.

I saw the plastic Santa Claus, he even nods his head,
And Rudolph too was prancing there, the one with nose of red.

The elves were loading up the sleigh; they never seem to pause.
They're working from a list that's held by smiling Mrs. Claus.

'Twas Frosty that was next to see, rolled in his garb of white.
I simply love the song he sings. It makes the Yuletide bright.

The lights are strung upon each tree. They glitter and they glow.
It's merriment for us tonight, good food helps make it so.

Oh, jolly, jolly time of year, with parties still in store,
Each day will bring more joy to me. How can I ask for more?

But I sense there's something missing. Some bauble or a chime?
Or could it be I've overlooked the "Why" of Christmas time?

Has all the sparkling tinsel, quite hid from me the star?
The manger and the shepherds, the wise men from afar?

I haven't paused to ponder, the gift that came to me,
For here began the lonely path that lead to Calvary.

He would die that we would live, oh, we of little worth,
Salvation starts that holy day, the day of Jesus' birth.

Oh, yes, there's more to Christmas than wreaths with ribbon red,
Or toys or song or holly, it's promised life instead.

When all the flashy trinkets have disappeared from sight,
We'll not abide in darkness, but revel in the light.

For though the season's trappings are boxed in storage place,
There still remains the wonder, the wonder of God's grace.

*December 1, 2004*

# Christmas Is Nigh

*In the spirit of the late J. Wilson Jones and written for the 178th meeting of The Upper Dublin Association of Montgomery County for the Recovery of Stolen Horses, Detection of Horse Thieves and Obtaining Other Stolen Property*

It's eighteen days 'till Christmas and so again we meet,
To talk of stolen horses, our friends to see and greet.

Noel is soon upon us, it comes but once a year,
Let our joy be unrestrained, the holiday is near.

There's parties and the shopping, so much to see and do,
Happy days and merriment, old times we must renew.

If eighteen days 'till Christmas, the seventh it must be,
Should not that date a memory stir, a date from history?

Do you recall a Sunday? It was in forty-one,
Pearl Harbor, calm and peaceful. Then came the Rising Sun.

The Sabbath barely dawned, when hell rained from the sky,
For near a hundred minutes. Three thousand men would die.

The Japs well knew their targets. They bombed and strafed the fleet,
And when their mission had been wrought, their vic'try was complete.

Our battle wagons blasted, had moored in tidy row,
Havoc spread across each one, on deck and then below.

*Arizona* torn in two; *Nevada* run aground.
We wept for *Pennsylvania* and *California* downed.

*Tennessee! Maryland! West Virginia*, fiery light.
Stripped away from us that day, the backbone of our might.

The tin cans and the cruisers felt fury red and raw.
*Helena* and the *Raleigh*. The bow blown off the *Shaw*,

That Sunday at Pearl Harbor, the ships were not at sea,
Roosevelt said the day would live as one of infamy.

Now the years have tumbled on, as tumble on they must,
Still hold in mem'ry's storehouse, the shed-blood and the lust.

Recall them not for hatred or ancient embers fan.
Recall them not for passion or ill feel toward Japan.

But yet there is a reason, that hallowed day to keep,
There's danger ever present so we must never sleep.

Let great resolve and courage, joined with a faith divine,
Be ours, these ancient virtues, our watchwords and our sign.

Vigilance and sacrifice our hallmarks too must be,
A price that's high, great demands, are those of liberty.

With eighteen days 'till Christmas, a message loud and clear,
The future we must bravely face to keep what we hold dear.

*December 7, 2005*

## A Christmas Day Recovery Fable

*In the spirit of the late J. Wilson Jones and written for the 179th meeting of The Upper Dublin Association of Montgomery County for the Recovery of Stolen Horses, Detection of Horse Thieves and Obtaining Other Stolen Property*

On the pages of our journals are writ of days long past,
Of horses we recovered then, and thieves to prison cast.

Both scallywags and bunko men were chased, our minutes say,
Each barn and shed was made secure at night as well as day.

Though pages all are flaked with age, such stories they relate,
How Upper Dublin came to be the envy of our state.

But of the tales these pages tell, there's one I'd like to share,
It's how our members Christmas day displayed their loving care.

A grieving father's fervent plea. How changed was evil's spell,
When all the members pledged to find a horse by Lionel.

Hushed was our party Christmas eve so could a stranger speak,
"I'm Revvy Brown. My story's sad. Your help is what I seek."

With tears he said, "I've scrimped and saved. I've gone without each day,
So I could buy my dying son a train with which he'd play.

"The doctor says there's little time before God's call he'll hear,
This Christmas surely is his last. He cannot live the year.

"From Sears and Roebuck I procured the perfect gift of love,
A train and track he wanted most before he goes above.

"But to my house a villain came, and stole the gift I'd bought,
You Upper Dublin men of law, I ask the thief be caught.

"Your purpose does include my wish, the father did explain,
The native red men from our west 'iron horse' will call a train.

"So if a train is horse of iron, a toy train too must be,
My prayer is that you'll all go forth to find that toy for me."

He silent stood, then added this, "No other hope is mine,
And well before your answer give, please seek advice divine."

This challenge from a grieving dad was lodged in every breast.
The party quit and some went north while some went east, then west.

The villain's trail in time was found, the toy he'd tried to vend,
At farmhouse here. Or tavern there. Now, just around the bend,

A surrey sped by whip so cruel, a man in des'prate flight,
Our riders quickly over took. He didn't dare to fight.

He lied and cried and shamefully tried to claim the toy his own,
He'd won it in a poker game or it secured a loan.

The troop returned to Dublin shire. The day was nearly gone.
They trotted to the father's house. They'd been on mount since dawn.

The tears the father shed that day were tears of joy, of course,
Said he, "I thought I'd never see an angel on a horse."

The men of Dublin headed home, but wondrous light was theirs,
For they all knew they'd done God's work by answer brought to prayers.

They gave the greatest Christmas gift, a gift of sacrifice,
Its joy came back to them tenfold, a joy that knew no price.

Our journal's closed. Its story told of men steadfast and true,
And how they banded Christmas day their savior's work to do.

Now still a postscript I would add of which I'm not assured
Was the boy so helped that day that he was fine'ly cured?

The father said, "I'm Revvy Brown, as surely you'll recall,"
So listen as I tell to you the strangest part of all.

Just come with me to later years and Reading Railroad lore,
In came a brand new president in nineteen forty-four.

His name was Brown, first name Revelle, the railroad his career.
He'd started as a water boy and risen every year.

Was he the lad our brethren served so many years ago?
Or is the name coincident? I simply do not know.

But miracles still have their place, though no one now can tell,
Perhaps the railroad chief's first train was made by Lionel.

*December 2006*

*Note: Revelle W. Brown was President of the Reading Company from 1944 to 1952.*

# How a National Day of Thanks Was Wrought

*In the spirit of the late J. Wilson Jones and written for the 180th meeting of The Upper Dublin Association of Montgomery County for the Recovery of Stolen Horses, Detection of Horse Thieves and Obtaining Other Stolen Property*

Tonight we meet to celebrate and tell our company's lore,
Since first our charter we obtained. The years we know, nine score.

We've served our local cit'zenry, just read our minute book.
But once we served the nation whole, 'twas by a ride we took.

The time was eighteen sixty-three, the country was at war,
"The union we'll preserve," said Abe, "what 'ere may be in store."

His brow was crossed with worry lines. The strife had taken toll.
The battle losses tore his heart, his mind, his very soul.

Came Simon Cam'ron in July, a question to relate,
"Shall we a day of thanks observe?" had asked his Keystone state.

"How can a day of thanks be named?" replied the president,
"When mis'ry binds our every task, our manhood's sadly spent.

"How can I choose a day of thanks, the land's so badly torn.
When sadness comes to crush each day and death bestrides the morn?

"Go tell your friends from Harrisburg, no day of thanks can be,
I can't proclaim Thanksgiving Day in eighteen sixty-three."

So Cam'ron sadly wrote his niece, who lived in Dublin shire,
This year no day of thanks we'll have, should any there inquire.

The maid said, "Honest Abe, I love, but with him disagree,
There's much for which we should give thanks in eighteen sixty-three.

"My brother lives to fight again, and I am only one,
In gratitude we pray each day, our thanks there just begun.

"Thanks for harvests, fruit and grain. For peace with foreign kings.
For Vicksburg and for Gettysburg, and countless other things.

"Thanks for a God who doth bestow, who welcomes offered prayer,
Who'll heal the wounds that rend our land, and soon with peace repair.

"Thanks should be ours, though wounded grave, our flag still flies the same.
So, Mr. Lincoln, we beseech, a day of thanks proclaim."

Then quill she took and wrote her words and to her father went.
"How can these thoughts of mine," she asked, "get to the president?"

He said, "My Upper Dublin troop!!! To Washington we'll ride,
A time to meet with Abe we'll seek. We cannot be denied."

Next day at dawn, they mounted up: a dozen from our corps,
Patriots all, but all too old, to fight in Civil War.

The trip, a week, with stops for rest—then to the chief straightway.
He read the words and said, "She's right, we'll have thanksgiving day.

"From plow and shuttle, ship and ax, have come our might and wealth.
Our freedom's in resurgence now as is our nation's health.

"Yes, we shall have a national day, a day when work shall cease,
We'll thank and pray that soon our land will rest again in peace.

"So thanks to her who's brought to mind, we live abundantly,
And thanks to you who rode so far, her message brought to me."

Then Lincoln smiled and shook each hand. The rest is history,
A national day of thanks began, in eighteen sixty-three.

To Upper Dublin they returned, glad tidings told the maid,
How she'd persuaded Honest Abe to grant for what she'd prayed.

I wish her name was mine to tell, our minutes do not say,
But at least you know our part, in that Thanksgiving Day.

And ever since when autumn comes, a day of thanks is set,
Reminder of the blessings ours that we must not forget.

For Father Abraham, give thanks, he saved the Union cause,
Give thanks for all our membership who've helped enforce the laws.

Give thanks for warmth on chilly nights, and thanks for friends we share,
Give thanks for grace from God above. His Son He did not spare.

And thanks for loved ones now at rest, who brightened many years,
And thanks for mem'ries still we keep as nurtured by our tears.

Thanks for harvest, fruit and grain, and thanks for liberty.
And thanks for those who still will strive, our people to keep free.

*November 28, 2007*

*Note: Simon Cameron of Pennsylvania was Lincoln's Secretary of War. Lincoln's proclamation of Thanksgiving Day was issued on October 3, 1863. It was the first time a national day of thanks was designated.*

# Gettysburg

*In the spirit of the late J. Wilson Jones and written for the 181st meeting of The Upper Dublin Association of Montgomery County for the Recovery of Stolen Horses, Detection of Horse Thieves and Obtaining Other Stolen Property*

This day in 1863, he rose, his speech to give,
"We'll honor those who died," his theme, "By how we choose to live."

"Four score and seven," he began, "A nation new was brought,
Equality and liberty, the ideals that it sought."

He went on:
"Can such a nation long endure? Men died to meet that test.
Upon their battlefield we meet to hallow where they rest."

"But in a larger sense we lack, the means to dedicate,
The valiant who so nobly died, did this ground consecrate."

He paused and concluding said,
"But rather should we here resolve this nation takes new birth,
So rule by people shall remain unperished from the earth."

And so,
Hark to the words that Lincoln stressed. "Devotion" and the "Brave."
"Unfinished Work" that they "Advanced" who now are in each grave.

"Shall not have died in vain those dead," no vow more sacred be,
That vow should still all hearts bestir, as back in sixty-three.

Be thankful for the words he spoke, may they still echo clear,
Be thankful for their sacrifice who hold our freedoms dear.

*November 19, 2008*

## This Company's Early Days

*In the spirit of the late J. Wilson Jones and written for the 182nd meeting of The Upper Dublin Association of Montgomery County for the Recovery of Stolen Horses, Detection of Horse Thieves and Obtaining Other Stolen Property*

In broad daylight from Paxson's barn, thieves stole a mare and sleigh,
They broke into Ike Ambler's place and both got clean away.

Ed Williams was the next to find that he was missing cash.
Brigands were working Dublin Shire. Hit too were Moore and Nash.

George B. Conway and Jarrett Kirk, Will Wood and Liv'zey too,
Were victims of some night-time rogues, by whom there was no clue.

The time was 1828. The prexy, John Q. A.,[1]
Determined were these honest men: No more would thieves hold sway.

An end to stealing was their goal, with ev'ry rascal caught.
Insurance was another need, for then, none could be bought.

"Our forces we must join as one. None else is near enough.
United we should make our stand. "These words from Dr. Hough.

The day of Valentines they met at nearby Three Tons Inn,
A girl and eight and twenty men, this company to begin.

Lew Jones the minutes carefully kept, Fitzwater did preside,
The fisc was in Jim Rutter's hands. These men, the first to guide.

A constitution they drew up, committees for each task,
And when they found a missing horse, the questions they should ask.

If getting back the stolen goods was not to be achieved,
A payment from the members' dues, the loss in part relieved.

It wasn't long until one night, a call for action rose,
From Howard Mullin's house it came: They'd taken all his clothes.

His Sunday meeting shirt and vest, his pants of buckskin brown,
And though he was to preach next day, they stole his preaching gown.

Since Howard had no shirt or gown, he wore his wife's red shawl,
He preached that never Peter rob so you can give to Paul.

He preached about forgiving sin of those who did repent,
But first, about their being caught, no matter where they went.

Tom Tomlinson and Simmers ("Joe") were told to go toward Trappe,
"Go past Blue Bell and keep going west, as guided by your map."

---

1 John Quincy Adams.

They did what they were told to do, but stopped at Center Square,
For there they saw a peddler's cart all filled with things to wear.

They thought they might just take a look at what he had to vend,
He told them he had shirts and more, if money they would spend.

They ruffled through the wares he showed and pants spied, buckskin brown,
A shirt and vest and leather coat wrapped in a parson's gown.

They tied the man and Joe rode off, a constable he found,
The magistrate said, "Lock him up and send him to the pound."

**Postscript**

The first call to our membership was crowned with great success,
And through its days this worthy group would never stand for less.

Though many years have hurried by, these first men all asleep,
'Tis well that we recall their deeds, their names in rev'rence keep.

*November 18, 2009*

## Of Keisel Fame

*In the spirit of the late J. Wilson Jones and written for the 183rd meeting of The Upper Dublin Association of Montgomery County for the Recovery of Stolen Horses, Detection of Horse Thieves and Obtaining Other Stolen Property*

The year was 1828, they met at Three Tons Inn,
A girl and 8 and 20 men, this company to begin.

It was the day of Valentines, but Cupid not their thought,
But rather how protect their barns and how could thieves be caught.

Paxson and Kirk and Dr. Hough, their kin you'll find still here,
This company they set on its path, its mission they made clear.

But of the girl, the only lass, what's there in mem'ries store?
What reason hers? What could she add? What brought her to the fore?

By Anna Keisel she was known, a widow, mother too,
Her husband had been killed by thieves, repayment was her due.

She told the men that she would ride and she'd no quarter ask
Of villains that she'd help to catch or any other task.

"Two blooded pups are mine," she said, "and you can count on me,
If ever tracking is required, for they would useful be."

Her name the men were quick to add to our initial list
When only seven months went by, Fate took a funny twist.

Some thief who'd heard of Anna's loss thought her an easy prey,
Into her shed he crept one night and stole her one-horse chaise.

The next day was the Sabbath, with church 'till half past one,
So Anna did not learn the theft 'till long the deed was done.

A crimson hue was Anna's chaise when taken from her shed
The thief quick painted it dark black to hide its fiery red.

Our company gathered Monday morn to search each route they'd set
T'ord north and south and east and west, an ever spreading net.

But Anna had another scheme, her hounds, no puppies now,
She'd named one Seek the other Find, were trackers she'd taught how.

From in the shed they got the scent, the thief would be their grail,
With Anna and two well-armed men who vowed they would not fail.

Past farm and village, through a woods and there a run-down shack,
No door to stop the baying hounds, inside a chaise of black.

Upon the ground a cringing man whose hands with paint were stained,
"Call off the dogs. I stole this rig," was what he then explained.

But when he rolled as if to rise, a gun was in his hand,
Which Anna quickly kicked away and foiled what he had planned.

The rest, of course, you well can guess. The thug went to the pen
While Anna was revered by all, a true-blue heroine.

Our company called her many times to aid and apprehend,
And she was always there for us, a helping hand to lend.

But there's a postscript I must add of Keisel, her last name,
Christopher, her older son, a justice of the peace became.

Through all the years, the Keisel name's been honored and no stain
In Dublin shire it's no surprise you'll find there's Keisel Lane.

*December 1, 2010*

# Forget Not the Holiday Just Past

*In the spirit of the late J. Wilson Jones and written for the 184th meeting of The Upper Dublin Association of Montgomery County for the Recovery of Stolen Horses, Detection of Horse Thieves and Obtaining Other Stolen Property*

I now give thanks for many things,
Some only I may know.
The way the sun, reflecting makes
Those di'monds on the snow.

My thanks for sorrows and for joy,
And loved ones now at rest.
My thanks for warmth on chilly nights,
And books that led my quest.

For children's children when they come,
Too soon they say goodbye,
For knowledge that my prayers are heard.
For triumphs when I try.

My thanks for sunset's reddish glow,
The promise of each dawn.
For ev'ry star and pale moonlight.
A mother and her fawn.

Oh, thanks for mountains. Fruited plains.
For trees, their majesty.
And those who serve in forces armed
To keep our nation free.

*November 30, 2011*

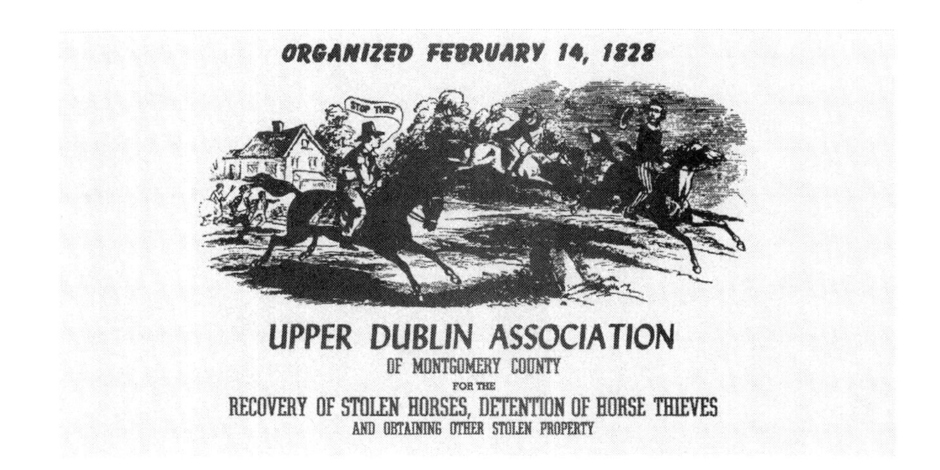

## A Tribute and Thanks

*In the spirit of the late J. Wilson Jones and written for the 185th meeting of The Upper Dublin Association of Montgomery County for the Recovery of Stolen Horses, Detection of Horse Thieves and Obtaining Other Stolen Property*

It's well to study his'try, to learn of ventures past.
Of those who built our nation, and how the die they cast.

Not all who merit honor are found in scholar's tome,
Some tend the flame of heritage, of country and of home,

And such a man's Bill Paxson, a son of Dublin's soil,
He's ever close to forest glade, its bounty for his toil.

He's studied all the struggles, its troubles and its strife,
And how by will were overcome, to give our land its life.

He has preached America, its virtues are his theme,
Hard work with all integrity, he's been the pa'trit's dream.

Our company's of Bill's lineage, Sire Charles helped create
With others at the old Three Tons, 'twas 1828.

Four decades and even more, Bill's been this company's guide,
Our yearly meetings were his task and a program helped provide.

Now our glasses raise on high, to Bill our thanks we give,
He's shown to all throughout the years just how a life to live.

*November 28, 2012*

## A Few Words of the Past

*In the spirit of the late J.Wilson Jones and written for the 186th meeting of The Upper Dublin Association of Montgomery County for the Recovery of Stolen Horses, Detection of Horse Thieves and Obtaining Other Stolen Property*

'T is fine to study hi'stry of places far away
About the European kings and when and where their sway.

The British have great tales to tell. I also went to Rome,
But then I thought I'd had enough. I'd study home sweet home.

To 1684 I turned: Ed Tanner bought a tract.
He then named it Upper Dublin. 'T was nothing that it lacked.

Its rolling hills were blessed with loam. Abundant rills with fish.
Iron ore and other min'rals too left nothing man could wish.

As you'd expect, the settlers came to farm the fertile soil
And reap the benefits that come from hard and honest toil.

Soon roads were laid and grist mill built, while limestone burned to lime,
Limekiln Pike reminds us all of what took place that time.

To Emlen's house came Freedom's cause, and to the nearby mill,
George Washington headquartered there, his army at Camp Hill.

Where Butler Pike met Horsham Road, Three Tuns a tavern there,
A store, a school, and sev'ral shops around the village square.

The year was 1828 and they met there at the Inn,
A girl and 8 and 20 men, this company to begin.

It was the day of Valentines, but Cupid not their thought,
But rather how protect their barns and how could thieves be caught.

*December 2013*

# In Faith They Did Abide

*In the spirit of the late J. Wilson Jones and written for the 187th meeting of The Upper Dublin Association of Montgomery County for the Recovery of Stolen Horses, Detection of Horse Thieves and Obtaining Other Stolen Property*

When first we met so long ago (It was on Cupid's day),
The business said, the business done, our founders knelt to pray.

There, one by one, they asked of God, protection when they'd ride:
No mount grow lame, no shoe thrown off, and sure of foot each stride.

Divine assistance so was sought, tradition came to be,
They'd pray before they'd gallop forth, then go stout heartedly.

In 1848 they met, an invitation theirs,
The Baptist church would honor them, with thanks and special prayers.

That day of choice in early fall, they to the church repaired,
Their task was blessed, a tribute read, no words of praise were spared.

"Apprehension and Recovery," was Rev'rend Humphrey's theme,
He said a Dublin freed from thieves, made ours a noble dream.

A yearly custom thus did start, for Dublin's churches each,
A diff'rent one would give a call, "Come hear our pastor preach."

The Luth'rens, Friends, and Dunkards, sincere in diff'rent ways,
Thanks would give for brigands caught, our worthy members praise.

Renewed, made strong, by what they heard, it helped them through the year,
Though danger lurked in ev 'ry ride, they said, "There's naught to fear."

Our members did not hesitate to say, "In God we trust.
He's ridden near us dark of night. His judgments all are just."

So of this heritage be proud, our privilege to trace,
And represent all those who made their world a better place.

*December 3, 2014*

# The Great Train Wreck

*In the spirit of the late J. Wilson Jones and written for the 188th meeting of The Upper Dublin Association of Montgomery County for the Recovery of Stolen Horses, Detection of Horse Thieves and Obtaining Other Stolen Property*

That summer day in '56 – each coach with children packed.
The inbound train. The outbound train approached on single track.

St. Michael's Church, a picnic planned for those in Catholic school,
The City's heat they'd gladly trade for time in country's cool.

The Camp Hill curve kept each from sight, unheard their whistles' cry,
The brakes were set, but far too late. No way they could pass by.

The older girls and older boys were joined by Father Dan,
The leading car was where they rode so fun and games could plan.

Hot steel tore steel and showered fire. Inferno quickly spurred.
With cannon roar the boilers blew—For miles the din was heard.

Their wooden coach was on its side. To it the embers sped.
They perished in the burning car; Priest Dan among the dead.

John Spencer of our ancient troop, from mount he saw it all,
And knew that he must gallop forth to other members call.

"Bring bandages, but one must go, to Chestnut Hill pell-mell,
Their Horse and Engine Comp'ny come, the ter'ble fire to quell."

Twelve of our group assembled there to rescue and to save.
The groans and screams of those still trapped tore even hearts most brave.

They bore the ones who could not walk and with the dying prayed,
And did what little could be done to comfort and to aid.

From out the City parents came, and some would find their dears,
But others searched and called in vain, for them the worst of fears.

That day of horror sixty died, Injured: one hundred more,
The grief that gripped the land around was never felt before.

The Widow Ambler ev'rywhere, no task too great or small,
A heroine, she led the way, our members did recall.

Throughout the day those members toiled, Dame Mary's want to heed,
Her asking did without delay on foot or sturdy steed.

Because she led while most stood back, her townsmen did proclaim
From this day forth and ever more this village bears her name.

But little known and should be told, our comp'ny's work that day,
Made possible what Mary did, the thanks that came her way.

*December 2, 2015*

*Note: "The Great Train Wreck" poem recounts the story of the horrible tragedy of the Great Train Wreck of 1856, particularly the role of the members of the Upper Dublin Association and the heroic actions of Mary Ambler, a 50-year-old widow who was one of the first on the scene. As the poem points out, the town of Ambler was named in tribute to her heroism on that awful day.*

# Independence Day

## Introduction by J. William Ditter, Jr.

*. . . these United Colonies are, and of right ought to be, free and independent states . . .*

*And for the support of this Declaration with a firm reliance on the protection of Divine Providence, we materially pledge to each other our lives, our fortunes and our sacred honor.*

There were fifty-six men who staked all that they had to the cause of a free America. In the words of John Adams, one of the fifty-six, this defiance and courage, this reliance, made that day in July the most memorable in the Epoch of America. He went on,

> *It ought to be celebrated as the Day of Deliverance by the solemn Acts of Devotion to God Almighty. It ought to be solemnized with Pomp and Parade, with Shews, Games, Sports, Guns, Bells, Bonfires and Illuminations from one End of this Continent to the other from this Time forward forever more.*

And so it should be.

Each year a poem featuring an image of the Liberty Bell and the Declaration of Independence's pledge of life, fortune, and sacred honor called family and friends to spend the afternoon of the Fourth with us.

And come they did—to enjoy the pool, badminton, quoits, and conversation. Bunting, flags, and flowers provided a patriotic stage and a bit of pomp.

We may not have had any guns or bonfires, but what we lacked in pomp was more than made up by knowing that we were celebrating the most memorable day in our nation's history.

## Our Resolve: Liberty

*...And for the support of this Declaration,*
*with a firm reliance on the protection of Divine Providence,*
*we mutually pledge to each other*
*our Lives, our Fortunes, and our sacred Honor.*

Of years two hundred twenty-nine
since Freedom's bell was heard.
The message dear. The challenge clear.
By which our hearts are stirred.

Our firm resolve must ever be
that liberty hold sway.
We celebrate. We dedicate.
On Independence Day.

*JWD, 2002*

## You Too Can Keep the Promise of the Bell

*...And for the support of this Declaration,*
*with a firm reliance on the protection of Divine Providence,*
*we mutually pledge to each other*
*our Lives, our Fortunes, and our sacred Honor.*

They heard the words. They heard the Bell.
And when were old they still would tell,
*That day of glory, in July,*
*On Providence we would rely,*
*Our Lives, our Honor, Fortunes all,*
*Pledged to that Declaration's call.*
Then they'd talk of those who fell,
To keep the promise of the Bell.

Perhaps no footprints in the snow
Were stained with blood, your path to show,
No empty sleeve from saber's slash,
No mem'ry kept of Yorktown's clash.
But still there comes for freedom's need,
A clarion call for you to heed:
To country, bravery, honor give,
Your children teach, by virtues live,
So when you're old, you too can tell,
"I kept the promise of the bell."

*JWD 2003*

# Freedom's Price

*...And for the support of this Declaration,*
*with a firm reliance on the protection of Divine Providence,*
*we mutually pledge to each other*
*our Lives, our Fortunes, and our sacred Honor.*

Silent stands the old bell now
While thousands come to see,
The voice that once cried through the land,
"These people shall be free."

They knew, who heard that day the bell,
Its message loud and clear.
To only them would freedom come,
Who'd meet its price most dear.

Hark to the echoes of the past,
Let us reminded be
A terrible price we still must pay
If we would still be free.

*JWD 2005*

*In my office on the* USS Amycus *(ARL 2), October 1945*

# Echoes from the Bell

*. . .And for the support of this Declaration,*
*with a firm reliance on the protection of Divine Providence,*
*we mutually pledge to each other*
*our Lives, our Fortunes, and our sacred Honor.*

You oft have heard the story of how the bell was tolled,
The pledge to independence of honor, life, and gold.

Yet know ye of the echo that filled the State House square?
"Freedom can be ours," it spoke, "if we will only dare."

Again the bounding echo, its words both loud and clear,
"Freedom for all time is ours, but oh, the price is dear."
Resounded last the clamor, to each its voice does cry,
"The torch be yours to take from them
whose due was cost most high."

Doubt not that toll should mind us
of Freedom's endless strife.
It seeks all those whose pledge will be
their honor, wealth, and life.

Friend, now fall upon your knees
and pray that God above
Brings ever from that echo
brave men who country love.

*JWD 2006*

# Can You Doubt?

*...And for the support of this Declaration,*
*with a firm reliance on the protection of Divine Providence,*
*we mutually pledge to each other*
*our Lives, our Fortunes, and our sacred Honor.*

Is there a doubt God blessed the pledge the signers that day made,
A pledge of honor, life, and gold, a pledge that none betrayed?

Is there a doubt God patri'ts graced, who icy river crossed,
To rout at Trenton, Hessian foe when all but hope seemed lost?

Is there a doubt at Valley Forge God heard the Gen'ral's prayer,
And wrought into an army bold from hunger and despair?

At Yorktown as surrender came and war to end was brought,
Is there a doubt that God revered the men who'd bravely fought?

Through darkest threats and fright'ning strife our portion comes to be,
Still God gives might to those He tests. Doubt not, on bended knee.

If we'll but follow, God will lead the nation He so blessed,
Faith and valor ours to prevail in freedom's endless quest.

*JWD 2007*

*The USS Amycus (ARL-2), Subic Bay, Luzon, the Philippines, October 1944.*

## Do We Need Another Bell?

*. . .And for the support of this Declaration,*
*with a firm reliance on the protection of Divine Providence,*
*we mutually pledge to each other*
*our Lives, our Fortunes, and our sacred Honor.*

Do now we need another bell
on Independence Square,
To tell that freedom shall be lost
unless our people dare?

Do now we need another bell
to say in cadence clear,
That lurking evil'd strip from us
whatever we hold dear?

Do now we need another bell
to keep us strong and proud,
With courage from our heritage,
defiant and unbowed?

Do now we need another bell?
Our brave we've sent 'a field.
Should we now turn the other cheek
and so to evil yield?

Do now we need another bell?
Pray God it is not true,
But seek resolve to stay the course
Until the task is through.

*JWD 2008*

## Who?

*...And for the support of this Declaration,*
*with a firm reliance on the protection of Divine Providence,*
*we mutually pledge to each other*
*our Lives, our Fortunes, and our sacred Honor.*

"How toll the bell?"
The pa'trits asked, who stood in State House Square.
No rope to pull. The portal locked that led to tower stair.

The lofty belfry gained the sky, no way there to be found.
But then as though it knew their thoughts, the bell began to sound.

In cadence slow it seemed to say, "Oh, people, gather near,
A solemn message will be yours, a challenge you shall hear."

And when that final pledge was spoke, of honor, life, and gold,
The bell began to peal again with words of glory bold.

"Freedom's yours to gain and keep. And freedom's worth the cost
Cry vigilance for ever more for freedom can be lost."

Who voiced the bell?
Who blessed this land?
Who blessed that sacred day?
In whom did pa'trits place their trust?
And who should lead our way?

*JWD 2009*

*Captain J. William Ditter, Jr., USNR, 1966*

## Blessings from the Heavens

*...And for the support of this Declaration,*
*with a firm reliance on the protection of Divine Providence,*
*we mutually pledge to each other*
*our Lives, our Fortunes, and our sacred Honor.*

The echoes of the sounding bell on wafting breeze did quickly dwell,
And too the words of freedom's call were triumphed o'er the city wall.

To farm and hamlet far beyond, the challenge went. But who'd respond?
Here one. Here two. Here even three, who joined the cause for liberty.

How honor those who gave their heed and suffered long for freedom's need?
What laud for heroes bravely fought and with their lives our country bought?

No plaque of stone. No flights of speech reflect the tribute we would reach,
But heaven trust and let it tell what wreath for those who heard the bell.

Two constellations in the sky shine bright each fourth day of July,
Greet Perseus and Hercules, recalling valor, both of these.

And though they speak from time long gone they're skyward found from dusk to dawn.
So too our paean there behold, a song that swells with glory bold.

Look past the tree and worship's spire, for pa'trits each an orb of fire.
To heaven ever turn our gaze for there we'll find our hymn of praise.

*JWD 2010*

# Not One. Not One.

*...And for the support of this Declaration,*
*with a firm reliance on the protection of Divine Providence,*
*we mutually pledge to each other*
*our Lives, our Fortunes, and our sacred Honor.*

The fifty-six who signed that day knew well the price that they might pay.
These men of substance and renown knew treason theirs who'd crossed the crown.
The order came: "Find each and kin.
Let torment,
capture now begin.
No mercy show.
No quarter give.
Let prison house if any live."
The dictates of the king were done, the signers harried one by one.
When came the day the war was through, how had the signers paid their due?

Lives and fortunes:
They'd pledged their lives and some were dead. The homes of some the torch had fed.
Some once of wealth now rags they wore, their shops and ships seen never more.

Sacred Honor.
With lives and fortunes though they paid, Not one, Not one, the cause betrayed.
Not one, Not one, renounced the pact. Not one, Not one, did pledge retract.

From these brave men a message clear,
Though lives and fortunes are most dear
Our guiding star should honor be
If self and country we'd keep free.

*JWD 2011*

## Words from Long Ago

*...And for the support of this Declaration,*
*with a firm reliance on the protection of Divine Providence,*
*we mutually pledge to each other*
*our Lives, our Fortunes, and our sacred Honor.*

"Oh, Mama we have just come back, we went to State House Square,
My Grandpa said to hear the bell, the one that's way up there.

"My Grandpa only has one arm while all of us have two,
'A Yorktown cannon ball,' he said, What ever did he do?

"He showed me how I should salute each time they read a name,
My Grandpa said because of them a country we became.

"Next came a promise that we made, our honor, lives, and gold,
Will serve the cause of liberty what e'er the future hold.

"The last thing was a prayer we said, when comes the day of need,
With help from God, brave men we'll know to follow and to lead.

"Then we came home."

Dear Friend, these words from long ago,
Bestir like souls today.
Ourselves to freedom dedicate,
And let God show the way.

*JWD 2012*

## Our Task: To Uphold

*...And for the support of this Declaration,*
*with a firm reliance on the protection of Divine Providence,*
*we mutually pledge to each other*
*our Lives, our Fortunes, and our sacred Honor.*

With shining words and noble thoughts the Declaration rings,
To every age and every one, abundant hope it brings.

There's right to freedom here and now our pat'riot sires proclaimed
The marks of free men that they spoke had all been carefl'y framed.

What means this freedom that they sought, for which they'd die and kill.
The Declaration specifies and so sets forth their will.

The right to life and liberty, pursuit of happiness,
To all mankind are gifts from God, unail'n'ble, no less.

These rights secured by governments, its powers as agreed,
By those who would be governed and care the nation's need.

A president who'll laws obey and give them his support,
With judges free from every whim who'll sit in nearby court.

No taxes save there be consent from those who'll burdened be,
The right to trade in distant climes and freedom of the sea.

Our task, uphold these lofty words for they are staunch and true,
We'll pass the torch of freedom's light so all will know their due.

*J. W. Ditter, Jr. 2014*

# In Conclusion

## Introduction by J. William Ditter, Jr.

You probably remember the time when the newly minted ensign was drilling his division on the flight deck of their carrier. His orders were crisp—Naval Academy crisp: "Forward. March." "In cadence. Count." "By the right flank. March." "By the left flank. March."

But as the men neared the edge of the flight deck, the ensign froze. He couldn't remember, "To the rear. March." And now they were only a few paces away. A grizzled chief with hash marks up to his elbow, noting the lash-up, called out, "If you can't think of anything else, at least tell them good-bye."

I'm like that ensign. I can't think of the right words to introduce the miscellany that follows but at least—well, I hope—there's no danger to come if you venture further.

*I helped out building the barn.*

## Uncle Sebastian and Once Upon a Time

Uncle Sebastian sighed. It was what Aunt Minerva called a "Sebastian Sigh." It started around the top of his boots, rippled his leather vest, and came out under his big handlebar mustache like—as Aunt Minerva said—"Like the time the ferry that was there before the bridge was built had a leak in the boiler—only sadder."

Now Aunt Minerva wasn't old enough to remember before the bridge was built, but Grandma Fowler had told her about the ferry and the boiler and how it sounded and that was good enough for Aunt Minerva. She became the town chronicler on the time the ferry had a leak in the boiler, the time the ferry hit the dock and split open five barrels of molasses, and the way Captain Boig could skip a silver dollar from the dock all the way over to Bearne Point. And then find it.

It was a Sebastian Sigh.

Tiger the Kitten Now a Cat opened his eye and tapped one paw nervously. Romper the Dog looked behind him to see whether Tiger the Kitten Now a Cat was awake.

Out in the kitchen, the curtains rippled in harmony with Uncle Sebastian's sigh, and Aunt Minerva, who was making cookies, looked into the living room.

"Well?" she said, holding one hand under the batter spoon so it wouldn't drip on the new rug.

"Well!" Uncle Sebastian replied.

"Why the sigh?"

"Well, if you want to know," said Uncle Sebastian, "the Nice Little Boy From Across the Way hasn't been here all week and I've thought of a story to tell him."

"Well, really, Uncle Sebastian," she said. "You know it's been raining since Monday and he is in first grade now. When did he have time to come see you?"

Uncle Sebastian began to breathe in, gathering his breath for another sigh, but Aunt Minerva held up her hand just the way Constable Brown held up his hand when he was directing traffic out of the fairgrounds during the first two weeks of August.

Uncle Sebastian knew the signal. He didn't sigh.

"It's Friday now, and the rain has stopped," he said, half to himself and half to Aunt Minerva.

And just then, the doorbell rang. A short and two longs.

"Now I wonder who that could be," Uncle Sebastian muttered, a smile beginning to make his eyes crinkle and shine.

"I wonder who that can be."

"Oh, I'll bet you wonder, all right," replied Aunt Minerva.

They both knew that a short and two longs was the special ring of the Nice Little Boy From Across the Way.

"Well," said Uncle Sebastian, trying to sound surprised when he opened the door, "Look who's here. Come on in, George. Aunt Minerva, look who's here. We have a visitor."

The Nice Little Boy From Across the Way shook hands and said, "I've had a busy week at school. First grade isn't for the faint at heart. Do you know," he asked Uncle Sebastian, "that every word in the English language is spelled from letters in the alphabet? Or that every letter is either a valve or a continent? And did you know that fish can breathe under water because they have scales? I'll tell ya, there's a lot to first grade."

He waited for his words to sink in. And then he sighed. It was a first-grade version of a Sebastian Sigh. Tiger the Kitten Now a Cat tapped his paw. Romper the Dog checked to see if Tiger was awake.

"I was hoping for a story," he went on, seating himself at the stool near Uncle Sebastian's chair. "Do you have one?"

"As a matter of fact, I do. Are you ready?"

"Ready."

"Once upon a time," Uncle Sebastian began, only to have the Nice Little Boy From Across the Way interrupt with a question.

"Why," he asked, "do stories always begin 'Once upon a time?'"

"All I can tell you," Uncle Sebastian answered, "is that it has been that way since time immemorial."

"Is time always 'immemorial?'" the young visitor asked.

"Oh, no," replied Uncle Sebastian. "Time is usually fleeting and together with the tide, it waits for no man. People have it on their hands, pass it, and then can't imagine where it goes."

"What else do they do with time?" asked the first grader.

Uncle Sebastian thought a moment and replied, "Some people kill it and some people save it. They try to find it for something. Often when they have it, they take it. Or they take it even if they don't have it. Others ask what it is and the ones they ask look at their clocks so they can tell it. There are people who take time out and have the time of their lives. They talk about that 'old-time religion' even though times were tough then. Sometimes people say something's true because they read it in the *New York Times*."

"Uncle Sebastian," said the small guest, "I don't know what you're talking about."

"Maybe you should ask your father. He's a lawyer, and I read once that a lawyer's time and advice are his stock in trade."

At this, the Nice Little Boy From Across the Way howled with laughter.

"Why," he said when stopped, "would my father want to trade his stockings with anyone? You're funny."

"You'll have to ask him complicated questions like that—sometime. And remember, it's always been a long time since you've seen someone and you never have time to do what you want to do—like playing golf or reading a good book. Then too, it's always time for something: lunch, dinner, or a cookie—or to go to bed."

"I know about that," said the youngster, "although I can't remember about what it's like when it's time for a cookie."

At that juncture, Aunt Minerva, who had been listening at the doorway bobbed out of sight for a moment and reappeared with a plate of freshly baked cookies. "I can take a hint," she said and winked at the Nice Little Boy From Across the Way, "but these cookies better not spoil your dinner."

"Never," cried the small one.

"Never," echoed Uncle Sebastian, as he also took a cookie. For a few moments all was silence. Both host and guest knew that you should never talk with your mouth full. It showed a lack of respect for Aunt Minerva's cookies—and Aunt Minerva's new rug. Besides, Aunt Minerva's cookies deserved to be savored. So they savored.

When both had finished a second cookie, Uncle Sebastian said, "And now I will tell you how Duke the Duck ducked the Doc."

"Duke the Duck?"

The very one. Duke the Duck. You've never heard of him?"

"Never."

"Well, it's about time. Anyone who's in first grade should know about Duke the Duck and his friend, Gus the Goose. Ready?"

"Ready."

And then it happened. The phone rang. Aunt Minerva picked it up, looking at her watch. "Fine. How are you?" There was a short pause and then, "Right away," she added. And then, turning to the Nice Little Boy From Across the Way, Aunt Minerva said, "It's your mother, darling. Guess what."

"I can't," said George, starting to get off the stool.

"I suspect," commented Uncle Sebastian, "that time has done something again—it's come all too quickly. I forgot to tell you it does that too."

"Or that it latches onto dinner to make dinner-time, which is what it is for you," Aunt Minerva said to their small visitor.

"But what about Duke the Duck and Gus the Goose? Will they wait 'til another time?"

"If it's not too long a time," said Uncle Sebastian replied. "I'll be back soon—and bring my sister too. Soon." And he gravely shook hands with Uncle Sebastian and gave Aunt Minerva the hug she bent over to receive.

When George got to the door, Uncle Sebastian said, "Thanks for coming to see us."

"Anytime," the boy replied with a wink. Then he was gone—almost before Tiger the Kitten Now a Cat could open his eye or Romper the Dog knew it.

"What a nice little boy, "Uncle Sebastian commented. "What a nice family," echoed Aunt Minerva.

## What's in a Name?

Uncle Sebastian put down his brush and stepped back to see if there was any dust to mar the finish on his latest project, a redwood sign. Satisfied, he turned toward the Nice Little Boy From Across the Way who sat cross-legged at the end of the workbench.

"Well?" he asked.

"Well, uh-yes," was the reply.

"You don't sound very enthusiastic," said Uncle Sebastian, a note of disappointment coming into his voice. "Don't you like it?"

"Well," said his young visitor, "*enthusiastic* is a big word for someone who is only six, but it's a neat sign and I know Aunt Minerva will like it. But..." and his voice trailed off. Then, when there was no response, he went on, "Read it to me again."

"What's in a Name?" said Uncle Sebastian, checking each letter for the twentieth time. "What's in a Name?"

The Nice Little Boy From Across the Way got down from his perch and looked up. "I thought you said it was for Aunt Minerva's rose garden. It doesn't say, 'This way to the Rose Garden' or even 'Rose Garden' or 'Aunt Minerva's Garden'. What kind of a sign is it if it doesn't tell you 'Rose Garden' or 'Rose' or anything?"

Uncle Sebastian turned out the light and led the way toward the living room. While they walked, he explained, "It's a subtle sign. It uses a familiar quotation to suggest a rose, rather than just coming out and saying 'rose'. That's the beauty of it. Do you understand?"

"'What's in a name?' suggests a rose?" the youngster queried. "I never know when you're kidding me," he went on. "Are you now?"

"Let me explain and you'll see that I'm not," countered Uncle Sebastian. "The quotation comes from a play called *Romeo and Juliet* by William Shakespeare. In the play, the hero and heroine come from families that were fighting each other. He wants her to know that their family names don't—and shouldn't—keep them apart and from being in love. So he explains that if we called a rose by another name, it would still be a beautiful flower. Here's what he says, 'What's in a name? That which we call a rose by any other name would smell as sweet.' Now do you understand the sign?"

By now they were in the living room. Uncle Sebastian thought for a moment, and then taking his old Bible from the nearby table turned to Ecclesiastes. "Let's see what we can find about names," he said. "Oh, here it is, 'A good name is better than precious ointment.'"

"What was that fellow's name that said you don't have to know the names of flowers to smell them?" came the next question.

"Well," said Uncle Sebastian, "That's not exactly what he said, but you're getting the idea. His name was William Shakespeare and he lived a long time ago." "In England," he added.

Uncle Sebastian was now in his favorite old leather chair while Tiger the Kitten Now a Cat and Romper the Dog kept an eye on each other.

"Tell me more about names," said the Nice Little Boy From Across the Way from his favorite spot on the three-legged wooden stool. "But no big words."

"Well," was the reply, "why don't you tell me? What's your favorite name?"

"George," came a quick rejoinder. "That's dad's name. And I'm named for him. Were you named for somebody?

"Oh, yes indeed," said the old man. "I was named for my father's brother. My Uncle Sebastian. And he was named for his father's brother, who was his Uncle Sebastian. But as far as I know, he was named for Saint Sebastian. At least there weren't any other Sebastians in the family."

"Saint Sebastian?"

"Yes, he was a Roman soldier who became a Christian, helped other Christians escape, and was himself killed by the Romans for doing so. He lived about 1700 years ago," the old man said, his mustache bristling, his eyes flashing at the thought of Christian martyrs. "But," he went on, "we were going to talk about you. Do you know of any other Georges?"

The boy thought and after a few moments said, "Well, there's my grandmother's brother. He's Uncle George, but I never see him. He lives too far away. And George Washington. He was the first president and the first general."

A moment later another thought struck him and he went on, "Wow. You were named for a saint. At least you were named for your uncle who was named for his uncle who was named for a saint. That's like your being named for a saint."

"Well," said Uncle Sebastian, "on that basis, you were named for a saint too."

"I was?" the youngster said, and he stood up to be sure he heard every word.

Leaning forward, Uncle Sebastian went on, "I thought you knew about Saint George. He's the patron saint of England, but what really interests me is that he and Saint Sebastian lived at the same time. George grew up as a Christian and became a distinguished Roman soldier. He told the emperor—Emperor Diocletian—of his Christian beliefs and the emperor had him killed. That was the same emperor who had Sebastian killed." And his mustache bristled and his eyes flashed again.

The young lad was impressed. "Wait 'till I tell my dad about that," he said.

"George is a great name," said Uncle Sebastian, warming to the task. "Six English kings were named George. There's a Lake George in New York. And there are cities named Georgetown in a lot of states. There's a George School and a Georgetown University.

"And there used to be a cartoon called 'Let George Do It.' As I recall, Louis XII of France originated the saying. He had a prime minister named Georges d'Amboise. When someone suggested the king should do something, he said, 'Let Georges do it.' In other words, 'let someone else do it,'" Uncle Sebastian added. "Do you see how famous your name is?" he concluded.

"How about my sister's name? Sarah?" the youngster asked.

"Well, Sarah was a Hebrew princess and the name Sarah now means princess. She's well named," came the reply.

"Boy, Uncle Sebastian, I almost forgot to ask where Aunt Minerva's name comes from. Do you know? I'll bet it means 'good-cookie-maker' or maybe just 'good cook.'"

Uncle Sebastian eyes twinkled. The Nice Little Boy From Across the Way had asked his question loud enough that the lady of the house, who was in the kitchen, must have heard it. "I checked on her many years ago," the man said with a big grin. "Minerva was a Roman divinity—that means goddess—and was believed to have invented numbers and musical instruments. She was the patroness of the arts and trades. She taught warriors prudence, courage, and perseverance." Then dropping his voice to a whisper—but with an affectionate smile—he added, "And cunning."

"Cunning? What's that?" came the whispered rejoinder.

"It's being sly, tricky. And your Aunt Minerva has none of those qualities so I don't want her to know that the Goddess Minerva did. Catch on?"

"Got it," said the boy, feeling a sense of male bonding without knowing what it was. "I guess you don't know about my mother's name. Or do you?"

Uncle Sebastian thought a moment. "Well, I can try," he responded. "Mary was the mother of Jesus. The Bible doesn't tell us who her parents were, but according to legend, her mother was Anne, the wife of Joachim. In any event, the Catholic Church remembers her with a feast day on July 26. So your mother's name honors the Blessed Virgin and honors her mother too. That's even better than a saint—or a lot of saints. Do you agree?"

"Well, I agree that my mother's better than a saint. And she can cook too," he added loyally. "And ski."

There was a moment of silence, which made Romper the Dog raise one ear as though he was afraid he was missing something while Tiger the Kitten Now a Cat opened one eye. Finally, the young visitor said, "I have a nickname. My mother calls me 'Geordie' and so does my father. Where do nicknames come from?"

"Often they're a shortened form of a name—Tom for Thomas, Bill for William, or Jim for James. Sometimes it's an affectionate..."

"A what inate?" the boy interrupted. Then he added, "I thought there weren't going to be any big words today."

"*Affectionate* means loving. And the only way you'll get to know words is to hear and use them," the old man explained with a smile. Then he went on, "When your parents call you Geordie they are saying you are very special, greatly loved, their pride and joy."

"Really?"

"Really. But even your nickname comes down to us from long ago. The Scotch used a gold British coin, a guinea, back in the 1600s. They called it a Geordie. And then in 1815, a man named George Stephenson invented a lamp for miners."

"Miners?"

"A miner is a man who goes down deep in the ground and digs out coal, or gold, or silver. It's a tough life from all I've read about it. Anyway, there's a lot of gas that can explode down there, and before there were electric lights, miners often had to work in total darkness. That is, they did until George Stephenson invented his miner's lamp. Guess what he called it."

The young eyes flashed and a smile came quickly. "A Geordie?" he asked, being almost sure of the answer.

"A Geordie indeed," was the response. "So there you have it. You got a saint's name and a nickname that combines gold and the giving of light, light that makes darkness disappear," Uncle Sebastian said with a smile. A smile and a hint of a challenge.

At that juncture, Aunt Minerva appeared with some corn bread muffins. She said, "I made these for the church bazaar and need someone to taste one. Will you be a saint and do it for me?" She smiled, feeling pretty cunning. She knew more about Roman deities than her husband gave her credit for.

"You're on," said the boy and he helped himself to the dish that was extended to him. And a moment later, "Ummm," and later, "Ummmm again." Then he said solemnly "Aunt Minerva, these muffins are divine. I predict they'll be the hit of the day. And you can quote me."

Aunt Minerva smiled as she said, "Thank you, dear, and I will."

Just then, the phone rang. Aunt Minerva picked up the receiver, listened a moment, then said, "We've been having such a nice time we didn't realize it was so late. He'll be right there, dear. It's nice to talk to you."

"Maryanne?" asked Uncle Sebastian.

"No, it was the princess. But she was calling for her mother," replied Aunt Minerva.

Before she could say anything more, the Nice Little Boy From Across the Way came over and she stooped down for his hug. Uncle Sebastian got a hearty handshake—then, almost shyly, a hug too. And the lad was gone.

The old couple stood in the window and watched. Their young friend turned, waved his hand, and then disappeared down the driveway. "What a Nice Little Boy," said Uncle Sebastian.

"What a nice family," Aunt Minerva echoed.

## Random Thoughts after a Contemporary Worship Service

How silently. How silently, the wond'rous gift is sent,
Let speakers now reverberate so we'll know what it meant.

How silently. How silently, in Bethlehem OK,
Turn up the speakers one more notch, it's now a diff'rent day.

We contemplate. We celebrate, with great cacophony,
No rest ye merry gentlemen. No silent night for Thee.

We won't in solemn stillness wait to hear the angels sing,
Turn up the speakers one more notch to greet our gracious King.

Instead with noise proclaim our joy, the angel chorus drown,
We'll loudly shout O Holy Night as Mary's child we crown.

The angel chorus should be loud to tell of holy birth.
Turn up the speakers one more notch, no peace to men on earth.

What child is this who's fast asleep, a manger for his bed?
Turn up the speakers one more notch and wake Him up instead.

Let decibels proclaim our joy so all will know He's here,
We'll guide three kings from Orient with raucous loud and clear.

O holy night, the stars do shine as shepherds watch their flock,
Turn up the speakers one more notch, this is the time for Rock.

The quiet was the songsters' stress who wrote of Christmas eve
Turn up the speakers one more notch, to show that we believe.

No ear may hear Him coming to free the world from sin,
It's that we've all grown very deaf because of all the din.

Abide with us Emanuel as strident notes are played,
If this keeps on throughout the year I'll need a hearing aid.

*December 21, 2008*

# An Interesting Find, and So We Sing at Christmas Time

*by Jack W. Driett, Jr.*

Although my father, grandfather, and great grandfather were lawyers, I went to Drexel and became a mechanical engineer and spent years working for the Pardway Valve Company, the last fourteen as its president.

After my parents died, my wife and I moved into the family home and stayed there for seventeen years until the last of the children married and established homes of their own. We decided to move into a smaller place nearer the city. However, before we left, there was the problem of three generations of closed files: the older ones in tin bread boxes, then some in file drawers, and many of my father's in fiber board boxes.

In some instances, the files had already been purged and all that remained were the fruits of legal research and a paid bill. Then too, there were those that contained an opinion from the court, a hand-written notation of some sort, or in rare cases, a sketch. Realizing that I had almost seventy-eight years worth of Montgomery County history, I began to look carefully for documents that might be of interest to the Historical Society.

The enclosed was of special interest to me and I copied it carefully from the hand-written pages found in one of the first files I examined. What do you make of it?

*Christmas Sleigh Ride, 1963: from left to right, David, Bill, Bob, and George*

IN THE COURT OF COMMON PLEAS OF MONTGOMERY COUNTY PENNSYLVANIA

FANNIE BRIGHT by her guardian: No. 37
Henry B. Bright: Plantiff
v.
October Term
JAMES LORD PIERPONT,

Defendant: 1850

George B. Driett, Esq.: Appearing for the Plaintiff

Pro Se: J. Pierpont

An Excerpt from the trial. November 15, 1851

The testimony of J. Pierpont
(Witness Sworn)

(Questions by Mr. Driett.)

State your name for the record and spell your last name.

A. It's James Lord Pierpont. P-I-E-R-P-O-N-T.

Q. Married or single?

A. Yes.

Q. Well, which?

A. Oh, single.

Q. Your age?

A. I'm 19. I'll be 20.

Q. On the night in question, what did you do?

A. I thought I'd take a ride.

Q. In what?

A. In a sleigh.

Q. Was it an open or closed sleigh?

A. Yes.

Q. Well, which?

A. Oh, it was an open sleigh. It had runners—and two seats.

Q. What pulled it?

A. A horse.

Q. So it was a one-horse, open sleigh?

A. Yes.

Q. Describe the horse.

A. It had four legs and…

Q. Mr. Pierpont, we will get along a lot better if you try to restrain your sense of humor. What was distinctive about your horse?

A. He was lean and lank. And he had a bobtail. That means a previous owner had cut off part of the horse's tail.

Q. In your opinion, are some horses lucky and some horses unlucky?

A. Yes.

Q. And this one?

A. Unlucky. Misfortune seemed his lot.

Q. So on the night in question, you thought you'd take a ride in a one-horse open sleigh?

A. Yes.

Q. What did you do?

A. I hitched up Bob— that's my horse—and drove over to the Bright place and soon Miss Fannie Bright was seated by my side.

Q. What was the snow like?

A. It had snowed a lot the night before and on into the day so the snow was deep.

Q. Had the wind been blowing so the snow was drifted?

A. Yes, there were drifts.

Q. You did all the driving?

A. Yes.

Q. Did you have lights on the sleigh?

A. No, it was a moonlit night—I could see real well and there were bells on a ring on the horse's harness so you could hear us coming along.

Q. What do you mean?

A. Every time the horse moved, the bells jingled.

Q. And did the jingling of the bells make your spirits bright?

A. Yes, both of us.

Q. Were you driving fast?

A. Well, pretty fast. When the snow is deep like that you have to go fast to stay on top of it.

Q. Would you say you were dashing along?

A. Yes.

Q. Dashing through the snow in your one-horse open sleigh?

A. Yes.

Q. And your spirits were bright?

Q. Were you having fun?

A. Yes.

Q. What else were you doing?

Q. Laughing and singing.

A. What were you singing?

A. Sleighing songs.

Q. Were you laughing and singing all the way?

A. Yes—we were having lots of fun. As I told you, the bells seemed to make our spirits bright.

Q. You were driving the entire time. Were you geeing or hawing or using the reins?

A. I was using the reins.

Q. What road were you on?

A. We weren't on any road. We were going over the fields.

Q. Still laughing and singing?

A. Yes. All the way.

Q. Did anything unusual occur?

A. Yes, the horse got into a drifted bank of snow.

Q. So, while you were dashing through the snow—off the road—having fun laughing and singing—you drove the horse into a drifted bank?

A. I didn't see the drifted bank.

Q. It was night time—you had no lights—you were having fun, laughing and singing all the way—you were driving and the horse ended up in drifted bank. Maybe if you'd been paying attention to your driving, you would have seen the drifted bank—is that right?

A. I guess you could put it that way.

Q. This was Bob, your unlucky horse?

A. Yes, misfortune seemed his lot.

Q. What happened to the sleigh when the horse sent into the drifted bank?

A. Well, he thrashed around and the sleigh turned over.

Q. In other words, you and Miss Bright were upsot?

A. Yes. Upsot.

Q. And then?

A. I woke up in Dr. Bray's office. I think they took Miss Fannie Bright to Grand View or some hospital or someplace.

Q. Did you try to find out how Miss Fannie Bright was?

A. Yes, the next day I went around to see her, but her father came out and said he'd horsewhip me if I ever came on his place again so I left.

I didn't want to wear out my welcome.

Q. After you left the Bright place, where did you go?

A. To the Woxall Hotel—I knew some of my friends would be there.

Q. Were they?

A. Yes.

Q. Did you tell them about how you had driven the horse into a snow bank and turned the sleigh over?

A. Everyone seemed to know about it.

Q. And even though you didn't know Miss Bright's condition, you made light of it, didn't you?

A. Oh, I wouldn't say that.

Q. Well, let's see. Did you point out to everyone there in the bar that the ground was white—by which you meant there was snow?

A. Yes, I said now the ground is white.

Q. What else did you say?

A. I told them to get a horse and hitch him to a sleigh.

Q. In light of what had happened the night before, did you suggest a closed sleigh?

A. No, I said to get an open sleigh.

Q. Did you emphasize to your friends that they were young and that this was the time to get some girls and take them sleigh riding?

And that while they were dashing through the snow, they should sing sleighing songs?

A. Yes.

Q. What kind of a horse did you suggest?

A. I suggested a bob-tailed horse, two-forty for his speed.

Q. That would be a fast horse?

A. Yes.

Q. And did you tell them to use a whip to make the horse go faster?

A. I suggested one crack—one crack of the whip—that's what I said.

Q. And you said if they followed your advice, they'd take the lead. What did you mean by that?

A. The girls would like them.

Q. So, not knowing whether Miss Bright was alive or dead, you went to this tavern where you and the other loafers hang out all the time and you told them to do what you had done—to get a sleigh, a bob-tailed horse, drive the horse at top speed, sing sleighing songs, and in that way, seek success with the girls. Isn't that what you said?

A. Not all my friends are loafers and we don't hang out there all the time—we go to other places too.

Q. Is that what you said?

A. I guess so.

Q. I have no further questions at this time.

I attest this is a true transcript of the above proceedings.

*Hannibal A. Cobb, court reporter*

## The Lucky Little Girl

"Mama, can I play with my paper dolls now?"

"You're a big girl now and you should call me 'Mother'. Only little girls say *Mama*."

"Yes, Mother. Can I please play with my paper dolls now."

"Last night, Darling, you fell asleep when you should have been studying your Italian verbs so let's have some fun by going over them together. We do want to please Vito when he comes this afternoon for your Italian lesson and we only have about forty minutes before Emil will be here for your voice lesson."

"Do you know where my paper dolls are? I put some of them with my French book and now they're gone."

"Oh, they'll turn up. Maybe they're under something. Now about your Italian. You know that Emil said you want to learn Italian since it will help you sing with more expression if you know what you're saying. And here's some good news, he has two new songs for you to learn so he's going to give you an extra hour today. You can tell your father about them when you write to him this week."

"Do I have to practice for two hours this afternoon? I was hoping I could do some coloring in the book Aunt Mary sent me for my tenth birthday last week. But I can't find it either. And I can't find my crayons."

"Oh, they're probably in one of your drawers. Now, about these verbs."

"Mother, can Jenny come to play with me some day next week?"

"Dear, Jenny lives way over in the next block, and next week in addition to Vito and Emil and your regular practicing, you have a hair dressing appointment and you'll need time for make-up and—we mustn't forget that Pierre is coming on Tuesday and there'll be more fun in learning how to answer when you're being interviewed on TV."

"Sometimes I wish I didn't have such a good voice."

"Dear, I know you think you're working awfully hard but all of us are. And we're doing it all for you. When you grow up, you'll be rich and famous and you'll thank us then. Now let's get started with these Italian verbs."

"Mama, when I grow up and am rich and famous, I'm going to have paper dolls to play with, and crayons and a coloring book, and a best friend, and a pet kitten too."

"Yes, dear. Now let's have some fun right now with these Italian verbs."

# We'll Call You

G. We are a small group of traveling players. We go from place to place bringing entertainment and light into this dark and troubled world.

Our play tonight takes place in the personnel office of one of nation's largest companies. My job is to interview prospective employees. My friend here is seeking employment.

G. Please spell your last name and sit down.

B. Which do you want me to do first? I can do it either way.

G. I don't care. Just do it.

B. Which?

G. Spell your last name.

B. (Sits) D I T T E R.

G. All right, Mr. Dieter, what's your first name?

B. Ditter.

G. (Looks around). Did her what?

B. No, that's the way you say it.

G. Oh, I see. Well, Mr. Didderwhat, what's your first name?

B. It's Ditter.

G. Your name is Didder Didderwhat?

B. No my last name is ditter. D I T T E R.

G. Oh, I see. Well, what's your first name?

B. I don't use it.

G. Why not?

B. My father didn't use it.

G. Your father didn't use your first name? I can understand that. Your father took your first name but didn't use it. Is that it?

B. No, I have a first name. I just don't use it. I use "J."

G. Now we're getting somewhere. Your first name that you don't use is Jay. J A Y?

B. No, it's just plain "J."

G. Your first name is Justplainjay. I can understand why you don't want to be called Justplainjay. What's your middle initial?

B. I don't use it.

G. Did your father take that too?

B. No, I have it but I don't use it because I use my middle name. My middle name is William.

G. Now we're getting somewhere. People call you "William"?

B. No, I don't use William. I'm called…

G. (Interrupting) You use an alias? I get it now. You and your father both had trouble with the law. He took your first name and you've changed your middle name. Is that it?

B. No, no, no. My name is William but I'm called Bill.

G. Well, Bill, now we're getting somewhere. In which city do you live?

B. I don't live in a city.

G. Well, which town do you live in?

B. I don't live in a town. I live in a place that used to be called Hendricks.

G. Used to be? Did your father take that when he took your first name?

B. No, you see the John R. Young Oil Company was across the creek and they had a post office, but they are gone now.

G. Did your father take them too?

B. No, please leave my father out of it. You see John R. Young had a post office called Hendricks but they've left now and have gone to Green Lane.

G. Green Lane is now called Hendricks?

B. No, it's still called Green Lane. John R. Young Oil Company went to Kleinbach's lumber yard.

G. John R. Young Oil Company now sells lumber in Green Lane?

B. No, they sell gasoline and ice cream and fishing supplies out on Route 63. That's a main road.

G. Now, we're getting somewhere. From the John R. Young Fish Store, how do you get to Hendricks?

B. You'd take the first road to your left and then turn right at the hotel and take Hendricks Station Road.

G. What's the name of the hotel?

B. Well, it's not a hotel anymore.

G. Did John R. Young take it too—to Green Lane or to the fish store?

B. No, it's still there. It's called a hotel even though it's not a hotel.

G. You have a lot of strange neighbors, don't you? I take it that you live on Hendricks Station Road.

B. No, at the bridge it changes to just plain Hendricks Road. We live just on the other side of the bridge. On Hendricks Road where Hendricks used to be but it's now Woxall.

G. What's Woxall?

B. That's where we live.

G. When did you move from Hendricks to Woxall?

B. We didn't move. John R. Young moved.

G. And took Hendricks to Green Lane which is still called Green Lane and they don't sell lumber, they sell ice cream and fishing gear. Is that right?

B. Well, they sell oil too.

G. So, if I went out to 63 I could go to John R. Young and get ice cream, gasoline, and oil?

B. No, you'd have to go to Green Lane for the oil.

G. I see. Well, let's get back to you and Hendricks where you used to live.

B. Woxall.

G. Right. Woxall. Who are your closest neighbors there in Woxall?

B. Well, it's the Thimm's. They are right around the corner, but they live in Perkiomenville.

G. That's spelled T I M S?

B. No, it's spelled P E R K I O M E N V I L L E.

G. No, Thimms. T I M S?

B. No. T H I M M. No, S. Two Ms, and they don't use the H.

G. Well, that certainly plain enough—just like you, your father, John R. Young, at the lumber yard where they sell fish and ice cream, the hotel which isn't a hotel, Hendricks which isn't Hendricks, roads that change their name at the bridge. And, and...(Stands up). Look, if we have anything that will fit your particular talents, we'll give you a call. Don't you call us. We'll call you.

(Both exit)

*The red barn on our property.*

## St. Paul's

Again and again of Sir Christopher Wren
In England you're told and you find.

How this church and that he pulled out of his hat
And buildings of most every kind,

We went to St. Paul's, saw its crypts and its halls,
Read the heroes' inscriptions with awe.

How men of the realm had their trick at the helm,
And marveled at all that we saw.

There, far, far from home, we stood 'neath the dome
That withstood the bombs and the fire,

And said a brief prayer 'twould always be there,
A symbol, free men to inspire.

*During World War II, the Luftwaffe attempted to bomb Britain into submission. London was a prime target. Though buildings around it were destroyed, Saint Paul's Cathedral miraculously escaped major damage. Images of the cathedral's dome framed by smoke and fire came to typify Britain's indomitable spirit. Verna and I were filled with wonder by the cathedral, its history and magnificence, then too, we remembered those days when Britain stood alone and all Churchill could offer his countrymen was blood, sweat, and tears.*

# About the Contributors to the Introductions

### *Frank Boni*

Frank Boni graduated from the University of Michigan in 1947 with a degree in mechanical engineering. He enlisted in the U.S. Navy in 1943 and spent much of his professional life working on Navy design projects involving power generation. He retired in 1983 as VP of Engineering at the Yarway Corporation. He traveled extensively, following his stepdaughter, an Olympic rower, to competitions. He has volunteered with the Red Cross and for the past thirty years has painted landscapes, covered bridges, churches, and portraits. He first came to know the Upper Dublin Association and Judge Ditter by attending a UDA meeting as guest of his second wife, Julie. Twenty years ago Bill Ditter proposed him as candidate for secretary of the association, and he served in that role until its dwindling membership decided the 2016 meeting—the association's 188th—would have to be its last. Frank has three children, four stepchildren, and numerous grand- and great grandchildren. He lives in Ambler, Pennsylvania in a retirement community.

### *Patricia Furlong, Esquire*

Patricia Furlong, Esquire, has been a career law clerk in the Eastern District of Pennsylvania since 1990. A graduate of the Delaware Law School, Ms. Furlong worked in the 1980s as a Deputy Attorney General in Delaware. In that capacity, she worked at the intersection of legal, medical, and ethical issues facing the state. During the AIDs crisis she represented the Department of Public Health, working through issues involving the right to privacy, public health concerns, and the evolving medical understanding of the disease. She also worked on behalf of the state to protect the legal rights of families and ensure proper medical protocols were followed in cases of brain death. After moving to Pennsylvania, Ms. Furlong worked as an attorney for the Central Legal Staff of the Superior Court of Pennsylvania and as a law clerk for Judge James R. Melinson when he served on that court. When Judge Melinson accepted an appointment to the federal bench, Pat came with him and clerked for him for the next fifteen years. She has worked on a wide range of cases at the Eastern District and, for last eleven years, for Judge Ditter. Pat lives in Philadelphia with her husband, Judge Vincent W. Furlong, two dogs, and at any given moment, one or more of her four children.

### *The Honorable Gene E. K. Pratter*

The Honorable Gene E. K. Pratter is a judge on the United States District Court for the Eastern District of Pennsylvania. Prior to joining the bench in 2004, and becoming one of Judge Ditter's colleagues, she appeared before Judge Ditter on behalf of clients in professional liability and ethics cases during her 30-plus-year tenure at the Philadelphia office of Duane Morris LLP, where she also served as the firm's General Counsel. In addition to managing a diverse docket, Judge Pratter contributes her time to professional and educational organizations. Judge Pratter has particularly enjoyed serving as an ethics trainer/mentor for new judges in Bulgaria and Romania, as well as contributing as a member of the Judicial Conference's Civil Rules Advisory Committee for six years at the invitation of Chief Justice John Roberts. A transplant from California and after earning her undergraduate degree at Stanford University before pursuing her law degree at University of Pennsylvania, she is proud to call Philadelphia home and enjoys family time in Nantucket.

## The Reverend Alan Smith

The Reverend Alan Smith is a graduate of East Stroudsburg State College and has a Master of Divinity degree from the Eastern Baptist Theological Seminary.

He began ministry as a pastor in 1977, serving churches of various sizes and stages in development and growth in the Eastern Pennsylvania Conference of the United Methodist Church. In 1999 he, along with his wife Mary (Hower) Smith and their five children, moved to Woxall, Pennsylvania, where he became the pastor of the Tabor UMC and Mary became its choir director. After eleven years at Tabor, Pastor Al was appointed as lead pastor to the Church of the Good Shepherd in Lebanon, Pennsylvania, an active and vibrant congregation of about 850 members and attendance of approximately 450 in Sunday worship. Both he and Mary are accomplished musicians—enjoy camping and the outdoors—and seeing their grandchildren.

# About the Author

## J. William Ditter, Jr.

J. William Ditter, Jr. is a senior judge on the United States District Court for the Eastern District of Pennsylvania. Nominated by President Richard M. Nixon to a new seat on the court, he received his commission in October 1970. In 1986 Judge Ditter assumed senior status and continues to serve in that capacity.

On the federal court Judge Ditter has presided over high profile cases, including the Reading Railroad bankruptcy and one of the nation's first aircraft hijacking cases. He has heard civil rights cases, including one brought the Department of Justice against then–Mayor Frank Rizzo, the City of Philadelphia, and many of its officials, as well as patent, medical malpractice, and product liability cases, in addition to criminal trials. A student of American history, in 1984 Judge Ditter was one of the incorporators of the Historical Society of the United States District Court for the Eastern District of Pennsylvania. Judge Ditter serves on its board of directors and chairs the calendar committee, which distributes an annual calendar to all members of the federal bench.

A 1943 graduate of Ursinus College, Judge Ditter received his law degree from the University of Pennsylvania in 1948. He worked as a law clerk for the Court of Common Pleas in Montgomery County and as an assistant district attorney in the county while in private practice with his late sister, Mabel Ditter Sellers, in Ambler, Pennsylvania. From 1964 to 1970, he served as a judge on the Court of Common Pleas of Montgomery County.

In 1942 Judge Ditter enlisted in the United States Naval Reserve. Called to active duty during World War II, he was the disbursing officer of a repair ship in the Philippines and was again on active duty during the Korean War. Judge Ditter retired in 1968 having reached the rank of captain in the Supply Corps.

Judge Ditter serves on the Board of Consultors for the Villanova School of Law and has been guest lecturer on constitutional law in an undergraduate program of Villanova University. He received an honorary law degree from Ursinus College and has been honored by his high school, the Montgomery County Bar Association, and numerous civic organizations. An active participant in the work of his church, he has been a Sunday School teacher, a lay minister who has preached at Sunday services, including a sermon at Old Christ Church in Philadelphia, and chairman of numerous church committees, including the building committee.

For more than sixty years he was married to the late Verna B. Ditter, the mother of his four sons: J. William Ditter, III, Esq.; George B. Ditter, Esq.; Robert V. Ditter; and David B. Ditter. Mrs. Ditter was a skilled artist and one of her paintings is reproduced in the background of the judge's portrait on the cover of the book. Judge Ditter has eight grandchildren and five great grandchildren. Judge Ditter's father was a member of Congress from 1933 until his death in 1943.

The judge's hobbies have included beekeeping, photography, gardening, genealogy, softball, and skiing. Also known for his love of a good story, Judge Ditter authors an annual Christmas letter, hoping to add to the merry and happy of the season.